Unequal Political Participation Worldwide

Highly educated citizens vote at much lower rates than less educated citizens in some countries. By contrast, electoral participation exhibits no such bias in other countries as diverse as Spain, Denmark, and South Korea. This book describes the levels of unequal participation in thirty-six countries worldwide, examines possible causes of this phenomenon, and discusses its consequences. Aina Gallego illustrates how electoral procedures, party and media systems, unionization, and income inequality impact unequal participation through an original combination of cross-national survey data and survey experiments.

Aina Gallego is a Ramon y Cajal Fellow (Assistant Professor) at the Barcelona Institute of International Studies. She completed her doctoral dissertation at the Autonomous University of Barcelona in 2008, and she was a postdoctoral scholar at Stanford University and the Spanish High Research Council. Her research focuses on several aspects of democratic representation, including inequalities in voter turnout and political participation, the formation of political preferences, and the effects of electoral systems and income inequality on political behavior.

The **Centro de Investigaciones Sociológicas** (**CIS**) is an independent entity assigned to the Ministry of the Presidency. Its main remit is to contribute scientific knowledge to Spanish society.

The **CIS** gathers the necessary data for research in disparate fields, from trends in public opinion to applied research. Hence, the CIS is responsible for carrying out studies that provide accurate diagnoses to guide the work of the public authorities in charge of the different administrations.

The **CIS** is known mainly for carrying out surveys that allow advances to be made in the knowledge of Spanish society and its evolution over time. However, it also performs other tasks in supporting training and research within the sphere of the social sciences.

CIS publications (the *Revista Española de Investigaciones Sociológicas*, REIS) and various collections of books are a basic channel for research dissemination that contributes to scientific knowledge on society.

Unequal Political Participation Worldwide

AINA GALLEGO

Barcelona Institute of International Studies

Centro de Investigaciones Sociológicas

CAMBRIDGE
UNIVERSITY PRESS

32 Avenue of the Americas, New York, NY 10013-2473, USA

Cambridge University Press is part of the University of Cambridge.

It furthers the University's mission by disseminating knowledge in the pursuit of education, learning, and research at the highest international levels of excellence.

www.cambridge.org
Information on this title: www.cambridge.org/9781107023536

CIS
Montalbán, 8
28014, Madrid, Spain

First published 2015

Printed in the United States of America

A catalog record for this publication is available from the British Library.

Library of Congress Cataloging in Publication Data
Gallego, Aina, 1981–
Unequal political participation worldwide / Aina Gallego.
  pages cm
Includes bibliographical references and index.
ISBN 978-1-107-02353-6 (hardback)
1. Political participation – Cross-cultural studies.   2. Democracy – Cross-cultural studies.   I. Title.
JF799.G35   2014
323'.042–dc23   2014022606

ISBN 978-1-107-02353-6 Hardback

Contents

List of Tables	*page*	xi
List of Figures		xiii
Acknowledgments		xv
	Introduction	1
1	Unequal Participation Around the World	13
	Previous Research on Education and Voting	14
	Education Models and Measurement of Unequal Participation	18
	Voter Turnout by Education Around the World	23
	Implications of Variability in Unequal Participation	31
2	Heterogeneous Consequences of Contexts on Participation	35
	Why Citizens Vote	37
	Baseline Unequal Participation	40
	Homogeneous and Heterogeneous Consequences of Contexts	42
	Heterogeneous Effects by Education Level: Registration	47
	Ceiling Effects: Voter Turnout and Compulsory Voting	50
	Assessing the Link Between Contextual Features and Turnout Inequality	55

3   The Difficulty of the Voting Procedure   57
    Ballot Structure, Cognitive Costs, and Preference
        Expression   59
    Consequences of Ballot Structure for Participation   62
    Experimental Evidence on the Consequences of
        Changes in the Ballot Structure   65
        The Number of Votes Experiment   66
        The Open–Closed Ballot Experiment   70
    Cross-National Evidence on the Association of
        Ballot Structure and Participation   74

4   Government Fragmentation and Media Systems   87
    Government Fragmentation and the Cognitive
        Difficulty of Voting   89
        The Coalitions Experiment   93
        Cross-National Bivariate Association   101
    Media Systems and Ease of Access to Political
        Information   103
    Multivariate Analysis on Coalitions and Media
        Systems   108
    The Cognitive Costs of Voting Affect Poorly
        Educated People Disproportionately   112

5   Trade Unions in the Highly Educated Membership
    Era   114
    The Classical Mobilization Account   116
    Do Trade Unions Enhance Turnout Equality?   119
    Trade Unions and Their Composition   126
    Trade Unions and Turnout Inequality   131
    Mobilization by Political Parties   141

6   Income Inequality and the Participation of
    Lower-Status Groups   144
    Theories of Income Inequality and Participation   146
    Review of Previous Empirical Studies   149
    A Graphical Bivariate Description   151
    Multivariate Analyses and Political Attitudes as a
        Mechanism   154
    Income Inequality and Political Behavior   163

7   Consequences of Unequal Participation for
    Representation   168
    Heterogeneous Preferences Among Populations   171

Contents   ix

Full Turnout and Electoral Results   174
Policy Outcomes and Resource Targeting   177
Issue Opinions by Education and Voter
    Participation Across Countries   178
Opinion Gaps Between Voters and Nonvoters When
    Participation Is Unequal   188
Unequal Participation and Unequal Representation   191
Conclusions   193

Appendix   205
Bibliography   211
Index   233

List of Tables

3–1 Number of Names of District-Level
   Representatives Citizens Know   *page* 61
3–2 Reported Intention to Vote in the Number of
   Votes Experiment   69
3–3 Reported Intention to Vote in the Open–Closed
   Ballot Experiment   73
3–4 Ballot Structure by Country   77
3–5 Frequency of Individuals and Elections by Ballot
   Structure in the CSES   79
3–6 Multivariate Models of Voter Turnout: Ballot
   Structure and Education   80
4–1 Reported Intention to Vote in the Coalitions
   Experiment   98
4–2 Multivariate Models of Voter Turnout:
   Coalitions, Media Systems, and Education   110
5–1 The Educational Composition of Union Members
   and Nonunion Members   124
5–2 Multivariate Models of Voter Turnout: Trade
   Unions and Education   134
6–1 Multivariate Models of Voter Turnout: Net and
   Gross Income Inequality and Education   156
6–2 Multivariate Models of Political Attitudes: Gross
   Income Inequality and Education   159

6-3 Multivariate Models of Voter Turnout: Gross
Income Inequality, Political Attitudes, and
Education   162
6-4 Marginal Effects of Education and Income with
and Without Mediators   163
7-1 Percent Agreeing That Government Should
Reduce Differences in Income Levels   180
7-2 Percent Agreeing That Men Should Have More
Right to a Job Than Women   183
7-3 Differences in Issue Opinion by Education Level
and Voter Participation   186
7-4 Difference in Issue Opinion by Voter
Participation in High Turnout-Inequality
Countries   190

List of Figures

0–1 Reported voter turnout in the United States, 2004 election   *page* 4
0–2 Reported voter turnout in Spain, 2004 parliamentary election   6
1–1 Reported voter turnout and average education level by age   22
1–2 Reported voter turnout by education level in thirty-six countries   25
1–3 Predicted probability to vote by education in eighty-five elections   28
1–4 OLS estimates of turnout inequality in eighty-five elections   32
2–1 Homogeneous and heterogeneous effects of contextual characteristics   43
2–2 Equalization of participation because of ceiling effects   51
2–3 Voter turnout, turnout inequality, and compulsory voting   52
3–1 Text of the Number of Votes experiment   68
3–2 Text of the Open–Closed Ballot experiment   72
3–3 Predicted voter turnout by ballot structure   84
4–1 Question wording of the Coalitions Experiment   96
4–2 Turnout inequality and government fragmentation   102

4–3 Turnout inequality and share of the audience of
	public broadcasters							108
5–1 Strength of trade unions across country				128
5–2 Percent union members and nonunion members
	who hold a university degree						130
5–3 Predicted voter turnout by education, union
	membership, and union density					136
5–4 Turnout inequality and union density				140
6–1 Turnout inequality (education and income) and
	income inequality							152

Acknowledgments

I am in debt to many people and institutions for their help and support. First of all, I thank my dissertation advisor, Eva Anduiza. The members of my dissertation tribunal, Mariano Torcal, Laura Morales, and Gábor Tóka, provided outstanding comments and encouraged me to write this book. André Blais, Russell Dalton, and Karen Jusko provided help and guidance at different stages of this project. Paul Sniderman challenged me to test my theory using survey experiments. I owe special thanks to Paloma Aguilar because she made the publication of this book possible, along with the editorial teams at Cambridge University Press and the Centro de Investigaciones Sociólogicas.

Many other scholars discussed parts of this project and provided comments and encouragement including Guillem Rico, Mark Franklin, Xavier Fernandez, Eduard Bonet, Pedro Riera, Matthew Shugart, Alan Renwick, William Jacoby, Miki Caul Kittilson, Sarah Birch, Carol Galais, Mónica Méndez, Jennifer Wilkins, Nancy Bermeo, Laia Jorba, Michele Micheletti, Agustí Bosch, Mar Reguant, Zoe Lefkofridi, Willem Saris, Maria José Hierro, Daniel Oberski, Margarita Torre, Marta Cantijoch, Robert Lineira, Araceli Mateos, and the three anonymous reviewers.

Several institutions have supported my research. I wrote my dissertation while in the Institut de Govern i Polítiques Públiques thanks to a fellowship awarded by the Universitat Autónoma de Barcelona. I have been recipient of several fellowships that allowed me to spend research periods at Essex University, the University of California at Irvine, the European University Institute, and the Université de Montréal. I received invaluable comments on pieces of this project at conferences, seminars, and workshops in Nicosia, Helsinki, Pisa, Valencia, Montreal, Boston, Barcelona, Salamanca, and Seattle. I also received financial support from the Centro de Investigaciones Sociológicas and from research projects of the Spanish Ministry of Education (SEJ2007–60082), the Ministry of Science and Technology (CSO2010–18534), and the European Science Foundation (project "Voter Turnout and Abstention in Context"). I completed this book in February 2012 during my research stay as a postdoctoral visiting scholar at the Political Science Department of Stanford University, thanks to a Beatriu de Pinós fellowship (2009 BP-A 00014) awarded by the Generalitat de Catalunya.

    Finally, for their love and unconditional support, I am deeply grateful to Iban, my family, and my friends.

Introduction

Political equality is an essential political ideal and it is the corner-stone of moral justifications of democracy. Most people would agree with the proposition that the interests and preferences of each citizen must be given equal consideration in the political process because no person is intrinsically superior to others in ways that can justify preferential consideration. A second premise is that each person is the best judge of her own interests and pref-erences and is capable of expressing them, hence ruling out any version of an enlightened sovereign as the best interpreter of cit-izens' will. Taken together, these two claims provide a powerful case for democracy. Only in electoral democracies can all citi-zens, in principle, have an equal influence in the political process (Dahl 1971, 2008; Przeworski 2010).

The focus on equality of influence as a key ingredient of politi-cal equality is central to many theoretical perspectives. According to Robert Dahl (2008), in an ideal democracy, all members of the community must have equal opportunities to express their views about alternative policies, they must have equal influence on the agenda, and every vote must be counted equally. Relat-edly, for Sidney Verba political equality "refers to the extent to which citizens have an equal voice in governmental decisions" (2003: 663). In a third influential definition, political equality is the "requirement that democratic institutions should provide citizens with equal procedural opportunities to influence political decisions" (Beitz 1989: 4). Political equality demands that individual interests and preferences be expressed and aggregated in such a way that each member of the polity has an equal amount of weight at determining the collective outcome. The actual ability to influence the outcomes of the political process surely varies widely across citizens and relevant social groups in practice. In real democratic systems many citizens lack relevant resources and effective opportunities to participate in political decisions, interest groups are able to shape which issues make it onto the political agenda, and the influence of money in politics is pervasive. To the extent that equalizing access to all relevant resources, such as money, influence on the agenda, and political contacts, is unfeasible or undesirable, full political equality remains a distant goal.

When narrowing down from equal political influence to equal participation in elections, the prospects for political equality are less dismal. Despite the very real barriers to full political equality, elections provide a unique way in which large numbers of citizens can each have the same amount of influence on the selection of governments and induce politicians to be equally responsive to their interests and preferences. The principle "one person, one vote" effectively spreads political power among all the adult members of a polity. It simultaneously gives every member of the polity the option to participate and caps the amount of influence each citizen can have on the outcome of an election. Voting is thus "the one participatory act for which there is mandated equality; each citizen gets one vote and only one vote" (Verba, Schlozman, and Brady 1995: 304).

Equal participation in elections is perhaps the most important and feasible practical application of the democratic ideal of political equality. Yet not even participation in elections is equal. Electoral participation can be unequal if members of some politically relevant groups, typically lower-status groups, systematically fail to vote.

This book is about unequal political participation, or the lower participation of low-status groups in elections. Political scientists care about unequal political participation because it implies that low-turnout groups, who are likely to have different political needs, interests, abilities, and preferences than other groups, exert less influence on the selection of governments than they would if participation were equal. The preferences of abstainers not only fail to have an influence at the selection stage, but they are also disregarded at the policy-making stage. Elected political representatives have no incentive to be evenly responsive to all if some distinguishable groups have lower participation rates than others. Instead, it is rational for politicians to satisfy the demands of very participatory groups, whose votes they need in order to be reelected, but neglect the views of regular nonvoters. If policies neglect the wants and needs of the most disadvantaged, their situation relative to other groups may deteriorate even further. Unequal participation generates unequal responsiveness of governments to the preferences of different types of citizens, possibly leading to a vicious circle in which social and political disadvantages reinforce each other over time. These considerations have led Arendt Lijphart to declare that unequal participation is "democracy's unresolved dilemma" (1997: 1).

Empirically, it is a political science truism that voter participation is unequal in the United States. The influential socioeconomic status (SES) model of political participation builds on the observation that higher levels of education and income and having a higher-status occupation are associated with higher turnout rates (Verba and Nie 1972). Education, in particular, is perhaps the strongest individual level predictor of the decision to vote. In 1972, only 38 percent of those with four years of education or less voted, compared to 91 percent of those who had attended college for five years or more (Wolfinger and Rosenstone 1980). Rosenstone and Hansen (1993) estimate that the voter turnout rates of college graduates exceed those of the grade-school educated by almost 30 percentage points. Using the cumulative American National Studies file, Han (2009) found a 30 percentage points participation gap in the turnout rates of people with a grade school education and people with a college degree in 1952, which increased to 40 percentage points in 2000. The evidence

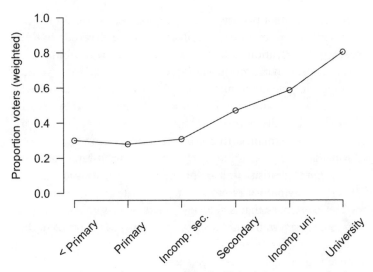

FIGURE 0–1. Reported voter turnout in the United States, 2004 election.
Source: CSES

that the poorly educated vote less frequently is so overwhelming
that scholars have claimed: "The relationship between education
and voter turnout ranks among the most extensively documented
correlations in American survey research. From the early work
of Merriam and Gosnell (1924) to today, literally thousands of
cross-sectional surveys have indicated that turnout rates climb
with years of formal schooling" (Sondheimer and Green 2010:
174).

There is no doubt that participation is highly unequal in
the United States, as seen in Figure 0–1, which uses data
from the cross-national Comparative Study of Electoral Systems
(CSES) for the 2004 presidential election.[1] About 30 percent of
Americans with less than a primary education and 28 percent of

---

[1] It is also well known that voter turnout is overestimated by surveys. For descriptive purposes it is useful to weight the data in order to correct for overreport-
ing. The weights are calculated as $W_{Vj} = \frac{V_{Oj}}{V_{Rj}}$ for voters and $W_{Nj} = \frac{1 - V_{Oj}}{1 - V_{Rj}}$ for
nonvoters, where V_O is official turnout rate and V_R is reported turnout rate in
country j. The official turnout data comes from the International Institute for

those with only a primary education voted in the last presidential election. By contrast, 47 percent of people who completed secondary education and fully 80 percent of those who had a college degree voted in the election.[2]

However, we know much less about unequal participation in other countries and very little about what drives differences in turnout inequality across countries. The aim of this book is to describe and explain unequal participation from a comparative perspective.

Political scientists often assume that lower-status groups universally vote at lower rates than higher-status groups, except perhaps in countries that use compulsory voting. If this were true, it would suggest that unequal participation is an unavoidable trait of democratic politics, a deep-seated flaw in an otherwise desirable political system.

In fact, however, the less educated *vote just as frequently* as the highly educated in many countries. Consider Spain, where voting is voluntary, as an example. Since the end of Franco's dictatorship, participation rates in parliamentary elections have ranged from a low of 68 percent of the voting-age population in 1979, to a high of 80 percent in 1982, one year after a failed coup d'état (Montero 1986). Besides these initial fluctuations, voter turnout has been very stable. On average, 74 percent of Spanish citizens vote in parliamentary elections, a figure typical

Democracy and Electoral Assistance voter turnout database (http://www.idea .int/vt/, visited June 2011). Voter turnout is always the ratio of voters to the Voting Eligible Population, except in the United States where it is the ratio of voters to the Voting Age Population.

[2] The gaps in the turnout rates of highly and poorly educated citizens can be somewhat exaggerated if, as research has found, the highly educated have a higher propensity to overreport their vote, that is, to say that they voted when in fact they did not (Bernstein, Chadha, and Montjoy 2001; Karp and Brockington 2005; Silver, Anderson, and Abramson 1986). However, some underprivileged groups, particularly African Americans, are also more likely to overreport voting (Abramson and Aldrich 1982; Sigelman 1982; Traugott and Katosh 1979). Unfortunately, the correlates of overreporting cannot be investigated in most countries because the actual turnout records are not available to researchers.

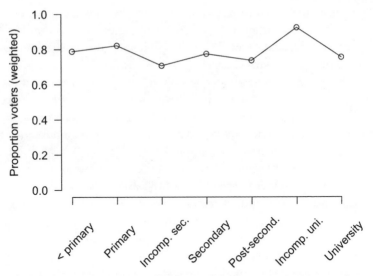

FIGURE 0–2. Reported voter turnout in Spain, 2004 parliamentary election. *Source*: CSES

of advanced industrial democracies (Franklin 2004). Figure 0–2 displays reported voter turnout rates by education level using weighted data from the CSES for the 2004 parliamentary elections, but the same pattern holds for other elections.[3] The contrast with the American case is striking. Fully 79 percent of citizens with less than a primary education and 82 percent of citizens who have completed a primary education report that they voted. The voter turnout rates of people who have higher education levels are very similar: 77 percent of respondents who have finished secondary education and 76 percent of those who have a university degree report that they voted in the parliamentary election.

The discrepancy between the American and the Spanish cases illustrates the claim that voter turnout is not unequal everywhere,

---

[3] The category "postsecondary education" is included in the Spanish graph, but not in the American. Because of differences in education systems, not all education categories coded by the CSES apply to all countries. For example, no distinction between vocational and university education is made in the United States.

which is to say that turnout is not necessarily unequal. The positive association between education and voter participation is not universal. Instead, it varies across countries, to the extent that education is perhaps the strongest predictor of participation in some elections, but there is no correlation at all in others. True, in the United States and a few other advanced industrial democracies, there are large gaps in the turnout rates of highly and less educated people. On the other hand, in many other contexts, there are literally no differences in turnout rates across education groups. Turnout-egalitarian contexts include very diverse countries in which voter participation rates are not particularly high, such as Spain or South Korea.

An accurate description of voter turnout rates by education level around the world is a necessary first step to understanding unequal participation. The mere existence of variation in the degree to which participation is unequal across contexts is relevant. Rather than being inevitable, unequal participation is contingent on institutional, political, or social characteristics. This insight opens the opportunity for comparative research to analyze why participation is equal in some contexts but not in others. A better understanding of unequal participation can perhaps even shed some light on what can be done to make participation more equal. Conceivably, better knowledge of this phenomenon may suggest ways of increasing the participation of low-status groups where they fail to vote and, in this way, bring us closer to the democratic ideal of equal participation.

Beyond description, the second aim of this book is to improve our understanding of why voter turnout is more unequal in some contexts than others. Only one previous study has attempted to explain cross-national variation in unequal participation at length. Verba, Nie, and Kim's (1978) classic "Participation and political equality: A seven-nation comparison" examined the degree to which socioeconomic status influenced political participation in seven nations. Their main claim was that unequal participation depended upon the degree to which lower-social status groups were affiliated with organizations such as trade unions, associations, and political parties.

This book builds on Verba, Nie, and Kim's (1978) contribution as well as on decades of accumulated comparative political behavior research. I present a general framework within which to think about unequal participation, which focuses on the interaction between individual characteristics and the contexts in which individuals participate in politics. The starting point is the micro-level resource model of political participation (Verba, Schlozman, and Brady 1995). People of low socioeconomic status vote less frequently in many contexts, because they have fewer resources and more negative attitudes toward politics. Participation is more costly and less rewarding for them. The second starting point is the macro-level approach to comparative voter turnout research, which claims that variation in aggregate turnout rates across countries can be traced back to a set of contextual characteristics, such as the electoral institutions, socioeconomic factors, or the party systems, that shape the costs and benefits of voting (Geys 2006, Blais 2006).

I propose that it is useful to make a theoretical distinction between contextual factors that affect the costs and benefits of voting in homogenous or in heterogeneous ways, depending on the individual availability of resources and motivation. Some costs and rewards of voting, such as the physical fatigue of going to the polls, affect citizens of all social groups roughly similarly, that is, homogeneously. On the contrary, differences in levels of available resources and motivations can make some individuals more sensitive than others to changes in other contextual features. For example, increases in the cognitive costs of deciding for whom to vote or of dealing with complicated voting procedures are easy to bear for people who have many cognitive resources. Any increases in complexity are, by contrast, much more cognitively taxing to bear for resource-poor individuals. Thus, a contextual-level characteristic that makes voting more cognitively costly should mainly demobilize less educated citizens and enlarge participatory gaps. Likewise, mobilization by political organizations is only a promising means of reducing turnout inequality if efforts to bring people to the polls are disproportionately focused on low-education groups. More generally, contextual characteristics to which highly and less educated people are heterogeneously responsive will affect turnout inequality, even if their impact on overall turnout rates is small.

A contextual characteristic can also equalize participation if it has homogeneous, but very large, effects on all types of citizens. For example, compulsory voting eliminates turnout inequality because it significantly raises the propensity to vote of all individuals and makes turnout rates approach their upper limit (Lijphart 1997).

By focusing on the interaction between individual citizens and the contexts in which they participate in politics, this work contributes to the growing literature that is progressively relating micro and macro theories of political behavior (e.g., Anduiza 2002; Van Egmond 2003; Franklin 2004; Anderson and Singer 2008; Karp and Banducci 2008; Kittilson and Schwindt-Bayer 2010; Klingeman 2009). This research program has already established that political behavior depends on both the characteristics of individuals and of the environments in which they live. I add to this literature by specifying under what conditions education, one of the most important individual-level characteristics, has a stronger or weaker influence on participation in elections.

Methodologically, comparative political behavior research on the interaction of individuals and contexts has almost always relied on a combination of survey data and contextual information for a relatively small set of advanced industrial democracies. The framework proposed by this book for understanding unequal participation can be used to generate numerous predictions, a few of which I examine through a combination of methods. I test hypotheses using a combination of survey experiments and cross-national data with a broad geographic scope. Specifically, the analyses conducted here draw on the pooled datasets of the CSES for eighty-five elections held in thirty-six countries.

Researchers increasingly rely on experimental methods, because they allow us to identify causal effects more accurately than traditional methods in the social sciences. In the last few years, there has been growing skepticism in comparative political behavior research about the validity of work that examines the effects of contexts based on cross-national data. In experimental studies, researchers control how units are assigned to treatments. Random assignment makes it possible to interpret any differences observed across treatment groups as causal effects. This work is one of the first comparative studies to use survey experiments specifically designed to examine how electoral institutions affect political behavior, and for whom.

Although experiments deserve much praise, it is also true that many contextual level variables of interest cannot be manipulated experimentally and the external validity of experimental results is often questionable. Hence, we also need to examine the extent to which the predictions of a theory correspond with the patterns we observe in actual elections. This book makes extensive use of observational cross-national survey data drawing mainly on a large dataset consisting of pooled data that comes from election studies held around the world.

The first chapter describes variation in the levels of unequal participation across countries. In addition, it discusses the results of previous research on education and voting, as well as some of the most relevant methodological considerations that need to be taken into account when studying unequal participation. Detailed description of the levels of unequal turnout in eighty-five elections held in thirty-six countries shows that there is a large degree of variation: Although participation is equal in some contexts, the turnout rates of highly and less educated voters are very similar in others.

The second chapter lays out a simple theoretical framework from which to think about the reasons of variation in unequal turnout that will be used in subsequent chapters. It presents a distinction between contextual characteristics that affect participation homogeneously and heterogeneously and discusses under what conditions turnout can be equal. The potential of contextual-level variables to make participation more equal or more unequal is illustrated by analyzing two relevant institutions that shape turnout inequality: compulsory voting and electoral registration.

Chapters 3 and 4 test predictions that follow from the argument that less educated citizens are particularly sensitive to changes in contextual characteristics that affect the cognitive costs of voting. These two chapters combine evidence from cross-national surveys and survey experiments, to show that the use of more difficult voting procedures, a high prevalence of coalition governments, and the presence of market-oriented media systems mainly reduce the participation rates of less educated people, while these factors do not have an impact on the turnout rates of highly educated people. These heterogeneous effects on the voter turnout rates of different education groups produce variations in unequal participation.

Chapter 5 makes a close examination of one classic explanation of unequal turnout, which is that strong trade unions mobilize the poor to vote and equalize participation. Although political economy models often assume that the main constituency of trade unions are the poor, I show that members of trade unions today are just as educated as or even more educated than nonmembers. Changes in the profile of members may have eroded unions' willingness to mobilize lower-status groups. The relationship between union density and turnout inequality across countries is, in fact, weak. At the micro level, trade unions mobilize both highly and poorly educated members to a similar degree. Hence, even if unions increase voter turnout, their impact on turnout inequality is very limited. In Chapter 5, I also discuss contemporary mobilization accounts of unequal participation that focus on the role of parties.

Chapter 6 departs from the general theoretical framework outlined in this book and turns to the question of whether income inequality is associated with inequality in voter participation. In recent decades, income inequality has risen in many countries, which has spurred worries about the consequences of this trend for democracy. Some authors claim that income inequality causes the poor to disengage from the political process, threatening the emergence of a vicious circle in which political and income inequalities reinforce each other. Other authors argue that turnout inequality is one of the reasons why income inequality has increased: When the poor don't vote, policies become increasingly biased toward the rich. Although I do not address the difficult issue of the direction of causality, Chapter 6 provides the first detailed description of the empirical association between income and turnout inequality and delivers some surprising findings. Gross income inequality before taxes and transfers is associated with turnout inequality, but net income inequality after taxes and transfers is not. This pattern is at odds with existing theories about the consequences of income inequality for participation and democracy and deserves further attention.

Chapter 7 moves from examining the determinants of unequal participation to assessing its consequences for democratic politics. Some researchers have claimed that unequal participation is empirically inconsequential, because voters and nonvoters have similar preferences about relevant political issues and support the same political parties. This chapter reviews the literature on the consequences of unequal participation for representation and adds new cross-national evidence. Differences in the political opinions of voters and nonvoters are nonexistent where participation is equal, but there are substantial gaps in opinion preferences in contexts where participation is unequal. This finding supports the claim that unequal participation can indeed have detrimental consequences for representation and the democratic process.

The concluding chapter discusses the contributions of this book, its implications and limitations, and further avenues of research.

Unequal Participation Around the World

Applying the principle of "one person, one vote" in elections was a historical step toward achieving more political equality. In spite of the existence of universal suffrage and the equal value of each vote, however, not every citizen actually uses the right to vote. This book studies unequal voter turnout, the systematic difference in the electoral participation of socially advantaged and disadvantaged groups.

Inequality in voter turnout does not automatically follow from just any difference in the characteristics of voters and nonvoters. For example, the fact that citizens who do not have clear-cut political preferences vote less frequently than citizens who have strong political beliefs does not necessarily generate unequal participation. Voting is, in most countries, a voluntary activity, and some people will freely choose not to vote. As long as voting is voluntary, a person who does not want to vote has the right not to do so. Individual decisions to abstain from participation in elections do not, themselves, constitute a source of inequality. Still, scholars worry about the consequences of lower-status persons, *as a group*, voting less frequently than higher-status persons. This is because the presence of systematic differences may result in a government's being unequally responsive to the interests and opinions of different groups, and may thus bias the representative process in favor of the privileged. Voter turnout is unequal only if the relevant social and political characteristics of voters and nonvoters differ (Verba, Schlozman, and Brady 1995).

While there are multiple sources of social disadvantage, this book focuses specifically on inequalities in participation related to education. There are theoretical and practical reasons to narrow the focus of this research from the wider concept of "unequal participation" to the more particular notion of "unequal participation due to education." Education is a particularly important individual characteristic for several reasons. First, the sheer strength of the impact of education on participation is unrivalled by other socioeconomic status (SES) variables. In the United States, education correlates strongly with virtually any individual level of political attitude and behavior. As Converse famously and succinctly noted, education is the "universal solvent" (1972: 324). A recent cross-national analysis found that in most countries, education outperformed other socioeconomic and demographic characteristics as a predictor of voter participation (Nevitte et al. 2009). Second, in most cases, education comes before occupation and income and influences the acquisition of both. People enter into different social positions based to a large degree on their educational attainment (Nie, Junn, and Stehlik-Barry 1996). Educational attainment affects employment and earning possibilities, as well as other nonmaterial manifestations of social status. While income fluctuates over the course of a lifetime, educational attainment is generally stable after full adulthood. Finally, on a more practical level, surveys always collect information on respondents' education levels, and such questions have high response rates. By contrast, low response rates to income and occupation questions generate data quality problems.

Previous Research on Education and Voting

Previous cross-national analyses have arrived at contradictory conclusions about the degree of inequality in turnout across democracies, and they have devoted little attention to questions of measurement.

One group of studies suggests that inequality in voter participation is an "American exceptionality." According to the Civic
Culture Study, in the mid-twentieth century only in the United
States was education a significant predictor of electoral participation (Nie, Powell, and Prewitt 1969; Burstein 1972). In
their study of participatory inequality in India, Japan, Nigeria,
Yugoslavia, the United States, the Netherlands, and Austria,
Verba, Kim, and Nie (1978: 120) reported that SES only had
a strong influence on voting in the United States and, to a lesser
extent, Yugoslavia. By contrast, the authors found no correlation
at all between SES and electoral participation in Austria, India,
and Japan. In a comparative nine-country study, Powell (1986)
found that education correlated with the probability of voting
only in the United States and, to a lesser extent, Switzerland. A
summary of cross-national and longitudinal differences in voter
turnout in sixteen European countries concluded that "in Western Europe, then, there is no significant correlation between educational attainment and electoral turnout" (Topf 1995: 48) and
another more recent comparison of European countries reached
a similar conclusion (Teorell, Sum, and Tobiasen 2007: 404–
409).[1] Hence, an important number of prior studies suggest that
turnout inequality is, or used to be, rare outside the United States.

Other research has noted that the correlation between education and participation varies widely across countries. This
variation is a matter of degree, rather than a sharp contrast
between the United States and other nations. For example, education affected nonvoting in nineteen of the thirty-three elections
examined by Neil Nevitte and colleagues (2009: 98) but had no
effect in the other fourteen. Wattenberg (2002) reports that the
bivariate correlation between education and voting is strongest

---

[1] One-country studies have also stressed null findings. For example, Parry,
Moyser, and Day reported that in Britain, "voting defies the general rule about
participation. In this instance, the least educated are more active" (1992: 76).
In a comparative analysis of presidential elections in the United States and
France, Pierce (1995: 119–121) found that one of the most striking differences
between the two countries was the inability of the socioeconomic model to
explain voting in France.

in the United States but is also substantial in other countries, such as Switzerland and the Netherlands, whereas it is nonexistent in Spain. Norris (2000) found that education was significantly associated with voter turnout in only nine of eighteen countries. Similar mixed findings have been reported by other authors (Anduiza 1999).

Finally, many scholars believe that education predicts voter turnout everywhere. For example, one textbook cites American studies as evidence of a general cross-national pattern (Clark, Golder, and Golder 2009: 707). Two recent comparative studies have asserted that "education has proven to be positively and significantly related to voter turnout in virtually every study of voter participation" (Chong and Olivera 2008: 394) and that: "Universally, wealthier and more educated citizens vote at higher rates than those of lower socioeconomic status" (Fowler 2011: 2). Even Wikipedia (as of July 2011) states in its non-geographically circumscribed entry on voter turnout: "The most important socioeconomic factor in voter turnout is education. The more educated a person is, the more likely he or she is to vote." These examples suggest that the notion that the well-educated always vote more frequently than the poorly educated is widespread.

Why have previous studies arrived at different conclusions about the impact of education on voting behavior? Three reasons may be offered to help reconcile the divergent views.

For one, the idea that education is universally associated with voter participation probably stems from the combination of two factors: Every political scientist knows that education and voting are correlated in the United States, and American perspectives are dominant in the field of political science, even if the American case is exceptional in many respects. In the absence of well-known, disconfirming studies, scholars assume by default that the rest of the world looks alike.

Second, the effects of socioeconomic variables on voter turnout may have grown larger over time in some countries, such that older studies find smaller gaps than more recent studies. Research on the determinants of turnout decline has found that participation is declining among younger generations and particularly among less-educated young citizens in the United States (Miller and Shanks 1996; Lyons and Alexander 2000: 1027; Wattenberg 2002: 69–79), Canada (Blais et al. 2004), Sweden, Norway, and Germany (Gallego 2008). More indirectly, other scholars have advanced reasons for the growth of educational biases. Putnam has concluded that "waning participation in elections, political parties, unions, and churches seems to be virtually universal. These common patterns are especially important because [. . .] these forms of social capital were especially important for empowering the less educated, less affluent portions of the population" (2002: 410). The predicted consequence is that certain vulnerable sectors of the population may increasingly fail to participate in elections. Dalton and Wattenberg predict that weaker ties between parties and citizens will lead to larger biases: "when parties make fewer and fewer efforts to mobilize citizens, they worsen inequality in participation" (2000: 284).

The third reason why previous research has come to different conclusions than contemporary research is that empirical works that examine the relationship between education and voting use different methods. Hence, their findings may not be comparable. Some analyses present differences in means or bivariate correlations. For example, Verba, Kim, and Nie (1978) compared inequality in participation by estimating the correlation between socioeconomic characteristics and political participation across countries. Other analyses report multivariate coefficients that control for a full array of sociodemographic and attitudinal factors. Powell (1986), for instance, controlled for political interest, party identification, and political efficacy. If political attitudes mediate the effects of socioeconomic variables on voter turnout, this multivariate approach will underestimate the relationship between the two. A different reason is that the inclusion of some omitted contextual variables may qualify the conclusions of previous research. For example, Arendt Lijphart (1997) reinterpreted the null results obtained by Richard Topf, arguing that once controls for compulsory voting were introduced, it became apparent that educational gaps also existed in

Europe. These different methodological choices are one plausible underlying reason for the disparity in the results.

Education Models and Measurement of Unequal Participation

There are two main theoretical perspectives that explain whether and why education is associated with the decision to vote in elections. The "absolute education model" is by far the dominant conceptualization in the literature (Emler and Fraser 1999: 259–260). It claims that education provides resources and values that facilitate and motivate participation (Verba, Schlozman, and Brady 1995; Rosenstone and Hansen 1993). Additional gains in education are thought to be associated with having more resources and more positive political attitudes, which make it easier and more rewarding to deal with politics. People develop the ability to gather and manipulate information efficiently through formal schooling. The highly educated learn more from the information they receive (Fiske, Lau, and Smith 1990; Tichenor, Donohue, and Olien 1970), and political knowledge is associated with higher levels of voting (Popkin and Dimock 1999; Milner 2002; Lassen 2005). Gains in education also increase the motivation to go to the polls. This is because schooling fosters a number of sentiments and attitudes that make people feel involved and willing to participate in politics, such as civic duty, interest in politics, and support for democratic institutions (Wolfinger and Rosenstone 1980; Nie, Junn, and Stehlik-Barry 1996; Delli Carpini and Keeter 1996; Campbell 2006; Blais and Achen 2010). Some experimental research confirms that one of the mechanisms that mediates the effects of education on voting is increased political interest (Sondheimer and Green 2010: 186).

The alternative view is the "relative education model," which claims that education sorts people into central or peripheral places in relevant networks. The more educational attainment a person has relative to others, the more central is her position in society, and the more likely she is to be mobilized to participate politically (Nie, Junn, and Stehlik-Barry 1996, see

Persson 2011 for an analysis of the Swedish case). Mobilization occurs in concentric circles, beginning at the center and expanding to the periphery. People in central network positions are more likely to have friends and coworkers who are active and who encourage participation. Because the schooling effect is relative to the attainment of others, rises in the average educational level deflate the value of education. The important factor, then, is how much education a person has compared to others.

The debate between the absolute and the relative conceptions has implications for the measurement of unequal participation. Advocates of the relative education model have proposed an alternative way to measure educational attainment, which explicitly takes into account the attainment of others. Rather than measuring education by the level attained, the relative measure estimates for each person if her level of education is higher or lower than comparable others. In the appendix to Chapter 1, I explain in more detail the operationalization of relative education models. The drawback of this proposal is that results from the relative operationalization are much more complicated to interpret. Nevertheless, if a relative measure has a stronger association with voting than an absolute measure, a case exists for using it. In my estimation, relative education models are not much more predictive of participation and they make the interpretation of the results obscure. Moreover, data on total years of education completed are not available in all CSES studies.[2] Adjudicating between the models theoretically and empirically is beyond the scope of this work, but this book takes the view that the absolute education model is dominant for a reason. Even critiques of the conventional approach concede the merits of the absolute conception in the case of voting. Because voting is an activity in which large parts of the population can take part, the mobilization efforts targeted at the center of networks, which are essential in the relative model, should not be as consequential for voting as for other forms of participation (Nie, Junn, and Stehlik-Barry

---

[2] The exploration in the appendix uses the European Social Survey.

1996: 75–76).[3] Because of both ease of interpretability and the-oretical considerations, this book builds on the conventional approach and uses absolute measures of education.

There is also intense debate on whether the correlation between education and voting is causal or spurious. Some authors argue that education is only a proxy for other unobserved char-acteristics, such as intelligence, which cause both political par-ticipation and the decision to continue one's education. Using natural experiments, such as the Vietnam War draft, matching, and controlled comparisons, some scholars have concluded that the relationship between education and voting may not be causal (Berinsky and Lenz 2011; Kam and Palmer 2008; Tenn 2007). However, other scholars have reached the opposite conclusion – that the education effect is, in fact, causal – using equally sophis-ticated and sensible research designs that include instrumental variables, alternative matching strategies, or educational exper-iments (Dee 2004; Sondheimer and Green 2010; Milligan et al. 2004; Henderson and Chatfield 2011; Mayer 2011). About half of studies on this topic have used the Political Socialization Panel Study, which tracks just one generation of Americans who were in high school in the 1960s over several decades. By contrast, we know very little about the causal status of the education–voting correlation in other contexts. The evidence thus far is split between findings that confirm or deny that the effect of education on voter participation is causal.

Important as this question is, the idea that the effect of edu-cation on voting is not causal does not undermine the polit-ical relevance of the correlation between education and voter turnout. Suppose that the elusive omitted variable that influ-ences both educational attainment and political participation is intelligence. Can the case be made that individual differences in intelligence are one legitimate reason why some citizens should have more political influence than others in the selection of the

[3] By contrast, the relative model may be better suited to explain participation in other political activities, such as signing petitions, participating in rallies, and the like.

representatives of all? Arguments along the lines that only the literate and knowledgeable are enlightened enough to know what is good for society have been used to exclude women, working-class men, and ethnic minorities from the electorate, but they are hardly defensible today. Moreover, to continue with this example, unequal participation due to intelligence is likely to produce biased representation as well. Intelligence improves the prospects of achieving a high social status and, therefore, the interests and preferences of people with high and low levels of intelligence are likely to differ: Bright people may prefer lower levels of unemployment insurance, for instance, if they anticipate that their probability of being unemployed is low. However, winning the genetics lottery is hardly a legitimate reason for a group to have a disproportionate influence on the selection of policies, with different implications for the rich and the poor. The possibility that education may be a proxy for intelligence or other underlying individual traits does not modify the substantive politically importance of the education–voting correlation.

A very important question when measuring turnout inequality is which variables confound the analysis of the extent to which education and voting are associated. Consider age, one of the most important predictors of voter participation across countries (Franklin 2004; Nevitte et al. 2009). The relationship between age and turnout is curvilinear: Young people are less likely to vote and voter turnout rates increase with age, up to a point. At older ages, people become less likely to vote, because their health worsens and they lose their social ties. Age, at the same time, correlates with education. Due to the continued expansion of enrollment in higher education, younger generations are, on average, more educated than previous generations. Figure 1–1 shows that age correlates positively with education and negatively with voter turnout in the CSES dataset.

Shall we control for age if we want to measure the association between education and voting behavior? Using Angrist and Pischke's (2008: 64–68) terminology, age is a clear instance of "good control," because it temporally and causally precedes education. Omitting age leads to underestimation of the relationship

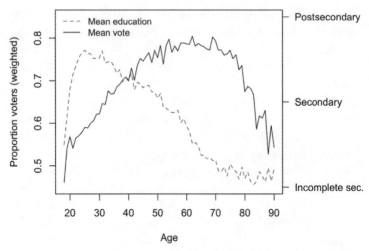

FIGURE 1–1. Reported voter turnout and average education level by age. *Source*: CSES. The left y-axis plots the proportion of respondents who report voting in the last election at each age group. The right y-axis plots the mean level of education of respondents at each age group. Education is a continuous measure which has five values: primary or less, incomplete secondary, complete secondary, postsecondary, or university education. The values are the means of this variable by age group.

between education and voting. If both the positive relationship between education and voting and the negative relationship between age and voting are strong, failing to control for age leads to the conclusion that education is uncorrelated with voter participation. Scholars can reach this misleading conclusion even if a relationship actually exists within each age group. Sex is less important as a predictor of participation, but a similar line of reasoning suggests that it is necessary to control for sex if we want to provide a summary measure of the association between education and voting.

On the contrary, we should not control for attitudinal variables when creating a measure of turnout inequality that estimates the relationship between education and voting in elections. The education–voting association presumably operates through attitudinal pathways: Education is positively associated with political interest, the belief that voting is a civic duty, political efficacy, and so on (e.g., Nie, Junn, and Stehlik-Barry 1996; Verba, Schlozman, and Brady 1995). These attitudes are mediators, not omitted variables, because they are at least partially affected by education. The inclusion of intermediary variables (if they are positively associated with the independent and the dependent variable) in analysis underestimates the correlation of education and voting. Thus, political attitudes are an instance of "bad control."[4]

Voter Turnout by Education Around the World

The main dataset used in this book contains the pooled three waves of the CSES.[5] Because of its global scope and the effort made to ensure the comparability of the variables, the CSES is one of the highest-quality academic surveys available for comparative electoral research. I excluded elections that are not fully democratic (defined as partial democracies, with a rating of three or less by Freedom House) from the database. The motives and incentives for voting or abstaining in partial democracies and in fully democratic countries differ, and generalizations that apply to democracies may not apply to other regimes. For instance, Blaydes (2011) reports that in Egypt, the illiterate are more than twice as likely to vote as the rich, because it is "cheaper" to buy their votes. The theory presented in this book applies to

---

[4] An additional note relevant to measurement is that inequality in voter participation is a characteristic of contexts, not of people. While decisions to participate in political activities are made by individuals, inequality is an aggregate phenomenon. Turnout can be very unequal in a country, city, region, or any entity that holds elections. On the contrary, the concept of unequal turnout cannot be applied to a single person. At the individual level, demographic and socioeconomic characteristics influence the decision to vote. It is when we pool individuals that we become capable of determining the extent to which socioeconomic characteristics are related to the decision to vote and whether or not inequality in participation exists.

[5] The CSES data are available for download at http://www.cses.org/.

free democracies in which instances of vote buying, if not completely absent, should at least be relatively infrequent and voters
do not receive direct compensation for their votes. The pooled
dataset contains data for 141,408 respondents who were inter-
viewed after 85 different elections held between 1996 and 2009
in thirty-six countries or, to be more precise, in thirty-five countries and in Taiwan.

Figure 1–2 describes the stylized relationship between voter
turnout and education. The graph displays the mean reported
turnout rates in each country, split by both education level and
age (distinguishing between people aged thirty-nine or younger
and people aged forty or older).[6] In the interest of space, it is useful to summarize information and collapse all surveys gathered
in the same country.

Education is coded into five categories. In many countries, at
least one of the original categories asked by the CSES is empty
or has very few cases, which motivated the recodification. The
lowest category, to which 22 percent of respondents belong, consists of respondents with a primary education or less. Another
20 percent have some secondary education but not a secondary
degree. Twenty-four percent of respondents have completed secondary education. Nineteen percent have attended postsecondary
vocational or university education but have no university degree.
Finally, 16 percent of respondents have a university degree. I use
this coding throughout the analysis. In the majority of countries
in which education is associated with voting, the relationship
is monotonic and increases approximately linearly. This pattern
allows us to make the simplifying assumption of linearity in multivariate analysis.

Actual voter turnout is 70 percent on average across elections
but, as is usual in election surveys, reported voter turnout is
considerably higher. I use weighting procedures in all analyses to
correct for overreporting.

---

[6] When data for more than one election were available for one country, the
individual datasets were merged. Throughout this book, the unit of analysis
will be election, not country.

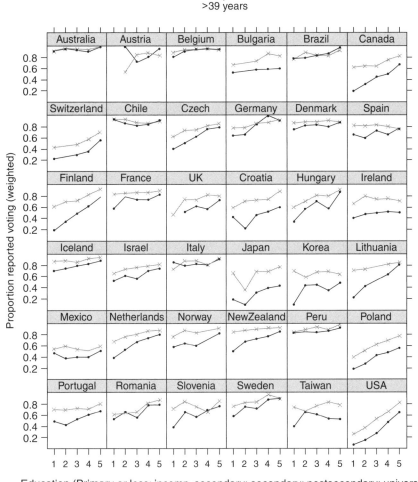

Education (Primary or less; incomp. secondary; secondary; postsecondary; university)

FIGURE 1–2. Reported voter turnout by education level in thirty-six countries. *Source*: CSES cumulative dataset. Entries are weighted mean reported voter turnout estimated for each education level.

This graph makes clear that, contrary to some characterizations, there is no United States–versus-the-rest dichotomy. Turnout is not unequal everywhere, either. Instead, there is wide variation across countries in the gradient of the education effect. For example, the relationship between education and voter turnout looks strikingly similar in Poland and the United States. The bivariate relationship between education and electoral participation is also large in Canada, Finland, Hungary, or Switzerland. This description also suggests that there exists no relationship whatsoever between education and voting in Peru, Chile, Spain, or Australia. In most countries, the highly educated vote at higher rates than the less educated, but the overall differences in the turnout rates of the education groups are moderate in size.

Furthermore, in a number of countries, including Canada, the Czech Republic, Finland, France, Korea, Lithuania, and Slovenia, the turnout gap between the highly and less educated is larger for young people than for older people. Voter turnout is frequently more unequal among younger generations.

After inspecting the actual data, the next question is how to create a summary measure of turnout inequality. One approach is quite simply to estimate the relationship between education and voter participation, controlling for age and sex, in a regression framework. Because the dependent variable can take on only two values (1 for voting or 0 for nonvoting), logistic regression is used.[7] The probability of voting (P) is modeled as:[8]

$$\ln \left(\frac{P}{1 - P} \right) = \alpha + \beta Education + \gamma Age + \delta Agesquared + \theta Sex$$

The β coefficient takes on a different value in each election survey. If education is not associated with the probability of voting, the value of the coefficient is close to 0, and participation is very equal. The gradient of the relationship between education and

---

[7] The logit link function transforms the predicted value of the dependent variable, to prevent it from adopting impossible values (probabilities higher than 1 or smaller than 0). The regression line is S-shaped. It becomes flatter at very high or very low probabilities of voting. Later, I will present estimations using Ordinary Least Squares models.

[8] Both age and age squared are introduced to model the curvilinear relationship between age and voting.

voting is flat. In elections in which the association between education and voting is strong, this coefficient takes on a positive value.

Estimating the strength of the association between education and voter turnout (controlling for age and sex) across elections provides a way to measure turnout inequality.[9] In an extension of this approach, in multilevel models used in later chapters, the coefficient of interest will be the interaction between education at the individual level and variables measured at the level of the election or the country.

Logistic regression coefficients, however, are not directly interpretable. Transforming them into predicted probabilities or into marginal effects allows us to assess the magnitude of the changes in voting associated with increases in education. Importantly, relatively large logistic regression coefficients are compatible with substantively small differences in the predicted turnout rates of the highly and less educated if overall turnout rates are very high and close to the 100 percent ceiling of turnout.[10] This implies that when using logistic models, coefficients should not be directly interpreted. Rather, it is necessary to transform the coefficients and interpret the results in terms of predicted probabilities. For this reason, I use a graphical approach to interpret the results of multilevel models throughout the book.

Figure 1–3 describes unequal participation defined as the relationship between education and voting as estimated from logistic

[9] For a discussion of similar data situations see the special issue of *Political Analysis* on "Multilevel Modeling for Large Clusters," Volume 13 Issue 4 Autumn 2005.

[10] The same logistic regression coefficient produces larger increases in the dependent variable when the predicted probability of voting is close to 0.5, but the effects get smaller and smaller as the predicted probability of voting approaches 0 or 1. Thus, if voter turnout is very high, large logistic regression coefficients are compatible with small, predicted differences in the voting rates of different groups. For a discussion of this in cross-national studies of voter turnout see, for example, Anduiza (1999: 230) and Franklin, Van der Eijk, and Oppenhuis (1996). As these authors note, the use of regular OLS or logistic regression can lead to somewhat different conclusions on the substantive magnitudes of the effect of individual variables when turnout rates are very high.

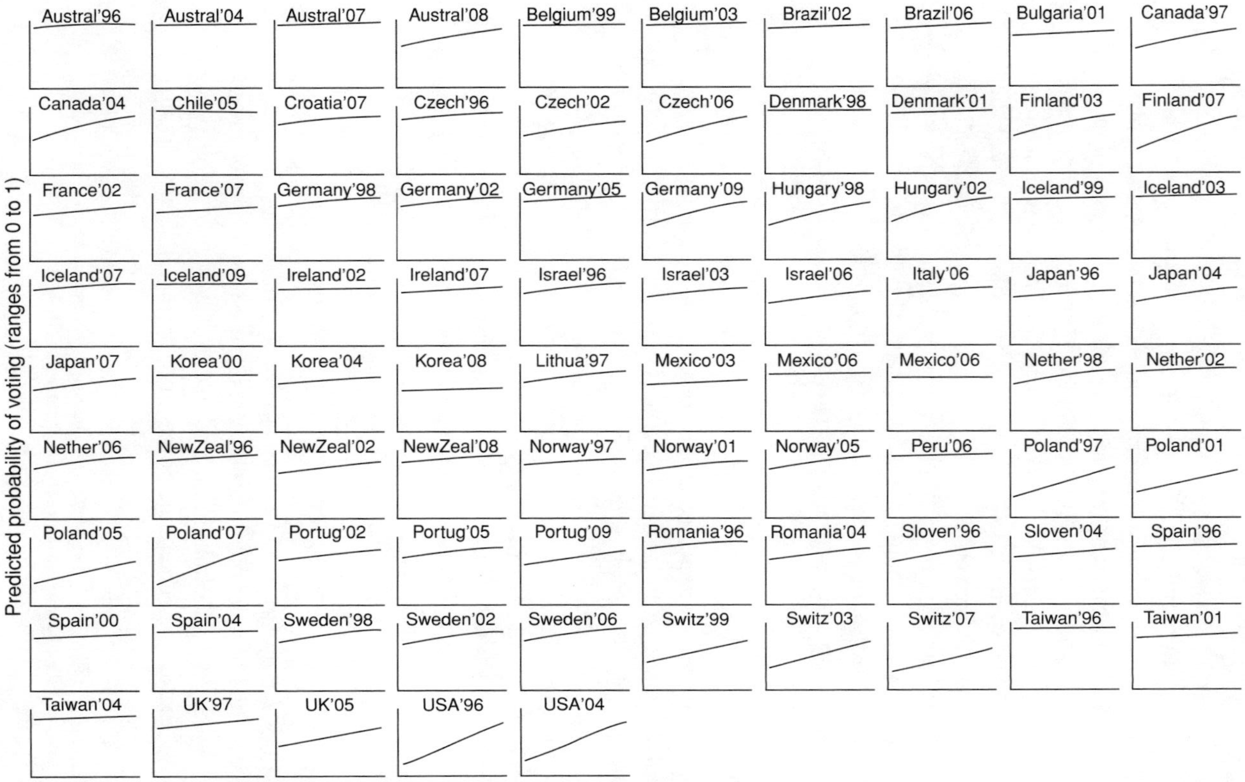

FIGURE 1-3. Predicted probability to vote by education in eighty-five elections. *Source:* CSES cumulative dataset. Predicted probability to vote by education for a forty-year-old woman. Calculated from logistic regression models including education, age, age squared, and sex as predictors. Weighted for actual turnout rates.

regression models for each of the eighty-five elections included in the dataset, controlling for age and sex. The lines are the predicted probabilities of voting plotted against education levels. Because the values of all the variables included in a model affect the probability of voting, we need to set the control variables at specific values. The predicted probabilities are calculated for forty-year-old women. Where participation is equal, the gradient of the relationship between education and voter turnout is flat. Conversely, highly unequal contexts exhibit steep gradients.

The association between education and voter participation is strongest in American elections. The predicted probabilities of voting of a forty-year-old female with primary education or less in the 1996 and 2004 election were 0.15 and 0.22, respectively. For a university degree holder (holding age and sex constant), these probabilities were 0.80 and 0.83. The estimated education gap in voter participation is thus, in both elections, over 60 percentage points.[11] Poland has also consistently very large turnout inequalities. In the four elections studied, the predicted probability of voting for a forty-year-old woman with less than primary education is between 0.25 and 0.34, whereas a similar person with university education has a much higher predicted probability to vote at 0.64 and 0.82. The estimated turnout gaps range from 35 to 58 percentage points. In Canada, Finland, Hungary, and Switzerland, the difference in the predicted turnout rates of the highly and less educated is also large at over 30 percentage points.

Conversely, the relationship between education and voting is weak to nonexistent in a rather large and varied group of countries. For example, the differences in the predicted turnout rates of people with the minimum and maximum level of education never exceed 10 percentage points in Australia, Belgium, Brazil,

---

[11] Probabilities always range from 0 to 1. Frequently, the results are converted into estimated voter turnout rates, which range from 0 to 100, for ease of interpretation.

Bulgaria, Chile, Denmark, Iceland, Korea, Peru, Spain, and Taiwan. In a few elections, the less educated even vote more frequently than the highly educated. Participation in these countries is roughly equal across education groups. In addition, the difference is never larger than 15 percentage points in Croatia, France, Ireland, Italy, and Mexico.

A third set of countries has medium-sized gaps in the estimated turnout rates due to education. The size of the gaps is not smaller than 10 percentage points and not larger than 35 percentage points across elections. These are sizeable differences, but not as large as those found in the countries with the largest inequalities in voter participation. The countries with moderate levels of inequality are Austria, Israel, Japan, Lithuania, Portugal, Romania, Slovenia, Sweden, Portugal, Romania, and the UK. Highly educated people, when controlling for age and sex, vote more frequently than the less educated in these countries, but the differences are not very large.

Finally, a set of countries is harder to classify because the size of turnout gaps varies from election to election. Reassuringly, this group of countries is small. Differences in the size of the gaps between elections can be due to idiosyncratic measurement variability, different mobilization patterns in the electorate, and specific characteristics of the election. Seeing huge discrepancies in the turnout gaps within the same country would shed some doubt on the validity of this measure of unequal turnout, but a scrutiny of this group indicates that the estimates are sensible. In the Czech Republic, the size of the estimated turnout gaps varies from a low of 12 percentage points in 1996 to a high of 41 percentage points in 2006. In the 2005 German election, there was very little difference in the reported turnout rates of the least and most educated (7 percentage points), but this gap was quite large in 2009 (40 percentage points). This pattern may reflect the demobilization of the social-democratic electorate in 2009, after the formation of the "grand coalition" government that followed the hard-fought 2005 election. Likewise, in the Netherlands, New Zealand, and Norway, there are both elections with very small turnout gaps and elections with moderate turnout gaps.

A similar approach to measuring turnout inequality involves calculating the gaps in the predicted turnout rates of people with the minimum and maximum levels of education using ordinary least squares models (OLS), as Jusko proposes (2011). In this approach, the linear regression models have the same specification as previously discussed. For convenience of interpretation, however, the education variable is recoded to range from 0, which is the minimum level of education, to 1, which is the maximum level. After estimating the models, the regression coefficients and standard errors of education are stored and they, by themselves, constitute a summary measure of unequal participation. The substantive interpretation of OLS coefficients is straightforward: They are the expected difference in the predicted proportion of voters among people with the highest and the lowest level of education. A point estimate of 0.2, for example, suggests that people with a university education vote at rates that are 20 percent points higher than citizens who have a primary education or less, on average. The estimated turnout gap is 20 percentage points.

Figure 1–4 displays the point estimates and confidence intervals of these alternative calculations for all elections.

The OLS approach provides a summary measure of turnout inequality that can be easily displayed graphically. This is a useful property because it allows us to plot the estimated size of turnout gaps against (continuous) contextual variables. As can be seen in Figure 1–4, the rank ordering of the elections from those in which turnout is equal to those in which it is more unequal closely resembles previous results.

Implications of Variability in Unequal Participation

This chapter has documented that there is large variation in the extent to which participation is unequal across elections. Turnout is very unequal in the United States, Poland, and Finland, where

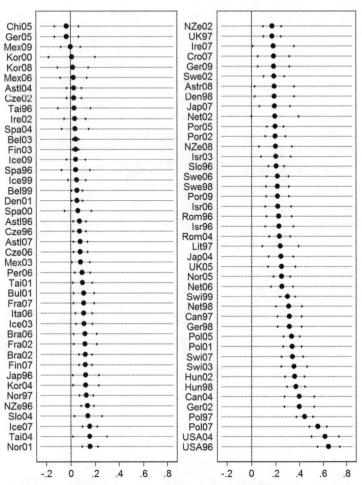

FIGURE 1–4. OLS estimates of turnout inequality in eighty-five elections. *Source*: CSES cumulative dataset. Entries are OLS coefficients of regression of voter turnout on education and confidence intervals. Age, age squared, and sex are included as controls, the data are weighted. The coefficients can be interpreted as the differences in the expected proportions of highly (university degree) and less educated (primary education or less) people voting, conditional on the values of the covariates. For example, a proportion of 0.4 means that the expected voter turnout rate of people who have a university degree is 40 percentage points higher than the expected turnout rate of people who have a primary education or less.

the less educated turn out to vote in elections at rates that are 60 percentage points lower than those of citizens with university degrees. Inequality in voting, on the contrary, is totally absent in other contexts, including in such heterogeneous countries as Chile, Denmark, South Korea, and Spain. The less educated vote just as frequently in elections as the highly educated, even in many countries that do not have compulsory voting. Many other cases fall in between, and the correlation of education and voting is visible but modest.

The fact that variation exists has relevant implications. If unequal participation were universal, we would perhaps conclude that it stems from in-built features of human nature and democratic political life, which are difficult to redress. The electoral systems, cultures, economic situations, and institutions of the countries included in this study are very diverse. The finding that no large degree of variation existed across contexts would hint that unequal turnout is something inherent to democratic societies. There would be less hope of redressing unequal participation. Even strong proponents of political equality would have to concede that some degree of inequality in participation is unavoidable. In a discussion on whether or not political equality is achievable, Dahl has noted that "a moral obligation would become irrelevant to human action if it obliged us to perform actions and behavior so far removed of our human nature [. . .] as to render the obligation completely out of reach of human attainment" (2008: 31). If achieving equal participation were impossible, there would be less reason to look for causes and remedies in the political, institutional, and economic environments in which people live.

Unequal participation is *not* universal. The fact that participation is equal in some places is the best possible proof that equal participation is within democracies' reach. For people concerned with political equality, this is good news. Accepting the normative claim that power should be spread as equally as possible among the members of a polity, this finding implies that there is room for improvement in societies that have large turnout inequalities. It becomes more important to understand what produces variation in unequal turnout. This is because knowledge about which features of political systems or elections are associated with large or small levels of unequal participation can guide steps directed toward coming closer to an attainable, as opposed to chimeric, political goal.

2

Heterogeneous Consequences of Contexts on Participation

While an extensive literature documents the link between socioeconomic status and voting, scant work has attempted to explain variation in the strength of this link. Three theories stand out, which offer insights but also present shortcomings.

First, the mechanical explanation of unequal voter turnout proposed by Arendt Lijphart in an address to the members of the American Political Science Association claims that the lower the turnout, the larger the inequality: "low voter turnout means unequal and socioeconomically biased turnout" (1997: 2).[1] He based this view on Tingsten's "law of dispersion" (1937: 230), which holds that the lower voter participation is, the larger the chances of dispersion are in the turnout rates of different groups. It is unclear, however, why every factor that increases voter turnout should also make participation equal. For example, engaged citizens, who are typically highly educated, use postal and early voting procedures more frequently than disengaged citizens. Introduction of these voting methods may simultaneously increase turnout and make it more unequal. This automatic, mechanical framework does not consider whether contextual

---

[1] For similar views see Rosenstone and Hansen 1993: 238–244; Franklin, van der Eijk, and Oppenhuis 1996: 316–319; Teorell, Sum, and Tobiasen 2007.

characteristics mobilize or demobilize educational groups in heterogeneous ways.[2]

The second theory claims that the degree of turnout inequality depends on the strength of organizations that mobilize lower-status groups such as left-wing parties and trade unions (Alford 1963: 302; Verba and Nie 1972: 340–341; Rosenstone and Hansen 1993; Verba, Kim, and Nie 1978) or on party incentives to mobilize lower-status groups (Jusko 2011). Of course, this explanation is compelling, and Chapter 5 discusses it at length. The main shortcoming of this theory is that little comparative research has assessed whether variation in the strength of specific organizations is associated with unequal participation cross-nationally.

The third theory names the burdensome registration procedure as the culprit behind the large turnout gaps in the United States (Kim, Petrocik, and Enokson 1975; Campbell et al. 1960, Chapter 11; Rose 1978; Wolfinger and Rosenstone 1980; Powell 1986; Piven and Cloward 1988). This explanation is unsatisfactory from a comparative perspective because this onerous registration procedure is an American exceptionality. We also need to understand the extensive variation in unequal participation across other countries in the world that do not have a voluntary and costly registration system.

This chapter briefly discusses why people vote, and then turns to an analysis of the conditions under which the gap in participation rates of highly and less educated people should emerge or disappear. I build on each of these previous explanations to present a more comprehensive framework to understanding unequal turnout. My central claim is that the most promising prospect to address this question is to identify contextual characteristics that affect the voting behavior of less and highly

---

[2] For example, Lijphart assumes that a number of institutional arrangements, such as concurrent elections, weekend voting, or proportional representation, will equalize participation because they raise voter turnout. However, the overall impact of such institutions on voter turnout is very small, and, without a clear understanding of who benefits the most from these institutions, we should be skeptical about their capacity to equalize participation.

educated people in heterogeneous ways. Next, I discuss what such characteristics may be.

Why Citizens Vote

The vast majority of voter turnout studies take Anthony Downs's economic model (1957) as their starting point (e.g., Aldrich 1997; Blais 2000; Franklin 2004; Gerber, Green, and Larimer 2008; Abrams, Iversen, and Soskice 2010). The economic model claims that a person will vote if the probability of her vote being pivotal in affecting the election result (P) times the difference in the utility she extracts from having her preferred party in power instead of having another party in power (B) exceeds the costs of voting (C).

This approach offers a useful analytical distinction between the costs and the instrumental benefits of voting, but the P-term is its Achilles' heel. On average, an individual voter in the United States has a 1 in 60 million probability of casting a decisive vote in the presidential election (Gelman, Silver, and Eldlin 2009). Though this probability is larger in other contexts, it remains negligible in all but exceptional circumstances. A systematic review of voter turnout studies concludes that the P-term has scant explanatory power (Mueller 2003). The most prominent piece of evidence in support of the claim that voters weigh their instrumental reasons against the probability of being pivotal is that turnout tends to be higher in competitive elections (Grofman 1993). However, competitiveness increases voter turnout by only a few percentage points (Blais 2006), and the positive correlation is partly due to the fact that political parties intensify their mobilization efforts in close elections (Cox and Munger 1989).[3]

---

[3] Extensive work that clearly adopts a social–psychological model perspective such as Gerber, Green, and Larimer (2008), starts from the basic model and adds a D-term for civic duty to vote. The consequence of keeping the P-term, instead of dropping it entirely, is of course that scholars need to claim that B does not affect the decision to vote *at all*. This amounts to stating that citizens who are indifferent between two parties should vote at the exact same rate as citizens who strongly prefer their party to win.

The main alternative approach to understanding why people vote is the more psychologically realistic social–psychological model model of political participation. I take this approach as the starting point for this examination of why voter turnout varies across countries and across types of citizens.[4]

A simple social–psychological model model of voter participation claims that people's decision to vote is a function of their motivation to vote, their ability to vote, and the difficulty of voting (Krosnick, Visser, and Harder 2011):

$$\text{Likelihood of voting} = f(\text{Motivation to vote, Ability to vote,}$$
$$1 - \text{Difficulty of voting})$$

After decades of research, we understand the *motivations* that encourage people to vote relatively well. Scholars have proposed dozens of predictors of voting (Teixeira 1992; Plutzer 2002; Fowler, Baker, and Dawes 2008), yet there are perhaps just two main proximate causes of voter turnout: the strength of one's preference for a party or candidate and the sense that voting is a civic duty (Blais and Achen 2010). Summarizing the empirical turnout literature, Blais and Achen report that those who care about the outcome of an election vote at rates more than 40 percentage points higher than those who care little or not at all. The belief that voting is a civic duty is an equally formidable predictor of voter participation, with most voters reporting that it is the single most important reason why they vote (Blais 2000, see also Campbell 2006). Either of these two motivations is sufficient for many people to go to the polls. A basic individual-level

---

[4] I assume that citizens are Humans, not Econs (for recent reviews see, for example, Anderson 2009; Thaler and Sunstein 2009; Marcus 2009; Kahneman 2011). Humans have a limited pool of mental resources, make most choices intuitively instead of computationally, learn the rules of logic imperfectly and with effort, and are quite bad at calculating probabilities. Humans try to make rational decisions and they are sensitive to changes in costs, benefits, and incentives. Nevertheless, their decisions frequently deviate from rationality. Systematic biases can come from contextual characteristics, cues, laziness, inborn tendencies, and many other sources.

specification, which includes a term for duty, a term for preferences, and the interaction of both terms, fits the data well in the United States and Canada (Blais and Achen 2010; Blais and Labbe-St-Vincent 2011). Adding covariates to the basic specification does not reduce the size of the core coefficients. This suggests that duty and personal preferences are the two most proximate factors that motivate people to vote and that either motivation is, on its own, sufficient to make people vote.[5]

The *ability* to vote in elections refers to the amount of resources a person needs if she is to perform the tasks required for voting, such as making sense of political information, understanding and fulfilling the administrative requirements to be eligible to vote, or actually casting a ballot (Krosnick, Visser, and Harder 2011). Some citizens have a greater ability to undertake political activity than others because they have more resources, such as time, money, and civic skills (Verba, Schlozman, and Brady 1995). People who have a large amount of the necessary resources to perform a specific political activity tend to participate more in that activity. This is because resources facilitate payment for the costs of participating, whether these costs are financial, cognitive, physical, or of another sort. Different resources can pay for different costs. For instance, money is an important predictor of donations, and civic skills help with conducting cognitively difficult activities.

The last component of the basic explanatory model of participation is the *difficulty* of voting. This difficulty refers generically to all contextual costs external to the individual.[6] Again, one can conceive of different types of difficulties, each shaped by specific

---

[5] The interaction term suggests that many people who have strong preferences, but do not think that voting is a duty, still do vote; conversely, many people who think voting is a duty vote in elections even if they do not have strong preferences.

[6] One may add that the external context also influences the benefits of voting, not just the costs. I keep the classification simple here but will occasionally discuss how contextual characteristics can make voting more or less attractive for different types of individuals.

contextual factors. For instance, the specific arrangements of electoral administration can affect the physical costs of voting, such as the time it takes a voter to get to the polling station. People who have to vote in new locations or who have to travel long distances to get to the polling station are less likely to vote (Dyck and Gimpel 2005; Brady and McNulty 2011; Haspel and Knotts 2005). In another application of this idea, voter participation is lower on rainy days (Gomez, Hansford, and Krause 2007), presumably because the physical costs of getting to a polling station are greater when it rains. Contextual characteristics can also affect the information and decision costs of deciding how to place one's vote. For example, it may be easier to decide which candidate to vote for if there are only two political parties than if there are many political parties. Consistent with this idea is the finding that political information is a stronger predictor of participation in contexts in which there is a large number of political parties (Jusko and Shively 2005). Finally, the specific procedure required to vote may be very easy or cognitively difficult. For example, the instructions for voting using machines can be very easy and straightforward or they can be confusing and cognitively challenging to understand (Calvo, Escolar, and Pomares 2009).

Baseline Unequal Participation

People differ in their motivations to vote and in their ability to vote. The less educated are, in general, less motivated to vote than the highly educated. Across countries, people with a low level of education are less likely to think that voting is a civic duty (Campbell 2006; Blais 2000; Blais and Labbe-St-Vincent 2011) and are less likely to have strong political preferences (e.g., Clarke et al. 2004; Dalton 2006). Besides motivation, less educated people have a lower ability to vote than highly educated people. This is because formal education is one of the ways in which people acquire the cognitive resources, information, and civic skills that facilitate voting participation (Verba, Schlozman, and Brady 1995; Rosenstone and Hansen 1993; Wolfinger and

Rosenstone 1980; Nie, Junn, and Stehlik-Barry 1996; Hillygus 2005).[7]

Even if there are differences in motivation and ability across education groups, we can expect most people with a low level of education to hold at least some weak political preferences or some vague sense that voting is a civic duty. If voting were a fully costless activity (say, for example, there are only two very distinct options and a citizen can vote through a computer or TV set simply by pressing a button), the participation rates of highly and less educated people would perhaps differ very little. Only the small fraction of people who are truly indifferent about the options and disagree with the idea that voting is a duty would abstain from voting.

Even if, in most contexts, voting has a rather low level of difficulty it is not costless. In a baseline situation, voting requires overcoming some moderate difficulties. People have to choose from a small set of options, the polling stations are reasonably close to people's homes, and the voting procedure is user-friendly. Highly educated people with sufficient ability and motivation to vote should be insensitive to small changes in the difficulty of voting; their propensity to vote is high and they have resources to pay for increases in costs. Hence, moderate difficulties do not discourage many of the highly educated from voting, and their turnout rates can be expected to be high.

People with low levels of education have, on average, fewer resources and less motivation to pay for small increases in the moderate costs of voting. If voting is not very burdensome, a sizeable share of less educated people will vote. However, there will be some with the lowest propensity to vote who will opt

---

[7] One finding of the analysis by Blais and Achen (2010) is that education predicts voter turnout even in models that include civic duty and preferences as predictors of voting. Part of the association of education and voting, as discussed in Chapter 1, is surely mediated through basic political attitudes. However, even when differences in attitudes are controlled for, education is in the United States or Canada an independent correlate of voting. This underscores that education does not only affect the motivation to vote but also the ability to vote.

for nonvoting. This is because the moderate difficulty of voting, along with a low ability and motivation to vote, offset the value of voting for these people. As a result of this different motivation and ability to vote, in the baseline case with small to moderate voting difficulty, voter turnout for poorly and highly educated people is unequal, but not by much. For example, the difference in the turnout rates of poorly and highly educated people may amount to 15 percentage points.

The difficulty of voting is, however, not constant but varies across contexts – and one may add that the benefits of voting are also context-dependent. The general thread in the comparative literature is that participation rates are lower in contexts where voting is difficult and less rewarding. Variation in the institutional and political environment of elections has consequences for overall voter turnout (Blais 2006; Geys 2006; Jackman and Miller 1995; Franklin 2004; Powell 1986).

Besides affecting aggregate voter turnout, contextual characteristics can also influence cross-national differences in turnout inequality. To understand how unequal turnout varies across contexts, we need to think about how and why contextual characteristics may affect the participation rate of each education group separately.

Homogeneous and Heterogeneous Consequences of Contexts

It is useful to make a distinction between characteristics that influence citizens in a homogeneous way and those that influence them in a heterogeneous way (see Verba, Nie, and Kim 1978). Contextual features that have heterogeneous effects on highly and less educated individuals have a stronger potential to account for variation in unequal participation than contextual features that affect all citizens in homogeneous ways.

Some contextual characteristics affect all types of citizens equally, that is, homogeneously. For example, imagine two types of polling stations that vary in the number of electors assigned to vote in them. In type I stations, the number of electors per polling station is large. Voters have to stand in a line for five minutes

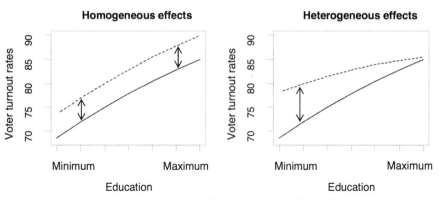

FIGURE 2–1. Homogeneous and heterogeneous effects of contextual characteristics

before voting. Some people strongly dislike queuing and upon seeing the line, they decide not to vote and leave the polling station. Type II stations have fewer eligible electors, and voters do not need to wait to cast a ballot. Highly and less educated citizens may differ in their reactions to a line but not by much. Suppose that the presence of a line in type I stations is associated with a 5 percentage points decrease in turnout rates across all education groups. This small, negative, and homogeneous effect on voter turnout would decrease overall voter participation, but it would leave inequalities in voter participation unchanged. In this example, the gaps in voter turnout rates between highly and less educated people would be identical in type I and type II polling stations, say at 15 percentage points, even if overall voter turnout would be higher by 5 percentage points in the absence of a line. The left panel of Figure 2–1 depicts the consequence of homogeneous effects like these for voter turnout and turnout inequality.

This simple example reveals the limitations of Lijphart's (1997) mechanical theory, which claims that any institution that increases turnout will also equalize participation. Most correlates of voter turnout have only small effects on turnout rates. Small or moderate increases in voter participation are entirely compatible with no change in turnout inequality. In fact, they are theoretically compatible with increases in turnout inequality.

The most promising avenue to understand variation in unequal turnout is to ask what factors may affect highly and less educated people's participation *heterogeneously*. The turnout literature has found that some citizens are more sensitive to contextual incentives or barriers to participation than others, and more generally that political attitudes and behavior depend on both individual and contextual characteristics.[8]

Any contextual feature that only mobilizes members of one educational group to vote, while not affecting members of the other, will have a strong potential to shape unequal participation. This type of feature may have a weak impact on overall turnout rates but can strongly modify turnout gaps in participation. The second panel of Figure 2–1 depicts a situation characterized by heterogeneous effects across education groups. In this example, the contextual feature mainly changes the turnout rates of people who have a low level of education.

The argument that heterogeneous effects are especially consequential for turnout inequality can guide toward formulating specific hypotheses about what may shape unequal participation. Which features may have heterogeneous consequences?

The most promising place to start is to ask which institutions or political contexts affect the information and decision costs of voting. Education provides or is associated with having more cognitive resources and skills that make it relatively easy for individuals to afford any voting costs that must be paid through mental effort. Poorly educated people should be more sensitive to increases in information or decision costs than highly educated people. Contextual features that make it more cognitively difficult to vote can be expected to have heterogeneous consequences. An increase in the cognitive costs of voting should

---

[8] For turnout studies, see, for example, Anduiza 2002; Van Egmond 2003; Norris 2004; Franklin 2004; Buhlman and Freitag 2006; Solt 2008; Soderlund, Wass, and Blais 2011; Quintelier, Hoogue, and Marien 2011. For other dependent variables, see, for example, Fisher et al. 2008; Bartle 2005; Anderson and Singer 2008; Karp and Banducci 2008; Kittilson and Schwindt-Bayer 2010; Klingeman 2009.

therefore mainly cause people with a low education level to fail to vote.

Many different contextual characteristics can shape the cognitive difficulty of voting. The empirical challenge to examining if this argument is valid lies in the fact that this difficulty cannot be directly observed or measured. Chapters 3 and 4 analyze several contextual features that arguably make voting more cognitively burdensome. They move from the general claim that increasing the cognitive costs of voting results in more unequal turnout, to making specific predictions and deriving testable hypotheses.

It is important to note, however, that the theoretical claim is more general and is not confined to the specific features that are analyzed empirically. If this argument is true, any characteristic of the election and institutional context that makes voting more cognitively burdensome should increase turnout inequality. In other work (Gallego 2008, 2010), I have examined further contextual characteristics that can modify the cognitive costs of voting and affect turnout inequality and found results consistent with the ones presented in this book.

The literature of American politics has made the argument that increases in cognitive costs produce more unequal participation. As reviewed in the introduction and developed in the next section, one of the main claims of voter turnout studies in the United States is that the existence of burdensome registration procedures affects highly and less educated people in heterogeneous ways. The explanation for this is lower-status people have a lower ability to deal with the steps required to register, such as obtaining the information on where to enroll and navigating an administrative task.

Other, noncognitive types of voting difficulties are less promising as potential driving forces behind unequal participation. Consider the amount of time it takes a prospective voter to get to the polling location. There are competing arguments on whether less educated people have more free time than highly educated people, and there are rival arguments on whether the value of time as a resource is larger for either group. It is theoretically unclear which group should care more about time costs. Presumably, having a high motivation and ability to vote can make small increases in time costs irrelevant. Other than this, however, there are no straightforward predictions on who is more sensitive to time costs.[9]

The distinction between contextual characteristics that can have homogeneous or heterogeneous consequences can also be applied to study how mobilization affects turnout inequality. In Chapter 5, I use this general framework to reflect on the conditions under which traditional lower-class organizations should mainly mobilize less educated people to vote. Mobilization theories claim that political organizations that mobilize the poor make participation more equal. Of course, this is an argument that organizations have heterogeneous effects on the voter participation of different education groups. Mobilization by political groups will only equalize participation if indeed they target and are effective at mobilizing less educated people to vote to a larger degree than they are able to mobilize highly educated people. In

---

[9] Electoral systems are one of the most important electoral institutions. Lijphart (1997) argues that introducing Proportional Representation (PR) in countries that have majoritarian systems would reduce turnout inequality because turnout is higher in PR systems. Indeed, turnout rates tend to be higher in proportional systems but only in advanced industrial democracies and only by a few percentage points (Blais and Aarts 2006). Some scholars have argued that majoritarian systems favor right-wing parties (Iversen and Soskice 2006, but see Jusko 2011). To the extent that poorly educated people are more likely to vote for left-wing parties, abstention among these voters may be stronger in majoritarian systems. However, we can also consider the reasons why highly educated people may be less likely to vote in majoritarian systems. Most importantly, voters of small parties tend to be more politically sophisticated than voters of large parties, and small parties tend not to be viable in majoritarian systems, which may discourage some educated people from voting. So, again, the predictions on whether electoral systems affect the turnout rates of different education groups in heterogeneous ways are indeterminate. In the CSES sample, the mean gaps in the turnout rates of highly and poorly educated people are 18 percentage points in elections held under PR systems, 19 percentage points in majoritarian systems, and 17 percentage points in mixed member systems. The differences are not statistically significant. Thus, it seems implausible that electoral systems per se are an important determinant of turnout inequality. Further results on electoral systems are provided in Chapter 3.

Chapter 5, I test empirically whether or not trade unions mainly mobilize citizens with a low education level to vote.

The distinction between homogeneous and heterogeneous consequences focuses attention on how and why any contextual characteristic may affect different people in heterogeneous ways. In the next chapters, considering unequal participation through the lens of the proposed framework forces us to test whether a feature does or does not have different effects on the participation of different groups.

Heterogeneous Effects by Education Level: Registration

Among contextual characteristics that may heterogeneously affect highly and less educated people, the one that has received the most attention in the literature is the registration procedure. This section reviews the registration literature because it is the most prominent application of the idea that the difficulty of voting tends to depress the participation of people with a low education level.

Having to register to vote imposes an additional cost on citizens. Educated people find it easier to understand and deal with administrative procedures. Therefore, registration is a requirement that should affect highly and less educated people in heterogeneous ways: the costs of registering should mostly prevent less educated people from being in the list of electors – and consequently from voting – because their ability and motivation for dealing with administrative procedures is, on average, lower.

Lopez-Pintor and Gratschew (2002: 25) classify voter registration systems based on four main criteria: whether registration is voluntary or compulsory, whether states or individual citizens are responsible for registering, whether the register is updated continuously, and whether there are voter-specific registers. In the United States, registration is voluntary and citizen-initiated, but the specific ways in which citizens can register vary substantially across states. In New Zealand, registration is compulsory and citizen-initiated. This compulsion seems to be enough to achieve registration rates that are as high as those in countries where the state is responsible for registration. According to official statistics, the registration rate in New Zealand is 94 percent. This figure is even higher than in countries in which the government takes an active role in registering citizens such as Germany, Australia, or Canada (Rosenberg and Chen 2009). The real straggler from a comparative perspective is the United States, where only 68 percent of the population is registered to vote. Based on this observation, scholars have long argued that one of the main reasons why voter turnout is low there and turnout inequality is large is the unique voter registration procedure (Powell 1986; Wolfinger and Rosenstone 1980).[10]

Much work has gone into attempting to estimate exactly how much a burdensome registration procedure reduces voter turnout rates, and which citizens are more sensitive to increases in registration costs. There is broad consensus that stricter registration rules correlate with lower turnout, but there is some disagreement about the magnitude of the effect. Early cross-state comparisons produced rather large estimates of the increase in voter turnout rates that would follow from eliminating early closing dates for registration, which ranged from 6 to 14 percentage points.[11] More recent work has found that reforms designed to ease the registration process did not increase turnout as substantially as proponents had hoped. For instance, Ansolabehere and Konisky (2006) use a longitudinal research design and look at the consequences of legislation change in New York and Ohio. They estimate that early registration reduces voter turnout by 3 to 5 percentage points. These findings have cooled academic optimism on the prospects of registration reform to affect both turnout and turnout inequality.

It is also well established that young people and lower-status people are more sensitive to the costs imposed by the registration

---

[10] Because of this uniqueness and the impossibility of estimating to what extent this high rate of inequalities in voter participation in the United States relative to other countries is due to registration or to other reasons, throughout the book most analyses are presented twice, once including and once excluding the United States.

[11] See, for example, Rosenstone and Wolfinger 1978; Mitchell and Wlezien 1995; Highton and Wolfinger 1998; Knack 2001; Brians and Grofman 1999, 2001.

procedure (Hershey 2009; Hanmer 2009; Rosenstone and Wolfinger 1978; Highton and Wolfinger 1998). In one of the most carefully conducted studies on this topic, Hanmer (2009) estimates that the adoption of Election Day Registration is associated with an increase of 8 percentage points in voter participation among citizens with low levels of education and income, but the increase is only 2.6 percentage points among citizens with high levels of education and income. The effects are heterogeneous, as the least educated gain the most from easier voting procedures. Similarly, the changes are larger in magnitude among young people than among older people.

The recent contributions that adopt a longitudinal strategy may, however, underestimate the true effects of registration on voter turnout. The American politics literature has not considered one important implication of the finding that young people are more sensitive to changes in registration procedures than older people. Voter turnout is path-dependent. Failing to vote in the three or four first elections in which a person is eligible to vote has durable consequences for future behavior. Voters and nonvoters are more or less fixed in their ways after their politically formative years (Franklin 2004).[12] One implication of this idea is that older people, who have taken a standing decision to vote or not to vote, barely react to institutional reform. Young people are more sensitive to reform, but it takes a long time for young generations, who learn to vote or to abstain under the new institutional setting, to replace older generations in the electorate. As a result, it may take more than forty years for a procedural change to unveil its full effects.[13] Longitudinal research designs that do not include a long time horizon will underestimate the true effects of institutional change. If this is true, the

---

[12] This realization has led scholars to talk about turnout as a habit (Aldrich et al. 2011; Plutzer 2002; Gerber, Green, and Schachar 2003; Fowler 2006).

[13] Franklin (2004) makes this point and applies it to the lowering of the voting age. In a recent paper, colleagues and I review other evidence of a time lag in the effect of institutional change on behavior, and we provide evidence that it takes time for both voters and parties to adapt to the institutional incentives provided by electoral systems (Gallego, Rico, and Anduiza 2012).

fact that there are only small increases in voter turnout after the introduction of a registration reform should not be a disappointment or deterrent for proponents of reform. Reducing barriers to registration may well have a larger positive impact on voter turnout than the more recent literature has suggested in the long run.

Ceiling Effects: Voter Turnout and Compulsory Voting

I have argued that contextual characteristics that shape the voter participation of highly and less educated people in homogeneous ways will generally not modify unequal participation. However, there is an important qualification to this claim: the one way in which contextual characteristics with homogeneous effects can reduce unequal participation is through ceiling effects (see Verba, Nie, and Kim 1978). Voter turnout rates among any group can never surpass 100 percent, and this simple fact has implications for our understanding of unequal participation.

A contextual characteristic with a strong homogeneous impact on turnout will equalize participation. In general, highly educated people tend to vote at high rates. If a contextual characteristic has a very strong effect on the voter turnout rates of all groups, highly educated people will quickly approach the 100 percent participation ceiling. Less educated people, on the other hand, can benefit from the entire upsurge. The consequence is, of course, more equal participation. The left panel of Figure 2–2 depicts this case. Relatedly, a contextual characteristic with moderate effects on voter turnout can equalize participation in contexts where the turnout rate of highly educated people is very close to the 100 percent participation ceiling. For instance, a feature that increases turnout by 7 percentage points can equalize participation in countries in which highly educated people vote at near-universal turnout rates. The right panel of Figure 2–2 displays this situation.

Compulsory voting is the only institution that, by itself, can achieve near-universal voter turnout rates. As is well-known, compulsory voting is the most forthright way to achieve equality

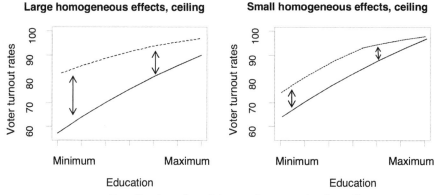

Large homogeneous effects, ceiling

Small homogeneous effects, ceiling

FIGURE 2–2. Equalization of participation because of ceiling effects

in participation by getting voter participation close to its ceiling (Lijphart 1997).

There can be little doubt that compulsory voting has a strong positive effect on participation rates.[14] Where compulsory voting is enforced, abstainers run the risk of having to pay small fines, having to justify their nonparticipation, or receiving other sanctions (Gratschew 2004). Even if no formal sanctions are enforced, social pressure to vote intensifies if voting is an obligation. Moreover, the institution of compulsory voting is often accompanied by regulations that make it easier to vote such as Sunday voting, easy registration procedures, and simple provisions for absentee voting (Jackman 2001). Through a variety of mechanisms, compulsory voting boosts turnout because it increases costs for nonvoting and decreases the costs of voting.

There is extensive evidence that compulsory voting equalizes participation. After the abolition of this institution in the Netherlands in 1970, the turnout gaps between education groups grew larger (Irwin 1974). Conversely, education gaps in voting

[14] See, for example, Blais and Dobrzynska 1998; Franklin 2001; Franklin, van der Eijk, and Oppenhuis 1996; Hirczy 1994; Jackman 1987; Jackman and Miller 1995; Powell 1980, 1988; Rose 2004; Siaroff and Merer 2002; Panagopoulous 2008; Birch 2009.

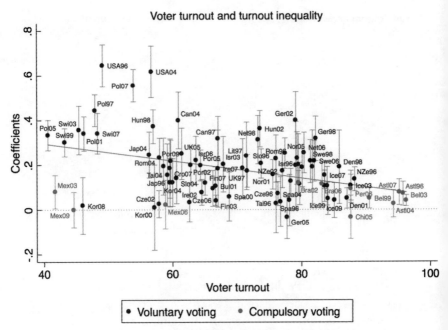

FIGURE 2–3. Voter turnout, turnout inequality, and compulsory voting. *Source*: CSES and IDEA turnout database. Some labels have been deleted. Official turnout rates are plotted against the regression coefficients of education on voting from OLS models. Age, age squared, and sex are included as controls, the data are weighted.

declined after the introduction of compulsory voting in Brazil (Power and Roberts 1995). If compulsory voting were abolished in Belgium, the socioeconomic gaps in voting would grow (Hooghe and Pelleriaux 1998). A recent comparative study with survey data from thirty-six countries, however, has found that gaps in turnout rates due to gender and education do not differ dramatically between countries with compulsory voting and those with voluntary voting (Quintelier, Hoogue, and Marien 2011).

Surprisingly, as far as I am aware, there has not been any study that examines the direct relationship between voter turnout and unequal turnout hypothesized by Lijphart. Figure 2–3 does just that. It plots official turnout rates, as collected by the

International Institute for Democracy and Electoral Assistance (IDEA) against turnout gaps, calculated as explained in Chapter 1. Elections in which voting is voluntary are colored in black and elections in which voting is compulsory are colored in gray.[15] There is a relationship between voter turnout and turnout inequality. Gaps in the participation rates of highly and less educated people are very small or nonexistent in countries in which turnout rates are near the 100 percent participation ceiling. The two countries with near-universal turnout rates are, unsurprisingly, compulsory voting countries: Belgium and Australia.

Elections in a number of countries with voluntary voting have voter turnout rates close to 90 percent. It is worth noting that high turnout is compatible both with nonexistent gaps and with moderate gaps in turnout due to education. For example, in the 2001 Danish election, 87 percent of the people voted and the difference in the estimated turnout rates of people with low and high levels of education was a mere 5 percentage points. In the 1996 New Zealand election, 88 percent of the population voted, but the estimated gap in the turnout rates of highly and less educated people was substantially larger at 14 percentage points.

At the other extreme, in a number of elections voter turnout is 55 percent or less. In most of these cases, turnout inequality is very high. In most of the low turnout cases, the difference in the turnout rates of the highly and the less educated is 30 percentage points or more. Korean and Mexican elections are, however, an exception to the pattern. Low voter turnout coexists with non-existent turnout inequality, at least as measured through self-reports in surveys.[16]

---

[15] Compulsory voting is enforced in some countries but not in others, though the distinction is blurry (Birch 2009). For a list of elections by voting system, see Appendix 1.

[16] The Mexican case is particularly intriguing because this country formally has compulsory voting, even if it is not enforced. To the extent that vote-buying and clientelism is common in Mexico, we should perhaps expect high turnout rates among lower-status groups. The puzzle in Mexico is why highly educated people report voting at the same low rates as poorly educated people. I have

The strong relationship between compulsory voting and turnout inequality confirms that this institution equalizes participation. Compulsory voting is a sufficient condition to achieve low turnout inequality. Thus, scholars who propose compulsory voting as a solution to unequal participation are no doubt correct (Lijphart 1997; Wattenberg 2006).

The fact that the presence of this institution is enough to have equal turnout in the set of countries that enforce it suggests that these cases should be dropped from the analysis. An alternative approach is to model this distinctiveness by introducing a variable for compulsory voting in multivariate analyses and another variable for the interaction between compulsory voting and education.[17]

At average levels of voter turnout, however, the relationship between voter turnout and turnout inequality is highly variable. At each level of voter turnout in this range, we can find both countries with no inequality in participation and countries with moderate or large inequality.

The correlation between voter turnout and turnout inequality (measured as the estimated gaps in the turnout rates of the highly and less educated) is −0.4 when including all elections. This is a large and statistically significant association. However, as the visual display suggests, the correlation is driven by the

searched for studies of electoral behavior in Mexico but I have not been able to find specific discussions about the topic of disparities in voter turnout rates across education groups. An exhaustive analysis of this case is beyond the scope of this study. In the empirical analyses, Mexico is coded as a compulsory voting country. Thus, this case is either modeled separately or excluded from analyses that do not include cases with compulsory voting.

[17] In Chapter 3, I show that keeping or dropping these cases does not modify the results in multivariate analyses. Analyses in later chapters exclude these cases entirely. All analyses presented in this book have been performed both including and excluding compulsory voting countries. When these countries are included, the models contain a variable in which enforced compulsory voting is coded as 1, nonenforced compulsory voting is coded as 0.5 and voluntary voting is coded as 0 (see appendix), as well as an interaction between compulsory voting and education. The model effectively captures the exceptionality of these cases. The results do not change when excluding the cases.

compulsory voting cases and by the United States, Switzerland, and Poland. After removing these countries, the correlation between voter turnout and turnout inequality is only −0.04 and not statistically significant.

In sum, as Lijphart argues, low voter turnout does mean socioeconomic biased turnout to some extent: Turnout is equal in countries with quasi-universal turnout rates, and most low-turnout countries exhibit large inequalities. However, this mechanical relationship cannot possibly tell the whole story. In the majority of elections, participation is neither very high nor very low, as turnout rates range from below 60 percent to almost 90 percent. In this very substantial set of cases, voter turnout is *entirely* unrelated to turnout inequality.

Assessing the Link Between Contextual Features and Turnout Inequality

In Chapter 1, I discussed how to measure unequal participation. In this chapter, I have argued that contextual characteristics that have heterogeneous effects on highly and poorly educated people hold the most promise in explaining turnout inequality. The next question is how to test arguments that follow from the theoretical framework. One way to assess whether a contextual characteristic has heterogeneous effects on participation is to examine if it moderates (i.e., intensifies or weakens) the association of education and voter turnout. Is the education–participation correlation smaller or larger in the presence of a contextual characteristic that affects the costs and rewards of voting? Contextual characteristics with homogeneous effects can influence the overall probability that each citizen will vote. In a multilevel model, this leads to a shift in intercepts. Characteristics with heterogeneous consequences mainly mobilize or demobilize one group – normally the one with a low education level. A change in slopes should reflect this. An interactive multilevel model with individuals at the first level and contextual characteristics at the second level can be used to test the hypothesis that a contextual characteristic modifies the association between education and voting:[18]

$$\ln\left(\frac{P}{1-P}\right) = \alpha + \beta Edu + \omega Context + \varphi Edu * Context$$
$$+ \gamma Age + \delta Agesq + \theta Sex$$

Here, the probability of an individual voting is predicted by education and other individual characteristics, by contextual characteristics, and by the interaction of education and contextual characteristics. The hypothesis that a contextual characteristic makes participation more equal is tested in multilevel models by examining whether the presence of this characteristic is associated with a change in the slope of education (coefficient φ). Finding this would support the hypothesis that effects are heterogeneous and therefore that the feature will be more likely to shape inequalities in participation. The presence of homogeneous effects should be captured by the coefficient ω, which allows the intercepts to shift when the contextual characteristic is present. Only in the presence of ceiling effects would contextual characteristics with no interactive effects result in less turnout inequality. In the analyses, all the results are transformed into predicted probabilities to assess the expected changes graphically.

---

[18] Because contextual characteristics have the same value for all respondents of the same election, we say that citizens are nested within elections. This fact violates the standard assumptions on the distribution of the error terms in regression. Regular regression models assume that the units are randomly sampled and, as a consequence of this, responses are conditionally independent given the covariates. However, people surveyed during a particular election in a country are more similar to each other because they are affected by unobserved common events. As a result, regular regression models produce incorrect standard errors. This book uses multilevel models because they relax the conditional independence assumption (e.g., Gelman and Hill 2007; Rabe-Hesketh and Skrondal 2008).

3

The Difficulty of the Voting Procedure

I have argued that less educated people are more sensitive to increases in the cognitive costs of voting because they have fewer resources to cope with them. Likewise, to the extent that highly educated people tend to be more involved in politics, they may be more responsive to increases in the benefits of voting. The procedure employed for voting in elections can affect how cognitively taxing but also how gratifying voting is. This chapter analyses whether the ballot structure, one characteristic of the voting procedure that affects the difficulty of voting and the motivation to vote, can modify turnout inequality.[1]

In some contexts, voting is very simple, but the expression of preferences is greatly constrained. Systems that allow distribution of several votes, rank-ordering preferences, or selecting candidates from a list put together by political parties within or across party lines, provide more freedom to choose than systems that do not allow these options (Pereira and Silva 2009). Voting

---

[1] It is worth noting that the aim of this chapter is not so much to test one stand-alone theory as to test one of the many possible predictions that follow from the more general theoretical framework, which states that anything that increases the cognitive costs of voting also increases turnout inequality. The particular prediction tested here is interesting because it is not obvious, and because it is readily testable. I test other predictions in the following chapters and have tested more implications in previous work (Gallego 2010).

is more difficult, if more rewarding, when voters can provide more detail about their political preferences. Poorly informed voters cannot take advantage of party identification, the most important cognitive cost-cutting device, when they have to make choices about candidates from the same party. Sophisticated people tend to know much more about politics than their partisanship. They may be frustrated about voting for a prepackaged set of candidates. They appreciate choice and they are willing to pay the price for it. The main hypothesis of this chapter is that the use of complex voting procedures increases the cognitive costs of voting and therefore reduces participation among less educated people but does not affect, or perhaps even increases, participation among the highly educated.

Can a minor feature of the electoral system such as ballot structure affect voter turnout and unequal participation? Ballot structure is an unlikely candidate predictor of turnout inequality. According to Shugart (2005), it is one of the least investigated topics of electoral systems research. While institutional factors are among the most important determinants of differences in voter turnout levels across countries (Blais 2006; Geys 2006), no studies have focused on the impact of ballot structure. Because researchers have examined electoral systems extensively, this omission suggests that ballot structure is not a very influential feature. Precisely because the effects of ballot structure are not self-evident, this is an excellent instance in which to test the theory that any feature that increases the cognitive costs of voting makes participation more unequal.

This chapter begins by reviewing why ballot structure affects the motivation to vote and the difficulty of voting, and discusses the implications of these arguments for unequal turnout. The argument's internal validity is assessed using two original survey experiments in which respondents could vote or abstain in hypothetical elections. This exercise helps to identify the effect on voter turnout of using a more difficult voting procedure and to establish causality. The cross-national analysis of the CSES data speaks to the external validity of the results.

The two strategies arrive at the same conclusion. Complex ballots decrease the electoral participation of less educated people. This group seems sensitive to even very small increases in the difficulty of voting, to which some of its members react by failing to vote. By contrast, the participation rates of highly educated citizens are unaffected. Taken together, the results provide strong evidence that the use of more difficult voting procedures intensifies turnout inequality.

Ballot Structure, Cognitive Costs, and Preference Expression

According to a standard classification, electoral systems can be distinguished along three lines of variation (Blais 1988; Lijphart 1990; Rae 1967): the electoral formula, district magnitude, and ballot structure. While the bulk of electoral systems research has concentrated on studying the consequences of the first two elements, we know much less about the effects of ballot structure on political outcomes. In representative democracies, elections necessarily involve selecting from a constrained number of choices. The specific ways in which voters select candidates, parties, or both, vary widely across the world.

Ballot structure determines how much detail citizens can convey about their political preferences when casting a vote. Scholars have criticized Rae's (1967) original classification between ordinal and categorical ballots as imprecise. A more recent proposal by Cox (1990) claims that ballot structure consists of the number of votes each voter is entitled to cast; whether voters are allowed to abstain from using some of their votes when they have more than one vote, or if they must cast them all; and whether voters can accumulate their votes. A fourth characteristic is whether voters can rank-order the candidates or parties.

In one extreme, voters may cast only one vote for one candidate in single-member districts or for a closed list of candidates predefined by parties, with no possibility of rank-ordering their preferences. This is not very burdensome in cognitive terms. If citizens know which party they support, voting in such systems is very easy. Partisanship is one of the main heuristics that help voters with low amounts of information to navigate the political landscape (Lupia, McCubbins, and Popkin 2000; Popkin 1991; Sniderman, Brody, Tetlock, and Brady 1991). Party identification is instrumental in cutting down the costs of gathering and processing political information. On the negative side, simple ballots do not allow citizens to express any further aspect of their political preferences beyond the party or candidate they support. This may be frustrating for highly motivated and knowledgeable citizens. Some analysts argue that sophisticated citizens are increasingly frustrated with electoral politics because they have limited opportunities for electoral participation (Norris 2000; Dalton 2006, 2008). Critical citizens should appreciate having more opportunities to participate.

Some voting systems allow citizens the ability to express nuanced choices. First, voters may be able to cherry pick or cross out one or more candidates from a party list in open list proportional representation systems, in the single nontransferable vote system, and in mixed member systems with open lists (Shugart 2005). They may even create their own list of candidates from different parties, as in Switzerland. Voting is more cognitively difficult when there is intraparty competition for several reasons. Party identification is useless as a cost-cutting heuristic when choosing between same-party candidates and thus a poorly informed voter can no longer rely on what was previously an important cost-cutting device. Learning about each additional candidate entails incurring some additional information costs. Moreover, candidates come and go from one election to the next to a larger extent than parties do, so information learned about candidates in one election may not be useful in the next.

Another way in which the voting procedure can be more difficult but more rewarding is that it sometimes allows voters to rank-order their preferences, as in elections conducted under the Alternative Vote or the single transferable vote system. In this way, if their most preferred party receives few votes, their second preference can still affect who is elected. This system allows citizens to vote both sincerely and strategically, revealing information about their favorite candidates and their second-best options. Voting is both about selecting candidates and about having one's preferences recognized in the public sphere (Przeworski 2003). Being able to achieve both aims should be gratifying for supporters of parties that have little prospect of obtaining

TABLE 3–1. *Number of Names of District-Level Representatives Citizens Know*

		Zero	One	Two or More	Total
Primary education	%	65	15	19	100
or less	N	5,902	1,391	1,765	9,058
Incomplete	%	48	21	32	100
secondary	N	3,983	1,724	2,651	8,358
Secondary	%	45	22	33	100
education	N	2,795	1,374	2,063	6,232
Postsecondary,	%	39	19	42	100
no univ.	N	2,133	1,055	2,303	5,490
University degree	%	31	21	48	100
	N	1,374	947	2,176	4,496

Source: CSES, first wave.

representation. At the same time, however, rank-ordering is more cognitively difficult than simply selecting one option.

A question included in nineteen countries participating in the first CSES wave allows us to assess unequal knowledge of the names of district-level representatives, and it provides some leverage to learn about what type of citizen may appreciate having more choices. Respondents were asked if they could remember the name of any candidate who ran in their electoral district in the last election. On average, 65 percent of respondents with primary education or less could not name a single candidate correctly. In sharp contrast, almost half of the respondents with a university education were able to name two or more representatives. Within most countries, there is a steep education gradient in knowledge, with the highly educated invariably able to name more candidates than the less educated.[2] Less educated people have scant knowledge about the names, let alone the characteristics, of competing candidates. Given this ignorance, it seems

---

[2] A majority of citizens could not name a candidate in Switzerland (59 percent of all respondents named no candidate), Germany (60), Spain (75), Mexico (83), Poland (65), Portugal (82), Romania (72), Taiwan (62), the United States (58), and Sweden (63). Countries in which name recognition is high are Canada (36 percent could not give a name), Czech Republic (47), Denmark (24), UK (43), Iceland (16), Japan (9), Korea (10), Norway (32), and New Zealand (20).

unlikely that they appreciate having the opportunity to express their preferences for specific candidates.

Admittedly, in many systems that use complex ballots, voters can opt out and instead vote using less burdensome alternatives. For example, voters may either vote for a party or else select specific candidates within party lists, as under flexible-list PR systems, or they may choose not to rank-order their preferences. Of course, if voters can vote using a simple procedure, the consequences of systems that grant choice for unequal turnout may be very small. Even in this case, however, we can perhaps expect a small reduction in the turnout rates of the less educated. In behavioral theories of elections (Bendor et al. 2011), people follow a trial-and-error process in which the results of previous experiences are taken into account to make future participation decisions. The fact of having the opportunity to choose or rank-order candidates when a voter lacks the information and expertise to take advantage of these options may turn out to be an uncomfortable experience. The recognition that one does not know how to answer to a question is not gratifying, even if one has the option of skipping the question. At an emotional level, poorly educated citizens may feel uneasy when confronted with a complex ballot. Referring to ballots in the United States, which ask about multiple offices and propositions, Martin Wattenberg (2002: 121) stated that voting in some contexts feels like taking an "SAT test." To be confronted with a complicated procedure, even if a simpler alternative is available, may cause some citizens to feel as if voting is an exam for which they are ill prepared. Thus, it is plausible that having even a mildly negative experience (such as the frustration of recognizing that one is not able to use a procedure that provides more choices) may tilt some voters with a low overall participation propensity to decide not to vote in future elections.

Consequences of Ballot Structure for Participation

If ballots that allow for more expression of preference increase the cognitive difficulty of voting, they should also decrease the turnout rates of the less educated. If such ballots increase the benefits of voting, they may increase the turnout rates of highly educated citizens eager for more opportunities to participate. If one or both assertions are true, more complex ballots will increase turnout inequality. Research on invalid voting and on the interaction of individual and contextual determinants of voter turnout provides supporting evidence for this claim.

Studies about the effect of ballot structure on invalid votes (blank or spoiled) show that complex ballot structures increase invalid voting among citizens with low cognitive resources.[3] The more difficult the ballot design and the voting procedure are, the larger the share of invalid votes. This finding has been replicated using observational data in the United States (Bullock and Hood 2002; Kimball and Kropf 2005) and in Latin American countries (Power and Garand 2007), as well as in an experimental study that examined the consequences of using four different voting machine prototypes in Argentina (Calvo, Escolar, and Pomares 2009). Besides ballot structure, the characteristics of the electorate predict invalid voting. It is more widespread in countries with low literacy rates (Power and Garand 2007; Reynolds and Steenbergen 2006) and, within the United States, in districts with a large percentage of African Americans, minorities, or poorly educated people (Bullock and Hood 2002; Herron and Sekhon 2003; Tomz and Van Houweling 2003). Finally, we know that characteristics of the electorate moderate the effect of ballot structure. Difficult ballots are associated with more invalid voting in districts with a large African American population (Kimball and Kropf 2005). Complex voting procedures also produced more unintentional split-ticket votes among less educated Argentineans, leading the authors to conclude that "where some

---

[3] Though it is typically assumed that voting is very easy, the difficulty of voting correctly may be substantial relative to the abilities of some citizens. In fact, invalid voting is surprisingly widespread in some countries. For example, Power and Garand (2007) report that more than 40 percent of the votes cast in some Brazilian or Peruvian elections were invalid. In the United States, research on invalid voting and its sociological and technological correlates became salient in the aftermath of the 2000 presidential election.

voters see increased political freedom to express more nuanced preferences, other voters see a navigation maze with candidate names and political propositions they hardly recognize" (Calvo, Escolar, and Pomares 2009: 230).

This evidence suggests that some people with low cognitive resources do not understand the instructions on how to vote when the ballots are complex. The experience of not being able to vote correctly is frustrating and displeasing and may discourage some persons from voting in subsequent elections.

Some previous voter turnout research has looked at this question more directly and has found that an open ballot structure reduces voter turnout among the less educated. Anduiza (2002) creates a composite index of individual incentives to vote, which contains information on the respondent's sociodemographic characteristics and political attitudes, and examines if it interacts with the ability to express preferences on the ballot when predicting voter turnout. She finds that although the chance to express preferences increases the likelihood of voting for people with a high level of individual incentives, this possibility decreases the likelihood of voting for citizens with a low score in the individual incentives index.

Other arguments suggest that a ballot structure that allows for the expression of preferences increases the benefits of voting, which should increase voter turnout. In a voting system that offers a larger palette of choices, it is more likely that citizens will be able to find a particular candidate who suits their personal tastes. Being able not to vote for a candidate from one's party may also be valued if citizens wish to punish specific politicians. For instance, one of the core demands of the "outraged" movement in Spain, which campaigned for a deepening of democracy in 2011, was precisely the introduction of open ballots to allow citizens to cross out corrupt candidates.

Second, an open ballot structure can increase the quality of candidates, which in turn increases incentives to participate. Candidates who run in systems that use open ballots are more likely to have been born in the district and to have previously held lower-level electoral positions (Shugart, Ellis, and Suominen n.d.). This is because when voters, rather than parties, have more influence on which candidates are elected, characteristics that make candidates attractive to voters, rather than to party leaders, are more important to decide who runs.[4]

Third, when citizens have more influence on the choice of candidates, representatives have greater incentives to be responsive to their constituencies. Open and flexible ballots promote constituency service and direct contact with voters (Bowler and Farrell 1993) as well as responsiveness to local interests (Carey 2007; Hix 2004; Norris 2004).[5]

Attentive voters should be more likely to perceive such beneficial consequences derived from more complex ballot structures than inattentive voters. To the extent that highly educated people are more likely to be informed and knowledgeable about politics, they can be expected to appreciate these positive aspects more than less educated people.

In sum, I have argued that the ballot structure can simultaneously affect the difficulty and the benefits of voting. Hence, the type of ballot structure can have a heterogeneous effect on different types of citizens. Highly educated citizens may perceive and enjoy the increased benefits of voting, and vote at higher rates when they have more choices. Difficult ballots, however, may dissuade some cost-sensitive, less educated citizens from voting.

Experimental Evidence on the Consequences of Changes in the Ballot Structure

Survey experiments allow us to assess whether or not a more difficult voting procedure has a heterogeneous impact on highly and less educated citizens. If the treatment is precise, the researcher can rule out the presence of other confounding factors. The randomized allocation of respondents to receiving different treatments ensures that the treatment groups contain individuals with similar characteristics on average. Experiments eliminate two

---

[4] The characteristics of candidates may depend on district magnitude; see Carey and Shugart (1995).

[5] For instance, open and flexible ballots are associated with larger budget deficits because legislators have more incentives to increase public spending targeted to their districts and pork-barreling (Hallerberg and Marier 2004).

concerns that plague observational studies: self-selection into treatment – because researchers assign units to treatments; and omitted variable bias – because, on average, covariates are balanced across groups. Any observed difference in the outcome of interest across treatment groups has a causal interpretation.

I designed two experiments to examine whether the use of a more difficult voting procedure increases turnout inequality. In both cases, the survey questions presented respondents with a hypothetical election and asked them what they would do in the situation. The experimental manipulations modified the ballot structure in a way that aimed to alter only the difficulty of the voting procedure. Otherwise, the descriptions of the election and the candidates were identical across the treatment conditions.

The Number of Votes Experiment

The Number of Votes experiment was embedded in an academic online survey fielded in April 2011 in Spain[6] and asked 902 respondents whether they would vote in a hypothetical election in which four candidates were running. The experiment modified the number of votes respondents could use. In the One-Vote condition, respondents could vote for one of four candidates with one vote, or else abstain.[7] In the Five-Votes condition, respondents had five votes, which they could use to vote for one of the exact same four candidates, or they could split between the candidates. They could also decide to abstain from voting. Thus, this manipulation modified two of the key determinants of ballot structure: the number of votes a voter is entitled to cast and the possibility to accumulate them (Cox 1990). Having more votes increases the number of options available to voters. For instance, they can give all the votes to one candidate, split the votes between candidates from the same party, or give votes to female candidates from different parties. Simultaneously, having

---

[6] The survey was jointly designed by the Spanish Centro de Investigaciones Sociológicas and the Elections and Democracy research group at the Universitat Autònoma de Barcelona.

[7] They were also told that 45 percent of people abstained in that particular election, in order to hold the descriptive social norm of voting constant at a relatively low level.

more votes makes it somewhat more difficult to vote, because it is necessary to think harder about how to allocate five votes from among a larger set of possible options.[8] See Figure 3–1 for the exact wording of the Number of Votes experiment.[9]

The choice of manipulating the number of votes a person had was motivated by the goal of achieving a high level of precision in the treatment. This treatment does not aim to reproduce any particular electoral system, but it was conceived to be more realistic than typical voting laboratory experiments (Duffy and Tavits 2008; Levine and Palfrey 2007) in which participants are told that they are members of a group and have the option to purchase a number of tokens with no reference to elections. In real elections, the amount of information on candidates and parties covaries with ballot structure, and there are more than two parties and four candidates. However, long survey treatments can increase partial noncompletion. The option of manipulating the number of votes, though not strictly realistic, allows a high degree of precision in the treatment and achieves the goal of making the voting procedure more difficult.

The experiment was embedded in a study that targeted adults aged forty-five years or less. The sample has a similar education level as the same-aged Spanish population. About 36 percent of the respondents have primary or lower secondary education,

---

[8] If respondents tried to skip the screen, a pop-up window warned them that they had not completed the question and asked them to fill it. In addition, in the difficult voting procedure condition, a pop-up warned respondents who had not cast exactly five ballots that they had not voted correctly. This did not allow for spoiled votes (if the count amounted to more than six) or undervotes (if less than five votes were cast) because these kinds of votes complicate the interpretation of the results. Though pop-ups may annoy some study participants, no respondent dropped out during or just after the administration of this question, suggesting that they were not strongly annoyed.

[9] The age restriction is because Internet use is not yet widespread in older age groups in Spain. The team that designed the survey feared that older Internet users are very different from the overall older population in terms of demographics and attitudes. Nonrepresentative samples can be used in experimental settings to test causal effects if the causal variable of interest has homogeneous effects or if the relevant heterogeneous effect is modeled (Druckman and Kam 2011). Here, the interaction of ballot type and education is directly examined in the analyses, thus heterogeneous effects are explicitly modeled.

Imagine that an important election is held. Two parties are running, one is left wing and the other is right wing, with the following candidates:

Party A (Left wing)	Party B (Right wing)
Candidate 1: Female, charismatic, liberal position on the issues of ecology, feminism, and human rights.	Candidate 3: Male, experienced in the private sector and good manager. Supports liberalization of the economy.
Candidate 2: Male, young, well-trained, with a technical profile. Opposes cutting down on social spending.	Candidate 4: Mature woman with a strong personality. Christian, with a long experience in religious organizations.

Treatment 1: Easy Voting Condition

Knowing that about 45 percent of the eligible voters choose not to vote, what would you do?

1. Abstain (not vote)
2. Vote for candidate 1
3. Vote for candidate 2
4. Vote for candidate 3
5. Vote for candidate 4

Treatment 2: Difficult Voting Condition

You have up to five votes, which you can give to one candidate or distribute between several candidates, even if they are from different parties.

Knowing that about 45 percent of the eligible voters choose not to vote, what would you do?

1. Abstain (not vote)
2. Vote for candidate 1 with [1,2,3,4,5] votes
3. Vote for candidate 2 with [1,2,3,4,5] votes
4. Vote for candidate 3 with [1,2,3,4,5] votes
5. Vote for candidate 4 with [1,2,3,4,5] votes

FIGURE 3–1. Text of the Number of Votes experiment

27 percent have upper secondary education, and 37 percent of respondents have some university education.

A randomization test (not reported) reveals no covariate imbalance between the two treatment groups. Classical predictors of voter turnout such as education, age, sex, interest in politics, the belief that voting is a civic duty, or close affiliation with a party are not associated with inclusion in the treatment conditions.

Table 3–2 displays the mean reported intention to vote in the election of respondents who fell in the One-Vote and the

TABLE 3–2. *Reported Intention to Vote in the Number of Votes Experiment*

	Easy Condition	Difficult Condition	Difference
Lower secondary	0.78	0.65	−0.12**
Standard error	0.03	0.04	0.05
Number of observations	156	156	
High secondary	0.84	0.82	0.02
Standard error	0.03	0.04	0.05
Number of observations	126	112	
Tertiary education	0.91	0.87	−0.04
Standard error	0.02	0.03	0.03
Number of observations	191	161	
All	0.85	0.78	−0.07**
Standard error	0.02	0.02	0.03
Number of observations	473	429	

* $p < 0.1$, ** $p < 0.05$, one-tailed test. The entries are proportions who respond that they would vote.

Five-Votes voting procedure conditions. The last column shows the mean difference in the reported intention to vote, which has a causal interpretation as the effect of voting with the more difficult procedure.

The reported intention to vote was higher in the One-Vote condition than in the Five-Votes condition. Eighty-five percent of respondents voted for one of the four candidates if they only had one vote. By contrast, 78 percent of those who had five votes used them, whereas 22 percent abstained from voting. The difference of 7 percentage points in reported turnout is significant at the 95 percent level. Though modest in size, effects in the one-digit range are typical of institutional predictors of voter turnout in cross-national studies, with the notable exception of compulsory voting (Blais 2006). Allowing voters the capacity to send more nuanced messages with their votes seems to decrease, rather than increase, their propensity to participate in an election.

When breaking down the participants by education level, it becomes clear that using a difficult voting procedure disproportionately depresses the electoral participation of the less educated, hence confirming my main hypothesis. Seventy-eight percent of respondents who had lower secondary education or less reported that they would vote in the One-Vote condition. This figure is just 65 percent for less educated respondents assigned to the Five-Votes condition. A difference of 12 percentage points in reported intention to vote due to the ballot structure is a large effect for an institutional characteristic. The difference is statistically significant at the 95 percent level. This result provides evidence consistent with the claim that, all else equal, presenting people with a ballot that increases the difficulty of voting will make some people with a low level of education decide not to vote.

On the contrary, there is no evidence that the voting procedure affects the willingness to vote among respondents with higher education levels. Respondents with upper secondary education voted at approximately the same rate in the easy voting and the difficult voting conditions (82 percent versus 84 percent). The voting procedure also did not have a significant effect on the reported intention to vote for citizens with some university education. The overall outcome of this heterogeneous effects on highly and less educated respondents is that turnout inequality was, in this hypothetical setting, larger under the more difficult voting procedure.

The Open–Closed Ballot Experiment

The Open–Closed Ballot experiment was embedded in a one-shot, stand-alone online survey fielded in December 2011 in Spain, and asked 500 respondents whether they would vote in a hypothetical election.[10] There were two treatment conditions, which modified only the ballot structure used for voting. Respondents were told that two parties competed in the election – one was center-right and the other was center-left. Each party presented three candidates. The description provided the

---

[10] Spain is a particularly good context in which to run an experiment on ballot structure because voters have experience with different ballot structures. While elections to the lower chamber of parliament use closed party list ballots, elections to the Senate use open list ballots. Thus, the procedures were not too far from the voters' actual experience.

names of the candidates (generated through a random online names generator) and some information on their backgrounds and political positions.

In the Closed-Ballot condition, the text containing a brief description of the candidates' characteristics was printed in light-gray color whereas all the other text on the screen was in black ink. The aim of presenting the information about the candidates in a lighter color was to subtly imply that it was unnecessary for respondents to read the whole text. In elections that use closed ballots, citizens have little reason to learn about the candidates because they cannot select specific names. Respondents were told that in this election citizens could vote for one of the two parties by picking a printed paper ballot and placing it in a ballot box. They had to indicate the likelihood that they would vote in this election on a scale from 0 to 10, with 0 being not at all likely to vote and 10 being very likely to vote.

In the Open-Ballot condition, respondents read about the exact same two parties and six candidates. This time, the entire text was printed in black ink, implying that they needed to read all the information about the candidates. The text claimed that, to vote in this election, voters had to write the name of one of the candidates on a white piece of paper (as done in elections in Finland). Again, respondents had to report the likelihood that they would vote on a scale that ranged from 0 to 10.

This manipulation, designed to modify the difficulty of the voting procedure, was intended to be as realistic as possible. As I have previously argued, it is easier to vote in a closed ballot system, in which citizens have to choose only between parties, than in an open ballot system, in which citizens have to learn about specific candidates and parties, and select candidates within parties. The exact wording of the Open–Closed Ballot experiment is in Figure 3–2.

This time, the sample contained people from all age groups. Because of the relatively small sample size, I decided not to sample respondents from the intermediate education categories. Thus, the sample included only people with a low education level (who have lower secondary education or less) and people with a high

Imagine that an important election is held. Two parties are running, one is left wing and the other is right wing, with the following candidates [in the Closed Ballot condition the information about the candidates was in black, in the Open Ballot condition it was in gray]:

Party A (Left wing)	Party B (Right wing)
Amaya Alfaro: Female, politically experienced and charismatic. Supports liberal economic reforms and has leftist positions on the issues of ecology, feminism, and human rights.	**José Centeno:** Middle aged male, experienced in the private sector and good manager. Supports liberalization of the economy. Liberal positions on social issues such as homosexuality or abortion.
Luís Pulido: Young male, well-trained, with a technical profile. Supports trade unions and opposes cutting down on social spending. More concerned about economic development than about green issues.	**Noemí Salazar:** Mature woman, energetic, with a strong personality. Christian, with a long experience in religious organizations and in campaigns in support of the family.
Iván Mercado: Party veteran, linked to the trade unions, able to negotiate in difficult situations. Has a pragmatic approach and a good record at attracting investment to his province.	**Esther Mota:** Party leader with extensive contacts and a great ability to negotiate, make deals, and convince others. Liberal in economic issues and takes moderate stances on social issues.

Closed Ballot Condition

You can vote in this election by inserting a paper ballot in a ballot box, or you can abstain from voting. What would you do in this election?.

Open Ballot Condition

You can vote in this election by writing the name of one of the six candidates in a white piece of paper and inserting the paper in a ballot box, or you can abstain from voting. What would you do in this election?

I would certainly not vote   I would certainly vote

0   1   2   3   4   5   6   7   8   9   10

FIGURE 3–2. Text of the Open–Closed Ballot experiment

education level (who have university or advanced vocational education). This decision allowed me to increase the sample size of the two education subgroups that are of more interest and to have more statistical power to test the hypothesis.

Table 3–3 displays the mean reported likelihood of voting (on the 0–10 scale) for respondents who fell in the Closed-Ballot and the Open-Ballot conditions. The last column is the mean

TABLE 3-3. *Reported Intention to Vote in the Open–Closed Ballot Experiment*

	Closed Ballot	Open Ballot	Difference
Lower secondary	5.65	4.61	−1.04**
Standard error	0.33	0.35	0.48
Number of observations	129	121	
Tertiary education	7.12	7.26	0.14
Standard error	0.29	0.30	0.42
Number of observations	125	125	
All	6.37	5.96	−0.41
Standard error	0.22	0.24	0.33
Number of observations	254	246	

* $p < 0.1$, ** $p < 0.05$, one-tailed test. The response scale ranges from 0 to 10.

difference in the reported likelihood of voting, which has a causal interpretation as the effect of a more difficult voting procedure on the reported propensity to vote.

The reported likelihood of voting was higher in the Closed-Ballot condition than in the Open-Ballot condition, but only slightly. In the Closed-Ballot condition, the average reported likelihood to vote was 6.4 on a scale from 0 to 10, and this figure was only 6 in the Open-Ballot condition. The 0.4 difference is very close to the 90 percent level of statistical significance (p-value $= 0.11$).

When breaking down the respondents by education level, the prediction that the use of open ballots depresses the reported electoral participation of the less educated is clearly supported. The mean likelihood of voting for poorly educated people was 5.7 in the Closed-Ballot condition but only 4.6 in the Open-Ballot condition. This substantively large difference is statistically significant at conventional levels. This finding provides support for the contention that poorly educated people are sensitive to increases in the difficulty of the voting procedure, to which some of them react by failing to vote. The mean likelihood of voting is, on the other hand, almost identical for highly educated people in both the Closed-Ballot and Open-Ballot conditions. The difference in the mean score across the two conditions is very small and statistically insignificant. Citizens who have a high level of education do not change their reported likelihood of voting depending on the type of ballot used.

The results of both experiments are consistent with the prediction that burdensome voting procedures tend to depress the electoral participation of the less educated. Increasing the difficulty of voting has heterogeneous effects on highly and less educated citizens and thus results in larger turnout gaps.

The experimental results are, however, not consistent with the hypothesis that ballots which offer a wider range of options increase voter turnout for the highly educated. One reason for this finding may be that the experiment is ill-equipped to fully test this claim. Part of the reason why ballots that provide more choices, and open ballots in particular, are hypothesized to increase turnout is that they increase the attractiveness and the perceived responsiveness of politicians. This positive effect of ballot structure on candidate qualities has been confirmed in the literature, but holding the characteristics of politicians constant makes it impossible to assess if turnout grows as a consequence of superior candidate quality. In other words, ballot structure may affect voter turnout indirectly through its effects on the characteristics and behavior of candidates and representatives, but the survey experiment cannot capture this indirect pathway. Moreover, the realism of a hypothetical situation embedded in a survey is low. To provide a fuller test of the hypothesis, the next section turns to observational data.

Cross-National Evidence on the Association of Ballot Structure and Participation

The observational study investigates the impact of ballot structure on voter turnout and turnout inequality using the cross-national CSES dataset. The CSES contains data on elections held under a wide variety of systems. Unfortunately, there is no wide consensus on the way to classify ballot structure, which is the main contextual variable of interest. As Norris (2002: 12) notes, there is overlap between ballot structure and electoral systems. Thus, this section also tests if electoral systems are associated with different levels of unequal participation. Here I follow Shugart's proposal (2005) and classify the systems as follows:

- *Closed party list* ballots in proportional representation (PR) systems: Political parties propose lists of candidates. Voters can vote only for the entire list; they cannot modify how votes are allocated to candidates from the same party.
- *Flexible* ballots in PR systems: Political parties propose ordered lists of candidates, but voters can overturn the order. Voters can select specific names, or cross out some candidates. In practice, the parties retain most of their influence on the election of candidates. The predefined list order constrains the effect of preference votes.
- *Open list* ballots in PR systems: Political parties propose candidates but there is no party-provided rank order. Preference votes alone determine the election of candidates.[11]
- *Nominal* ballots in majoritarian systems: Parties propose only one candidate and district magnitude equals one.[12] There is no option to rank order candidates from different parties. Used in first-past-the-post systems and in two-round systems.
- *Dual* ballots in mixed member systems: Voters can cast two votes, typically one for a party list and another one for a candidate. The exact system and allocation rules vary substantially from country to country.

---

[11] Though not strictly open list, Switzerland is included in this category. This country has one of the most complicated systems. It allows voters to express detailed preferences because votes can be distributed within or across party lines. Voters can cast a vote for a list and modify it by crossing out or repeating the names of candidates. They can also split their votes between candidates from different party lists and create their own list by writing candidates' names on a blank ballot. Another option is to vote for parties.

[12] Chile is a special case in legislative elections. It uses the binominal system with two-member districts and a majoritarian formula. If a list obtains more than twice the number of votes of the runner up list, its two candidates are elected. Otherwise, the two largest parties receive one candidate each (Zucco 2007). At the time of writing, there were intense discussions on electoral reform. In any case, Chile is coded as nominal because the presidential elections use a majoritarian system.

- *Other cases:* This category includes Ireland, Australia, and
  Taiwan in legislative elections. In both Australia, under the
  Alternative Vote (AV), and Ireland, under the single transferable vote (STV), voters are allowed to rank-order their preferences.[13] These two systems are similar except for district
  magnitude. In the single nontransferable vote (SNTV) system
  used in Taiwan before 2007, voters can vote for one of several
  candidates in multimember districts. Parties can propose more
  than one candidate. The candidates with the highest number of
  votes win.

This classification falls short of fully capturing the real concept
of interest, which is the difficulty of voting under different ballot
structures. However, it is an approximation and it is plausible to
argue that this difficulty increases monotonically along the three
types of ballots in PR systems.

Some of the elections included in the CSES are presidential contests or simultaneous presidential and legislative elections, which use different electoral systems (e.g., Taiwan or
Mexico). When elections are concurrent, the variable takes the
value of the structure used in the presidential election, that is,
nominal ballots. Table 3–4 presents the cases that fall in each
category.[14]

There are a large number of individual respondents in each
category. However, the number of actual elections in the open
ballots category and the "other" category is rather small.

In PR systems, the openness and difficulty of voting increases
ordinally. Closed party lists are the easiest system; flexible lists
have an intermediate level of difficulty; and open lists are the

---

[13] Under the AV, if a candidate has a majority of first preferences, he or she is
elected. If no candidate has a majority of first preferences, the next preferences
of voters who voted for the less successful candidate or candidates are counted.
Under the STV, the ballots list candidates in multimember districts alphabeti-
cally. Voters have to select at least one candidate and write the number one.
They may also rank one or more candidates using consecutive numbers.

[14] I thank Pedro Riera, Matthew Shugart, and Alan Renwick for comments on
how to classify the countries. The sources I used contain several important
discrepancies on how to classify the systems. Any errors left are my own.

TABLE 3–4. *Ballot Structure by Country*

Country	Election type	Ballot	Year(s)			
Australia	Legislative	Alternative Vote	1996	2004	2007	
Austria	Legislative	Flexible list	2008			
Belgium	Legislative	Flexible list	1999	2003		
Brazil	President (and legislative)	Nominal	2002	2006		
Bulgaria	Legislative	Closed party list	2001			
Canada	Legislative	Nominal	1997	2004		
Chile	President (and legislative)	Nominal	2005			
Croatia	Legislative	Closed party list	2007			
Czech Rep.	Legislative	Flexible	1996	2002	2006	
Denmark	Legislative	Flexible	1998	2001		
Finland	Legislative	Open list	2003	2007		
France	President	Nominal	2002			
France	Legislative	Nominal	2007			
Germany	Legislative	Dual	1998	2002	2005	2009
Hungary	Legislative	Dual	1998	2002		
Iceland	Legislative	Closed party list	1999			
Iceland	Legislative	Flexible	2003	2007	2009	
Ireland	Legislative	STV	2002	2007		
Israel	Legislative	Closed party list	1996	2003	2006	
Italy	Legislative	Closed party list	2006			
Japan	Legislative	Dual	1996	2004	2007	
Korea	Legislative	Dual	2000	2004	2008	
Lithuania	President	Nominal	1997			
Mexico	Legislative	Dual ballot	2003	2009		
Mexico	President (and legislative)	Nominal	2006			
Netherlands	Legislative	Flexible list	1998	2002	2006	
New Zealand	Legislative	Dual	1996	2002	2008	
Norway	Legislative	Closed party list	1997	2001	2005	

(continued)

77

TABLE 3-4 (*continued*)

Country	Election type	Ballot	Year(s)
Peru	President (and legislative)	Nominal	2006
Poland	Legislative	Open list	1997, 2001, 2005, 2007
Portugal	Legislative	Closed party list	2002, 2005, 2009
Romania	President (and legislative)	Closed party list	1996, 2004
Slovenia	Legislative	Flexible list	1996, 2004
Spain	Legislative	Closed party list	1996, 2000, 2004
Sweden	Legislative	Flexible list	1998, 2002, 2006
Switzerland	Legislative	Open list	1999, 2003, 2007
Taiwan	President (and legislative)	Nominal	1996
Taiwan	Legislative	SNTV	2001
Taiwan	President	Nominal	2004
UK	Legislative	Nominal	1997, 2005
USA	President (and legislative)	Nominal	1996, 2004

Notes:

Bulgaria: Changed to a mixed member in 2009 (Nikolenyi 2011).

Denmark: The parties themselves can decide which of four preferential list options want to employ. One of the options is an open list system (Elklit 2011).

Iceland: A reform of the electoral system was approved between 1999 and 200 with the aim of decreasing malapportionment and increasing proportionality (Hardarson 2002). Among other aspects, the ballot structure changed from closed party lists (Karvonen 2004), to preference lists (Renwick 2010). Although this reform may have been a suitable case study of changes in the ballot structure, the fact that malapportionment and disproportionality changed simultaneously makes it unsuitable as a case study, because each aspect can be expected to have a distinct impact on voter turnout and thus any effects are confounded.

Italy: Changed from mixed member electoral system to PR in 2005 (Baldini 2011).

Japan: Elections were to the lower chamber in 1996 and to the upper chamber in 2004 and 2007. Both use mixed member parallel systems, but with different features (for a description see, for example, Gallagher 2001).

Norway: It is possible to cross out candidates, but this option is rarely used (Shugart 2005). Most sources classify it as a closed party list system.

Romania: Changed to a mixed member in 2008 (Marian and King 2010).

Sweden: Changed from closed party list to preference lists in 1997 according to Karvonen (2004), though Renwick and Pilet (2010) claim that the reform had mixed effects on personalization, simultaneously reducing the freedom of voters to express preferences and increasing the influence of preference votes on candidate selection.

Taiwan: Changed from SNTV to a mixed member majoritarian system in 2007 (Chen 2006, Tan 2009).

Slovakia: The system of preferential voting was strengthened in 2006, the threshold was lowered to 3 percent of the party vote. Previously, for the preferential votes to count, a candidate had to receive at least 10 percent of the total votes cast for the party.

Source: CSES, Gallagher and Mitchell 2005; Pereira and Silva 2009; Shugart 2005; Colomer 2004; Johnson and Wallack 2011; Karvonen 2004; Renwick and Pilet 2010, the online Inter-Parliamentary Union database (visited in July 2011, available at http://www.ipu.org/parline), and http://electionresources.org/ (visited in July 2011).

78

TABLE 3–5. *Frequency of Individuals and Elections by Ballot Structure in the CSES*

Type of Ballot	Respondents N	Respondents (%)	Number Elections
Closed party list	27,089	19	18
Flexible party list	29,878	21	19
Open party list	16,871	12	9
Dual ballot (mixed system)	30,061	22	16
Nominal (FPTP and 2-round)	24,486	18	17
Other (AV, STV, and SNTV)	9,657	7	6
Total	141,408	100	85

most difficult to use. Thus, closed lists are coded as 0, flexible lists are assigned the value 0.5, and open lists are coded as 1. Closed party lists are the reference category. In addition, one of the models includes the three categories of PR systems as dummies in order to examine if the results are robust to different coding decisions. A dummy variable distinguishes between the values of each of the additional possibilities: dual ballots used in mixed member systems, nominal ballots in majoritarian systems, and other systems.

The models include controls for age, age squared, sex, compulsory voting,[15] and an interaction term of education and compulsory voting. The analyses are replicated for legislative elections only, for all elections, excluding compulsory voting countries and excluding Poland to check the robustness of the results.

Model 1 includes only legislative elections, which are arguably more similar to each other. The results suggest that, all else being equal, less educated citizens have a lower predicted probability of voting in countries that use an open ballot structure than in

---

[15] Compulsory voting is coded 1 for countries in which this institution is enforced, and 0.5 where it is not enforced. The coding (see appendix) follows Birch (2009).

TABLE 3–6. *Multivariate Models of Voter Turnout: Ballot Structure and Education*

	Legisl. Elections (Model 1)	All Eighty-Five Elections (model 2)	Ballot Dummies (Model 3)	Compuls. Vote Exclud. (Model 4)	Poland Excluded (Model 5)
Education	0.24*** (0.03)	0.24*** (0.03)	0.24*** (0.04)	0.25*** (0.03)	0.25*** (0.03)
Ballot openness in PR systems (0 closed, 0.5 flexible, 1 open)	-1.16*** (0.28)	-1.15*** (0.29)		-1.16** (0.30)	-0.78* (0.33)
Flexible ballots (ref. closed party lists)			-0.24 (0.20)		
Open ballots			-1.41*** (0.27)		
Dual ballot (mixed system)	-0.30 (0.23)	-0.30 (0.24)	-0.02 (0.22)	-0.19 (0.26)	-0.22 (0.23)
Nominal ballot (majoritarian)	-0.68[+] (0.35)	-0.59* (0.25)	-0.29 (0.23)	-0.69* (0.29)	-0.50* (0.25)
Other (AV, STV, and SNTV)	0.42 (0.37)	0.36 (0.37)	0.70* (0.34)	0.005 (0.47)	0.46 (0.37)
Ballot openness*education	0.18*** (0.05)	0.18** (0.06)		0.18** (0.06)	0.14** (0.07)
Flexible ballots*education (ref. closed party lists)			0.08[+] (0.05)		
Open ballots*education			0.18** (0.06)		
Dual*education	-0.004 (0.05)	0.001 (0.05)	-0.002 (0.05)	0.02 (0.05)	-0.006 (0.05)

	Model 1	Model 2	Model 3	Model 4	Model 5
Nominal*education	0.02	0.04	0.04	0.07	0.04
	(0.07)	(0.05)	(0.05)	(0.06)	(0.05)
Other*education	−0.13[+]	−0.11	−0.11	−0.18*	−0.11
	(0.08)	(0.08)	(0.08)	(0.09)	(0.08)
Constant	−0.93***	−0.91***	−1.18***	−0.94***	−0.99***
	(0.16)	(0.17)	(0.16)	(0.18)	(0.17)
Controls for age, age2, and sex	Yes	Yes	Yes	Yes	Yes
Controls comp. vote and interaction	Yes	Yes	Yes	No	Yes
Variance constant	0.69	0.72	0.64	0.75	0.70
	(0.06)	(0.06)	(0.05)	(0.07)	(0.06)
Variance slope (education)	0.02	0.14	0.14	0.14	0.14
	(0.14)	(0.06)	(0.01)	(0.01)	(0.01)
Correlation education, constant	−0.20	−0.24	−0.27	−0.34	−0.23
	(0.14)	(0.12)	(0.12)	(0.12)	(0.12)
N elections	74	85	85	73	81
N individuals	122,520	137,967	137,967	115,813	130,082

+ p < 0.1, * p < 0.05, ** p < 0.01, *** p < 0.001. Entries are multilevel logistic regression coefficients (standard errors). Models with random intercepts and random slopes for education. Education is a continuous measure that has five values: primary or less, incomplete secondary, complete secondary, postsecondary, or university education. Compulsory voting is coded 1 if sanctioned and 0.5 if not sanctioned. Ballot structure in PR systems takes on three values: 0 closed party lists, 0.5 flexible lists, 1 open lists. Closed party list is the reference category. No weights applied.

countries that use closed party lists. For less educated people, the probability of voting is also lower in mixed member systems and in majoritarian elections that use nominal ballots.

The interaction of ballot openness and education is positive, significant, and approaches the magnitude of the education coefficient. This suggests that the relationship between education level and voting is stronger in elections that use an open ballot structure than in elections that use closed ballots. In contrast, the interactions of dual ballot structure and nominal ballots with education level are not significant at conventional levels. This implies that the gradient of education is similar in majoritarian systems, mixed member systems, and PR systems with closed party lists. In other electoral systems, the relationship between education and voting is weaker than in closed-party-list PR systems.[16]

The individual level coefficients have the expected signs. Education (coded in five categories), age (modeled curvilinearly to account for the possibility that voter turnout declines at old age), and sex are all associated with voter turnout in the expected directions.

Next, model 2 provides additional support for the hypothesis that the gradient of the education effect is stronger in elections that use open ballots than in elections that use closed party lists, using all the information available in the CSES. This model includes all presidential elections, which use nominal ballots. The coefficients of most variables are very similar in size to the results found in the first model.

Model 3 uses a different codification of ballot structure. Instead of employing a three-category variable in PR systems, it includes closed party lists, flexible lists, and open lists coded as separate dummies. This allows us to rule out the possibility that the results are completely driven by the cases that use open

---

[16] In the CSES sample, the mean gaps in the turnout rates of highly and poorly educated people are 18 percentage points in all elections held under PR systems, 19 percentage points in majoritarian systems, and 17 percentage points in mixed member systems. The differences between the three groups are not statistically significant.

ballots. The results are clearly confirmatory because the coefficients of the flexible ballots dummy have the same direction but lower values than the coefficients of the open ballots dummy. In PR systems with flexible ballots the predicted probability of voting is lower for people who have a low education level than it is in closed-party-lists PR systems. This implies that there is indeed a monotonic relationship such that more open ballot structures lead to a lower expected voter turnout of poorly educated citizens and larger gaps in the turnout rates of the highly and less educated.

In model 4, the analyses are replicated excluding countries that use compulsory voting. Compulsory voting and the interaction with education were modeled explicitly in the previous analyses, but this model allows us to completely rule out the possibility that compulsory voting countries are influencing the results. Again, very similar results are obtained.

Model 5 further verifies the robustness of the results by excluding Poland. Poland uses open ballots and is one of the countries with the largest levels of turnout inequality. It is therefore necessary to reject the possibility that the results are driven by this particular case. The omission of this country generates slight differences in the estimates. The logistic regression coefficient of ballot structure is reduced when Poland is omitted. However, it is still a large coefficient and significantly different from zero, and the interactive coefficient between high education and ballot structure in PR systems remains similar in size. This suggests that, although the case of Poland is influential, it does not drive the results, which are robust to its exclusion.[17]

Logistic regression coefficients are not intuitively interpretable. In order to shed light on the magnitude of the estimated effects, I calculated the predicted probabilities of voting for different types of people using the estimates from model 2, which

[17] Additional analyses exclude Switzerland, which may also be an influential case. A similar pattern is obtained when excluding Switzerland; the uninteracted coefficient for ballot structure is smaller in size, but the interactive coefficient remains similar in magnitude and statistically significant.

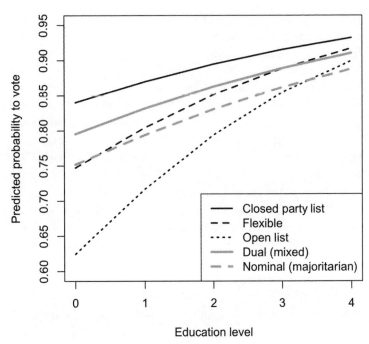

FIGURE 3–3. Predicted voter turnout by ballot structure
Predicted probability to vote by level of education and ballot structure calculated from model 2, Table 3–6. For a forty-year-old female, in countries with no compulsory voting. Education has five values: primary or less, incomplete secondary, complete secondary, postsecondary, or university education.

draw on data from all elections included in the CSES. Changes in probabilities for binary dependent variables are contingent on voter turnout levels.[18] The probabilities were estimated for a forty-year-old woman in a voluntary voting country. The education level varies from 0, which stands for having primary education or less, to 4, which stands for having a university degree. The results are displayed in Figure 3–3.

---

[18] For logistic coefficients, the magnitude of the changes is largest when the probability of voting is 0.5. The exact change in the predicted probability of voting depends on the value of all covariates. Therefore, a person with a specific kind of profile has to be selected.

In all systems, the highly educated have a higher probability of reporting that they voted than the less educated. However, the gradient of the relationship varies substantially depending on the ballot structure used. The probability that a respondent with a low level of education reports voting is 0.84 in closed party list systems, but only 0.62 in open ballot systems and 0.75 in flexible list systems. In contrast, at higher education levels the probability to report voting is very close to 0.9 in all three cases. Ballot structures are not associated with an increase or a decrease in the predicted probability of voting among the highly educated. This makes sense. Highly educated citizens may turn out to vote in any event, as for them, the costs of voting are largely irrelevant. They do not appear to vote more when ballot structures allow an expression of more nuanced choices. This may simply be a consequence of ceiling effects as their reported turnout rates of around 90 percent are already very high.

The size of the gaps in the turnout rates of the highly and the less educated does vary substantially across systems. In elections held in closed-party-list PR systems, the estimated gaps are relatively small at only 9 percentage points (93−84). They are almost twice as large (92−75 = 17) in systems that use flexible lists and the estimated gap widens to a staggering 28 percentage points (90−62) in countries that use open lists. It is likely that the estimates are biased. Beacuse these are very large effects, in all likelihood any biases are upward. However, the sheer magnitude of the differences across systems makes it very unlikely that the null hypothesis that ballot structure is not associated with turnout inequality is true.

The gradient of the education effect is also steep in majoritarian elections that use nominal ballots. Although the probability to report voting for a forty-year-old woman with less than primary education is 0.75, it is 0.89 if the woman has a university education, resulting in a sizeable gap of 14 percentage points. At 11 percentage points (91−80), the gaps are somewhat smaller in elections that use dual ballots in mixed member systems. These results are also interesting because they suggest that turnout inequality levels are not much larger in majoritarian electoral systems than in PR systems. Majoritarian systems do not seem to result in a demobilization of the poor and steep turnout inequalities.

In sum, both the observational, cross-national strategy, and the two survey experiments provide support for the hypothesis that the use of a more complex ballot structure, which allows citizens to express more nuanced choices but also increases the difficulty of voting, depresses voter turnout mainly among less educated people. The difficulty of the voting procedure is a clear instance of a contextual characteristic with heterogeneous effects on different education subgroups. The use of more complex ballot structures reduces the voter turnout rates of low education groups and results in larger levels of turnout inequality.

This finding qualifies previous optimistic views on the desirability of providing more choice in the ballot. Many analysts view the maximization of participation opportunities as an "indisputably" positive quality of electoral systems (Gallagher and Mitchell 2005: 570–1). However, only some citizens seem to benefit from electoral systems that allow for the expression of varied preferences. For the majority of citizens whose political engagement is low, and especially for less educated citizens, more opportunities to send nuanced messages may only add to the difficulty of voting and even dissuade participation.

4

Government Fragmentation and Media Systems

This chapter examines additional predictions that follow from the general claim that any contextual level feature that affects the cognitive costs of voting should also shape turnout inequality because highly and less educated people are heterogeneously sensitive to changes in cognitive costs. I focus on two of the many possible predictions. Although Chapter 2 discussed registration procedures and Chapter 3 examined whether the cognitive difficulty of the voting procedure, which is an institutional aspect of the electoral system, influences turnout inequality, this chapter concentrates on one characteristic of the party system and another of the media system. These very different factors have in common that they may shape the cognitive costs of voting. Their selection for analysis in this book is motivated by the aim of assessing whether the logic of the general argument holds across a wide range of applications. It is important to note, however, that the selection of these characteristics does not amount to cherry-picking convenient cases. In previous work (Gallego 2008, 2010), I have examined the impact of other contextual characteristics that affect the cognitive costs of voting and have found them to be associated with turnout inequality.

The first section of this chapter argues that coalition governments increase the information and decision costs of participating in elections. While in some political systems, only one large party governs, in other systems, parties need to build coalitions to form governments. When the winner of an election forms a coalition with smaller parties, voters must consider not only which party they prefer, but also how they feel about the other coalition partners, and how inter-party negotiations affect policy. Thus, understanding the political system is more cognitively taxing when governments are fragmented, and this should intensify turnout inequality. Confirmatory evidence for this prediction comes from the results of both an analysis with cross-national data and a survey experiment.

The second section of this chapter claims that a country's media system can shape its level of unequal participation. Citizens learn about politics mostly through the news content offered by the media. The amount, quality, and availability of the news that media systems deliver varies widely, depending on whether media systems are oriented toward public service or toward commercial purposes. In public-service-oriented media systems, citizens easily encounter large amounts of high-quality information, even when not actively looking for it. These systems reduce the costs of being informed about politics. Previous research suggests that in public-service-oriented systems, people know, on average, more about politics, and there are smaller knowledge gaps between interested and uninterested citizens. Besides affecting political knowledge, a decline in information costs should also foster the electoral participation of the less educated and reduce turnout inequality. Using cross-national data, I find evidence in support of this hypothesis.

Taken together, Chapters 2, 3, and 4 provide abundant evidence that various contextual features that increase or reduce the cognitive costs of voting have heterogeneous consequences for the political participation of citizens, conditional on their level of education. Finding support for quite diverse hypotheses that stem directly from the more general theoretical framework can increase our confidence about the validity of the general argument.

Government Fragmentation and the Cognitive Difficulty of Voting

Coalition governments in which more than one party holds executive power are the norm, rather than the exception, in electoral democracies. Several studies have shown that multiparty agreements are the most frequent outcome of democratic elections (Katz 1997; Hobolt and Karp 2010; Armstrong and Duch 2010; Vowles 2010). In recent years, there has been growing interest in comparative political behavior research on the determinants of vote choice in elections where coalition formation is likely. There is extensive evidence that voters in highly fragmented party systems engage in a variety of forms of strategic voting. Instead of voting for the party that they perceive to be closest to their position, some citizens vote for the weakest partner in their preferred coalition or for the member of a viable coalition that they dislike less[1] (Bargsted and Kedar 2009; Gschwend 2007; Blais et al. 2006; McCuen and Morton 2010; Meffert and Gschwend 2011).

Even if there is no shortage of theoretical speculation, scant empirical research has investigated how prospective or retrospective evaluations of coalitions affect voter turnout. There are several reasons why multiparty governments should be expected to reduce voter turnout.

First, coalition governments may reduce the benefits of voting, because such governments are less accountable and result in less policy change. Multiparty arrangements obscure responsibility for specific government action and thus make it more difficult for voters to hold parties in government accountable retrospectively (Strom 1985; Narud and Valen 2008; Kedar 2005; Powell 2000). When holding executive power, one party can blame its coalition partners for unpopular policies or for failure to implement proposed policies. More generally, it becomes more

---

[1] For example, left-wing voters who think that there will be a center-right coalition may vote for the centrist party in the coalition.

challenging for voters in multiparty governments than in one-party governments to know which coalition partner is responsible for which decision. Furthermore, the literature suggests that coalition governments are less able than one-party governments to implement policy changes (Lijphart 1999; Alesina, Roubini, and Cohen 1997; Franzese 2002), and this inability to produce clear change should reduce incentives to vote because who wins is less consequential. In established democracies, a larger number of parties in a government is associated with a lower level of agreement in surveys with the statement that who is in power makes a difference (Vowles 2010). This finding suggests that voters indeed are aware that coalitions result in less policy change.

A second reason why coalition governments may depress participation is that citizens become more averse to voting for their preferred party when they strongly dislike one likely coalition partners. For example, suppose that a conservative voter feels close to a Christian-Democratic party, but this party may form a coalition with a populist antiimmigrant party the conservative voter dislikes. The voter may prefer to abstain from voting, rather than support a coalition he opposes or vote for a left-wing party. Consistent with this idea, supporters of a party are more likely to vote for it when the party does not announce a preelectoral coalition than when it announces a preelectoral coalition with a party they dislike (Gschwend and Hooghe 2008).

Third, and most important for this work, coalition governments have long been hypothesized to increase the information costs of voting, because elections in which coalition governments are the likely outcome present additional complexity and uncertainty for voters (Downs 1957: 300; Jackman 1987; Hobolt and Karp 2010: 299; Brockington 2004: 473). When one party is able to form a government alone, there is a direct link between the outcome of an election and policy, as voters expect the winner to try to implement the policies proposed during the election campaign and can punish the incumbent government for failing to deliver. By contrast, policy outcomes are less straightforward when the number of parties in government is larger than one. Policies depend on how many seats parties get in parliament and on the outcomes of negotiations between government partners. Coalition partners need to compromise on policies, and the outcome of specific negotiations may be uncertain. Before voting, citizens need to decide on their preferred party and determine how likely it is that this party will enter a coalition government, what other parties might be part of such a coalition, what policies these other parties might defend, and what the likely outcome of interparty compromises will be. Retrospectively, they need to discern which party is to blame for each policy. Hence, prospective and retrospective voting is harder in multiparty governments than in one-party governments.

Some authors have argued that most voters may not be able to think about postelectoral pacts prospectively (Downs 1957). However, preelectoral coalitions and political history can somewhat assuage the difficulty. It is not unusual for parties to announce which coalition partners they would choose if their combined election results allowed them to form a government (Golder 2005). Preelectoral coalitions reduce the information and decision costs of voting, because they constrain the number of possible party combinations that voters need to evaluate. Similarly, the history of previous coalitions serves as a strong cue when voters guess which coalitions are likely to happen. Most combinations of coalition partners should be very predictable for the public, because the same political parties tend to negotiate similar agreements in successive elections (Armstrong and Duch 2010). In spite of this, deciding for whom to vote when elections produce coalition governments is more costly than deciding for whom to vote when elections result in one-party governments, because voters still need to evaluate what they think about coalition partners and what the product of negotiations between partners will be. The same argument applies to the retrospective evaluation of policies implemented by government coalitions.

The argument that coalition governments increase the information costs of voting suggests that government fragmentation may be one candidate predictor of unequal participation. The rise in information and decision costs should have heterogeneous consequences for the participation of highly and less educated citizens. While the former may find it easy to learn about likely coalitions, the positions of partners, and likely results of negotiations, this may be challenging for some people with a low education level. The first hypothesis of this chapter is that coalition governments depress participation among the less educated and thus result in larger turnout inequality.

Existing research provides mixed support for the notion that coalition governments depress voter participation. On one hand, some studies of the determinants of cross-national differences in voter turnout do not find voter turnout to be higher in elections that produce single-party governments (e.g., Blais and Dobrzynska 1998). On the other hand, the only study that has looked in depth at the importance of coalitions for voter turnout finds a negative correlation between these factors (Brockington 2004).[2] Interactions with individual-level characteristics reveal that supporters of large parties are particularly less likely to vote when elections result in multiparty governments. However, Brockington does not find that citizens with low levels of education or weak partisans are less likely to vote when elections produce coalitions.

The contradictory results may be related to differences in model specification. The relationship between electoral systems, number of parties, coalition governments, and voter turnout is complex and requires discussion. It is well known that several characteristics of electoral systems influence the number of electoral and parliamentary parties (Lijphart 1994; Laakso and Taagepera 1979). In majoritarian systems, the number of parties tends to be lower than in PR systems. The larger the number of parties that obtain parliamentary representation, the more likely it is that a government has to be formed by coalition. The literature on voter turnout has long noted that each of these three factors (electoral systems, number of parties, coalition governments) may have different consequences for voter participation. To summarize, disproportionality reduces voter participation, because it

---

[2] More specifically, the negative association between number of parties and voter participation is reduced when controlling for coalitions.

produces less competitive elections and a larger share of wasted votes (Selb 2009; Gallego, Rico, and Anduiza 2012). However, research has failed to find a consistent association between the number of parties and voter turnout (Geys 2006; Blais and Aarts 2006), which may be due to the fact that the negative and positive consequences of the number of parties cancel out. The presence of a larger number of parties increases the number of choices available to citizens and also increases electoral mobilization, which should increase turnout. But more parties should also produce coalition governments and increase the information costs of voting, which should reduce turnout. Finally, as previously reviewed, the evidence that coalitions reduce turnout is scant and, at best, mixed.

Because electoral systems, number of parties, and coalition governments are so closely related, observational research has limited ability to disentangle how each factor affects voter participation. The usual approach is to rely on regression methods to sort out the relative effects of individual factors on voter turnout but the results are very sensitive to model specification. In the next section, I look at the consequences of coalitions for voter participation and turnout inequality, and I contribute to existing research by analyzing a survey experiment that only manipulates the necessity to form coalitions, while leaving other aspects of elections constant. This strategy allows me to isolate the effect of coalitions. The existence of a positive association between government fragmentation and unequal turnout is supported in a bivariate analysis with cross-national data. The multivariate analyses in the last section of this chapter include electoral systems and the effective number of electoral parties as control variables.

The Coalitions Experiment

I designed an original survey experiment to examine whether the prospect of having a coalition government affects the voter participation of people from different education groups in heterogeneous ways. This experiment was embedded in an academic online survey conducted in Spain in November 2011, about ten days before a parliamentary election was held on November 20, 2011. The characteristics of the survey were similar to those of the first experiment described in Chapter 3.[3]

The survey experiment presented respondents with a fictitious election. In all treatments, the text reported that two large political parties and four small political parties competed in the election. The text also provided information about the characteristics of the parties and the shares of the vote they would obtain, according to preelectoral polls. The vignette described the two large parties as being center-left and center-right and the four additional parties as being a green party, a right-wing party from one of Spain's regions (*Comunidades Autónomas*), a left-wing regional party, and a liberal party.

The party system described in the survey resembled the actual Spanish party system, which has a large center-left and a large center-right party that obtain a plurality of the vote. There are also several smaller parties, some of which operate nationwide and some of which compete in only certain regions. There are two main dimensions of political competition in Spain. The most important is competition between left-wing and right-wing political options on economic issues such as redistribution. The second is a center-periphery cleavage; while some political parties want to maintain the territorial status quo or increase centralization, a number of regional parties endeavor to reclaim more self-government or even independence, as in Catalonia or the Basque country. Thus, respondents could relate to the imaginary party system presented in the experiment.

The experimental manipulation altered the level of electoral and government fragmentation. While the hypothesis to be tested was that the prospect of having a coalition government discourages some people with a low level of education from voting, it was necessary to provide some information about the

---

[3] Both surveys were part of a four-wave panel study. The second wave, which contained the experiment on ballot type, went to the field in April 2011, and the experiment on coalitions was included in the third wave of the panel in November 2011. This sample also contained only young people aged 18 to 45.

political parties and the likely election results, to contextualize the situation. In particular, the treatment modified the percent of votes that preelectoral polls predicted each political party would receive, as well as the number of parties that was necessary to form a government. In the first condition, respondents were told that, according to the polls, each of the two large parties would receive approximately 45 percent of the vote and that the winner would be able to form a government alone. The other parties would receive a combined 10 percent of the vote. The level of fragmentation was low, and there was no need to form a coalition. In the second treatment, the text reported that each of the two large parties would get 35 percent of the vote, while the other four parties would receive a combined 30 percent of the vote. The winning party was bound to form a coalition with one of the small parties. This was the intermediate level of fragmentation condition. In the third treatment, respondents were told that each of the two large parties would get only 25 percent of the vote, while the other four would receive a combined 50 percent of the vote. The text stated that the winning party would need to form a coalition with two of the small parties, in order to form a government. This was the high fragmentation condition.

After reading about the election, respondents had to report what they would do in the hypothetical situation: certainly vote, probably vote, probably not vote, or certainly not vote. Figure 4–1 displays the full question wording and the visual information provided in each experimental condition.

In all treatments, the popular vote was described as being approximately evenly split between the three left-leaning political parties and the three right-leaning political parties. This was necessary, in order to suggest that both a left-wing and a right-wing government could be formed and thus to leave the winner of the election open to interpretation. Of course, an even split of the vote was not a realistic situation in the actual political context. The conservative Partido Popular won the Spanish November 2011 parliamentary elections by a landslide, and a large number of electoral polls had forecasted the victory. Unfortunately, it is impossible to establish whether the lack of correspondence

Introduction to the three treatments

Two large parties run in an important election, one is center-left and the other is center-right. Moreover, there are four small parties with different political positions.

Treatment 1: Low Fragmentation Condition

According to the polls, each of the two large parties will receive 45 percent of the vote. The winner will obtain enough members of Parliament to be able to form a government alone. The small parties will together receive 10 percent of the vote. The winner will not need to form a coalition with any of these parties in order to govern.

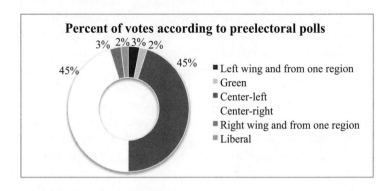

Treatment 2: Intermediate Fragmentation Condition

According to the polls, each of the two large parties will receive 35 percent of the vote. The winner will not obtain enough members of Parliament to be able to form a government alone. The small parties will together receive 30 percent of the vote. The winner will need to form a coalition with one of these parties in order to govern.

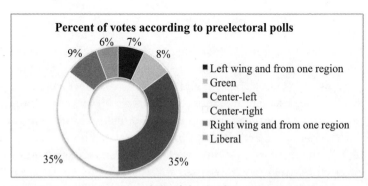

FIGURE 4–1. Question wording of the Coalitions Experiment

Treatment 3: High Fragmentation Condition

According to the polls, each of the two large parties will receive 25 percent of the vote. The winner will not obtain enough members of Parliament to be able to form a government alone. The small parties will together receive 50 percent of the vote. The winner will need to form a coalition with two of these parties in order to govern.

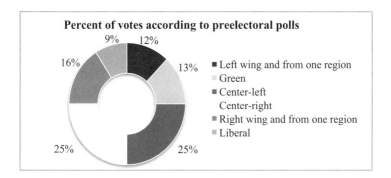

Percent of votes according to preelectoral polls

- Left wing and from one region
- Green
- Center-left
- Center-right
- Right wing and from one region
- Liberal

What would you do in this election?

1. I would certainly voting
2. I would probably vote
3. I would probably not vote
4. I would certainly not vote

FIGURE 4–1 (*continued*)

between the real election and the fictitious election biased the responses systematically.

The one way in which the preelectoral context probably affected responses to the survey question was reflected in the very high proportion of respondents who reported that they would vote in the hypothetical election. More than 85 percent of respondents claimed that they would certainly or probably vote. Social pressure to vote intensifies during electoral campaign periods, and such environmental pressure may have affected responses. In order to reduce the skewness of the data, I recoded the response options in two categories. The first category, coded as 1,

TABLE 4–1. *Reported Intention to Vote in the Coalitions Experiment*

	Low Fragmentation, One Party	Intermediate Fragmentation, Two Parties	High Fragmentation, Three Parties	Difference Low-High
Lower secondary	0.49	0.46	0.42	−0.07*
Standard error	0.03	0.03	0.03	0.04
Number of observations	214	204	209	627
High secondary	0.58	0.57	0.54	−0.04
Standard error	0.04	0.04	0.04	0.06
Number of observations	137	182	165	484
Tertiary education	0.61	0.61	0.60	−0.01
Standard error	0.03	0.03	0.03	0.04
Number of observations	241	230	263	734
All	0.56	0.55	0.53	−0.03
Standard error	0.02	0.02	0.02	0.03
Number of observations	592	616	637	1,845

* $p < 0.1$, ** $p < 0.05$, one-tailed test. Entries are the proportion of respondents who reported that they would certainly vote.

contained people who reported that they would certainly vote. The second category, coded as 0, contained respondents who claimed that they would probably vote, probably not vote, or certainly not vote.[4]

Table 4–1 presents the proportions of respondents who reported that they would certainly vote in the imaginary election. The figures are split by respondents' level of education and by treatment group. Respondents with low education have lower secondary education or less, those with an intermediate level of education have upper secondary education, and those with a high level of education have some university education. The hypothesis to be tested was that a high level of political fragmentation, which forces the formation of coalitions, depresses

---

[4] An alternative way to analyze the results is to calculate the mean value of the four response categories ("certainly vote" coded as 3, "probably vote" coded as 2, and so on). The same pattern as reported here holds.

the participation rates of only poorly educated people, whereas it does not affect the participation rates of people with higher education levels. The implication of such a heterogeneous effect should be that turnout gaps are larger in highly fragmented political systems.

The results confirm that highly and less educated people are heterogeneously sensitive to changes in level of fragmentation. In the low fragmentation condition, 49 percent of respondents with a low education level claimed that they would certainly vote, compared to only 42 percent in the high fragmentation condition. The 7 percentage points difference is statistically significant at the 90 percent level. In the intermediate fragmentation condition, reported intent to vote fell in between the two extreme categories, because 46 percent of respondents with lower secondary education or less were certain that they would vote. The gradual difference across the three conditions was reassuring.

Changes in the level of political fragmentation, by contrast, did not alter the reported intent to vote of highly educated people. In all three experimental conditions, about 60 percent of these group reported that they would certainly vote. The percentage reporting the same in the group with an intermediate level of education fell between the figures for the poorly and highly educated groups. In the low fragmentation condition, 58 percent of people with an intermediate education level reported that they would certainly vote, compared to 54 percent in the high fragmentation condition. The difference was not statistically significant.

Looking at the whole sample, a highly fragmented system conducive to coalition government seemed to reduce turnout only very slightly. Taken together, the level of electoral and governmental fragmentation only modified reported intent to vote by 3 percentage points. This difference came close to, but did not achieve, statistical significance at the 90 percent level (p = 0.12).[5]

---

[5] The analyses have been replicated first including only supporters of the two large parties in Spain (*Partido Popular* and *Partidos Socialista Obrero Español*, which together constituted 40 percent of the sample) and then excluded supporters of these two large parties. Some results are worth mentioning. Highly

Because of the heterogeneous effects of changes in level of fragmentation on highly and less educated respondents, turnout gaps varied substantially across the experimental conditions. When two large parties dominated the system and could form a government alone, the difference in the reported intent to vote with certainty of highly and less educated respondents was only 12 percentage points. In the very fragmented scenario, this gap grew to 18 percentage points. Thus, turnout inequality was larger when the election resulted in a coalition government than when it produced a one-party government.

The sample was more politically interested than the Spanish people generally. It is very plausible that any overall effects would be larger in a more politically disengaged sample.

In spite of the small overall impact of coalitions on voter turnout, the results of the experiment provided clear support for the hypothesis that the prospect of having coalition governments affects highly and less educated people heterogeneously. Because governmental fragmentation reduces participation only among the less educated, it can affect unequal participation, even if the general effect on voter turnout is trivial.

While the experiment in this study did not unveil the exact mechanism that produces a decline in the participation rates of the poor, the results are consistent with the general claim that unequal participation increases when participating in elections requires more cognitive effort. In high fragmentation scenarios, large parties have to form coalitions with smaller parties, and the relationship between voting and government formation and policy is less clear. Thinking through the logic of coalition formation is less straightforward for voters than choosing between two

educated supporters of the PP and PSOE reported that they would certainly vote more frequently in the high fragmentation treatment than in the low fragmentation treatment. What is more, the finding that poorly educated respondents were less likely to vote in the highly fragmented scenario replicated well. In fact, the difference was somewhat larger among poorly educated people who were not supporters of the two large parties (difference in proportions $= 0.1$, $p = 0.06$).

large and well-defined policy options. Turnout inequality grows when voting is more cognitively costly.

Cross-National Bivariate Association

Experimental results are internally valid, but there may be doubts about their external validity. To assess whether political fragmentation is associated with larger turnout inequalities in real elections, this section turns to the CSES data.

The measure of political fragmentation that I use is government fractionalization, or the probability that two randomly chosen deputies from government parties are of different political parties. The data come from the Database of Political Institutions (Keefer 2010). This measure is available for a wide range of years and cases that cover all CSES elections, with the exception of those in Taiwan. Government fragmentation captures the degree to which a government is composed by different political parties. A score of 0 is given if a government is formed by members of only one party and a score of more than 0 (with a theoretical maximum of 1) is given if a government is formed by more than one party. The values refer to the fragmentation of the incumbent government, that is, the government in power prior to the election. However, all analyses were replicated using the fragmentation of the government formed after the election and the results obtained were very similar.

The analyses reported in this chapter excluded countries with majoritarian electoral systems. These systems are different to others in that only one party is typically in charge of the governments and because uninominal districts greatly constrain the number of viable parties. As discussed, low competitiveness, wasted votes, and few parties, all of which are typical of majoritarian systems, may depress participation for reasons other than the presence of coalition governments. Of course, the bivariate relationship between fractionalization and turnout is weaker if we include the cases of the United States, Canada, and the UK. These countries have both high levels of turnout inequality and governments that are typically formed by just one party. The multivariate analysis

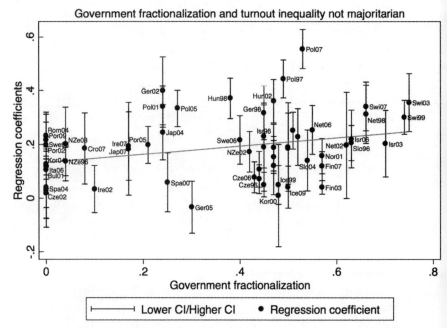

FIGURE 4–2. Turnout inequality and government fragmentation. *Source*: CSES and Database of Political Institutions. Government fragmentation is plotted against the regression coefficients of education on voting from OLS models. Unreadable labels were deleted. Elections held under majoritarian systems were excluded.

presented at the end of this chapter include elections held in majoritarian systems and controlled for confounded variables.

Figure 4–2 plots the size of the gaps between the predicted voter turnout rates of highly and less educated people against measures of government fractionalization in countries with proportional or mixed member electoral systems.

The gaps in the turnout rates of highly and less educated people are typically rather small in countries with low levels of government fragmentation. For example, if government fragmentation has a value of 0.2 or lower, the difference in the turnout rates of highly and less educated people is never larger than 25 percentage points. At intermediate and high levels of government fragmentation, there is considerable variation in turnout inequality, but the turnout gaps tend to become higher, on average, as governmental fragmentation grows. Thus, the bivariate relationship is clearly positive. The results suggest that in countries with proportional and mixed member electoral systems, a larger degree of government fragmentation is associated with more unequal voter participation.

Media Systems and Ease of Access to Political Information

A very different type of contextual characteristic that can modify the cognitive costs of voting is the media system. Traditional research on political knowledge and communication has focused on the individual-level determinants of knowledge and media consumption (e.g., Delli Carpini and Keeter 1996), but recent scholarship has increasingly emphasized that the structure of a media system profoundly shapes levels of political awareness and political behavior (Prior 2005, 2007; Aalberg and Curran 2011; Baek 2009).[6] This is because media systems influence how costly it is for citizens to encounter high-quality political information or, conversely, how easy it is for them to avoid encountering information. This section argues that public-service-oriented media systems are associated with smaller participatory gaps, because the abundance of high-quality news in these systems reduces the costs of learning about politics for all citizens and increases the ability and motivation of uninterested citizens to vote.

The concept of media system refers to the set of organizations, regulations, and common journalistic practices that characterize the supply of media contents in a country. There are different classifications of media systems. For example, Hallin and Mancini (2004) distinguish between the liberal media model, found mostly in Anglo-Saxon countries; the polarized pluralist

---

[6] This literature focuses on broadcasting because television is the type of media through which a larger share of the population obtains political information. This may be changing due to the widespread use of the Internet, but I follow this convention in this chapter.

model typical of Mediterranean countries; and the democratic corporatist model, found in Northern Europe. I employ here the distinction between a private, market-oriented model; a public-service-oriented model; and a mixed model (Baek 2009; Aalberg and Curran 2011). This simpler classification situates the types of media systems on a continuum and has the advantage of containing relevant information for a large set of countries.

In market-oriented media systems, most news organizations are privately owned and have mainly commercial goals. The state plays a light role in regulating the content of emissions. By contrast, in public service systems, a larger share of news organizations are publicly owned, and states regulate actively, with the aim of making sure that both public and private media organizations deliver high-quality political information. The assumption in these systems is that the social function of the media is to educate, not just entertain, audiences. This aim follows from the idea that the correct functioning of democracy requires the public to be informed about public affairs. The differences in ownership, orientation, and regulation between these media systems have important consequences for the types of content that these systems offer (Iyengar et al. 2010; Curran el al. 2009; Aalberg and Curran 2011). In market-oriented systems, compared to public-service-oriented systems, broadcasting focuses more frequently on soft news (such as crime, sports, or accidents), domestic stories, and entertainment. Conversely, public systems deliver an abundance of hard news and information on international affairs, and the share of news content relative to entertainment content is larger.

Citizens learn about politics mainly through the media. How much they end up absorbing depends not only on their motivation to learn, but also on the characteristics of the supply of political information. Importantly, the individual motivation to learn is a more important determinant of political knowledge in some media systems than in others. Some citizens actively seek to learn about public affairs in the media, but exposure to political information also happens unintentionally, depending on how available and avoidable news is in the information environment.

The degree to which exposure to information depends on individual decisions to search for it largely depends on the characteristics of the information environment (Prior 2007). For example, prior to the spread of cable television, all news channels used to broadcast news during prime time, and anyone who watched television at this time had no option but to watch the news. This changed with the introduction of more channels that offered entertainment content during prime time and thus provided alternatives to news to citizens who were not interested in politics or current affairs. Curran et al. (2009) report that in Denmark, Finland, and the UK, about three quarters of poorly educated people report watching news regularly. This figure compares favorably to the meager one-third of less educated Americans who report watching news. The authors attribute this difference to the fact that American channels offer many more options than European channels. This literature shows that individual interest in political information becomes a more important determinant of exposure to news content as the set of programs from which citizens can choose grows larger.

Market-oriented media systems offer more entertainment options and lower quality news than public-service-oriented systems. This difference in the supply of news produces differences in the amount and distribution of political knowledge in society. Citizens who live in market-oriented systems know, on average, less about politics than do citizens in public-service-oriented systems (Dimock and Popkin 1997). Furthermore, in market-oriented systems, there are larger knowledge gaps between highly and less educated people (Iyengar et al. 2010). The easier it is for uninterested citizens to avoid political information, the more ignorant about public affairs they become. It is noteworthy that, according to a study conducted by Iyengar and colleagues in Denmark, where the media has a strong public service orientation, the level of political knowledge is very high, and there are no differences in political knowledge between highly and less educated people *at all*. This suggests that a media system that provides high-quality information can compensate for differences in prior knowledge and for cognitive resources obtained through the education system.

The amount and distribution of political knowledge in a society is important to understanding voter turnout, because political knowledge is one of the most important correlates of political behavior. Citizens who know a lot about politics are more likely to vote and to participate in other political activities (e.g., Delli Carpini and Keeter 1996; Holtz-Bacha and Norris 1999; Aarts and Semetko 2003). Furthermore, increases in the supply of information cause increases in voter turnout (Lassen 2005). In the United States, a larger supply of entertainment contents has widened the gaps in political knowledge and participation between citizens who are interested in politics and citizens who are not (Prior 2007).

In spite of the importance of political information to political behavior, macro-level comparative research has paid very little attention to how the characteristics of media systems affect cross-national differences in voter turnout. The one exception is Baek (2009), who shows that media systems and the laws that regulate political campaigns positively correlate with differences in political participation in 74 countries. She argues that this is because institutional settings that lower the information costs of voting have higher turnout rates.

The characteristics of a media system can be expected to affect not only aggregate voter turnout rates, but also turnout inequality. The literature reviewed above argues that the costs of being exposed to news is lower in public-service-oriented systems than in market-oriented systems, and that lower costs result in higher levels of knowledge and smaller knowledge gaps. If this is true, the difference in the ability and motivation to vote between highly and less educated citizens should also be lower in the former systems. Consequently, I expect the gaps in the turnout rates of highly and less educated citizens to be smaller in public-service-oriented systems than in market-oriented systems.

To test the hypothesis that media systems shape levels of turnout inequality, I first examined the bivariate correlation between these factors. The type of media system was operationalized using two measures, following Baek (2009). One measure used was the percentage of the audience that follows public broadcasters, relative to the total audience share of the five largest broadcasters. Via multivariate analysis, I also examined whether an alternative measure of type of media system, which categorically distinguished between private, mixed, and public systems, was associated with turnout inequality.[7]

This analysis has shortcomings. The measure does not vary over time, and the identification strategy is very simple. There is no obvious way to manipulate the media system in a survey experiment, and thus the analysis here was limited to observational data. However, the choice of media system as a contextual characteristic over other possibilities is justified by the aim of examining characteristics that are as varied as possible. The results have to be taken with caution, but they are interesting nevertheless, if only because we know so little about the relationship between media systems and voter participation.

Figure 4–3 displays the bivariate relationship between the audience share of public broadcasters and turnout inequality. The United States and Switzerland have a disproportionate influence on the bivariate correlation, and thus the graph includes two fitted lines with and without these two cases.

The relationship between the audience share of public broadcasters and unequal participation is moderately negative. On average, turnout inequality is somewhat smaller in countries in which public channels have a large share of audiences. The relationship is clearly influenced by the United States and Switzerland, but excluding both countries from the analyses still yields a negative correlation. This suggests that gaps in the voter participation of highly and less educated people may be somewhat reduced in contexts where a large share of the population watches public broadcasters offering more and better quality news.[8]

---

[7] All data are taken from Baek (2009). Data about public audience share are missing for Iceland and data about the type of media system are missing for Taiwan.

[8] The relationship may, of course, be endogenous if all education groups are more likely to participate in politics and also demand more political information in some contexts than in others. Then, differences in political engagement may

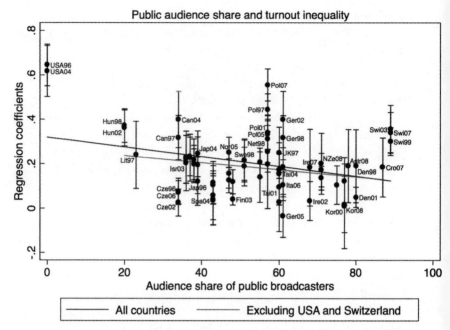

FIGURE 4-3. Turnout inequality and share of the audience of public broadcasters. *Source*: CSES and Baek (2009). Audience share of public broadcasters is plotted against the regression coefficients of education on voting from OLS models. Unreadable labels were deleted.

Multivariate Analysis on Coalitions and Media Systems

I used multivariate analysis to examine more systematically whether coalitions and type of media system are associated with the gradient of the relationship between education and voting. The multilevel regression models tested, in particular, whether the presence of the contextual variables of interest moderated (i.e., intensified or weakened) the relationship between individual

drive exposure to public channels. It is plausible that political attitudes and, in particular, demand for political information shape the types of media systems that prevail in societies, instead of media systems being the determinants of political attitudes. I follow here the literature on political communication, which takes media systems as exogenous. In any case, as I have pointed out, the bivariate correlations should not be interpreted as causal.

education level and voter participation. In this analysis, I included two alternative measures of media systems, a continuous measure of the audience share of public broadcasters and a categorical measure that classified media systems as private, mixed, or public. When first run, the models included only the government fractionalization and media systems measures. Thereafter, they also included controls for the variables examined in Chapter 3 (ballot structure and electoral system) and for the effective number of electoral parties.[9] It is important to recall that the focus of this book is not so much what affects overall levels of voter turnout as what moderates the relationship between education and voting.

Model 1 examines whether lower government fractionalization and larger public broadcasting audience share are associated with a reduced association between education and voting. Model 4 has a similar specification but includes the categorical distinction between media systems instead of the variable audience share. Models 2 and 5 replicate models 1 and 4, adding controls for ballot structure, and models 3 and 5 add controls for effective number of electoral parties. All models include controls for sex, age, and age squared. Countries in which voting is compulsory are excluded, but the results replicate well when these countries are introduced and when compulsory voting and interaction with education are introduced as separate variables.

Education is correlated with reported voter participation in all models. Government fragmentation always has a negative sign, as hypothesized, suggesting that poorly educated people vote less frequently in fractionalized systems. However, only two of the coefficients reach statistical significance at the 90 percent level. Likewise, only one of the uninteracted coefficients of the media system variables is significant at conventional levels.

More important, however, is the finding that the contextual variables of interest interact with individual education, as

---

[9] For a discussion of this indicator see Laakso and Taagepera (1979). The data come from Gallagher and Mitchell (2005), updated.

TABLE 4–2. *Multivariate Models of Voter Turnout: Coalitions, Media Systems, and Education*

	Media Indicator: Audience Share			Media Indicator: System Type		
	No Controls (model 1)	Ballots (model 2)	ENEP (model 3)	No Controls (model 4)	Ballot (model 5)	ENEP (model 6)
Education	0.42***	0.42***	0.51***	0.40***	0.38***	0.52***
	(0.06)	(0.06)	(0.09)	(0.02)	(0.06)	(0.09)
Government fractionalization	−0.16	−0.65+	−0.43+	−0.10	−0.59	−0.42
	(0.40)	(0.27)	(0.54)	(0.41)	(0.39)	(0.56)
Audience share public broadcasters	0.01	0.01*	0.01+			
	(0.01)	(0.005)	(0.006)			
Public broadcasting system (private=0; mixed=1; public=2)				0.15	0.06	0.28
				(0.22)	(0.21)	(0.25)
Ballot openness in PR systems (0 closed, 0.5 flexible, 1 open)		−1.62***			−1.38***	
		(0.30)			(0.30)	
Dual ballot (mixed system)		−0.23			−0.12	
		(0.23)			(0.24)	
Nominal ballot (majoritarian)		−0.66**			−0.79*	
		(0.27)			(0.29)	
Other (AV, STV, and SNTV)		−0.10			−0.17	
		(0.49)			(0.50)	
Effective number of electoral parties			0.04			0.05
			(0.11)			(0.11)
Government fract.* education	0.18**	0.05	0.24**	0.17*	0.13+	0.26**
	(0.08)	(0.08)	(0.10)	(0.08)	(0.08)	(0.10)
Audience share*education	−0.003***	−0.004***	−0.003**			
	(0.001)	(0.01)	(0.01)			

110

	(1)	(2)	(3)	(4)	(5)	(6)
Public broadcasting*education				−0.12**	−0.13**	−0.14**
				(0.04)	(0.04)	(0.05)
Ballot openness*education		0.24***			0.18**	
		(0.06)			(0.06)	
Dual*education		0.05			0.05	
		(0.05)			(0.05)	
Nominal*education		0.06			0.06	
		(0.06)			(0.06)	
Other*education		−0.05			−0.15	
		(0.10)			(0.11)	
ENEP*education			−0.02			−0.03
			(0.02)			(0.11)
Constant	−1.78***	−0.98***	−1.96***	−1.55***	−1.21***	−1.82***
	(0.30)	(0.31)	(0.50)	(0.30)	(0.30)	(0.53)
Controls for age, age2, and sex	Yes	Yes	Yes	Yes	Yes	Yes
Variance constant	0.80	0.66	0.81	0.81	0.66	0.82
	(0.07)	(0.07)	(0.08)	(0.07)	(0.06)	(0.02)
Variance slope (education)	0.14	0.12	0.13	0.14	0.12	0.13
	(0.01)	(0.02)	(0.02)	(0.02)	(0.01)	(0.02)
Correlation education, constant	−0.41	−0.16	−0.43	−0.45	−0.28	−0.46
	(0.12)	(0.16)	(0.12)	(0.11)	(0.13)	(0.12)
N elections	66	66	62	66	66	62
N individuals	105487	105487	100228	105487	105487	100228

+ $p < 0.1$, * $p < 0.05$, ** $p < 0.01$, *** $p < 0.001$. Entries are multilevel logistic regression coefficients (standard errors). Models with random intercepts and random education slopes. Compulsory voting countries are excluded from the analysis. Education is a continuous measure that has five values: primary or less, incomplete secondary, complete secondary, postsecondary, or university education. Ballot structure in PR systems takes on three values: 0 closed party lists, 0.5 flexible lists, 1 open lists. No weights applied. Missing data: government fractionalization for Taiwan; media systems for Iceland; ENEP for Japan, Lithuania, and Taiwan.

expected. Larger degrees of governmental fractionalization intensify the correlation between education and reported participation in all but one of the models. These interactions suggest that the gradient of the relationship between education and voting is steeper in highly fractionalized contexts and hence voter turnout is more unequal when more than one party is in government than when only one party is in government.

The relationship between education and voting is weaker in public-service-oriented systems than in market-oriented models. First, the negative coefficient of the interaction term between education and audience share of public broadcasters suggests that the association between education and voting becomes, on average, weaker as public audience share increases. Second, when including the alternative categorical measure, the results also suggest that the relationship between education and voting is less steep in public-service-oriented systems than in market-oriented systems. In all six models, the interactive coefficients are of the expected direction and statistically significant.

The interactive coefficients are robust to the inclusion of controls for ballot structure, the factor examined in Chapter 3, and are also robust to controlling for effective number of electoral parties. Thus, even if the identification strategy employed here is not powerful and the results need to be taken with caution, the multivariate results provide additional support for the two hypotheses of this chapter.

The Cognitive Costs of Voting Affect Poorly Educated People Disproportionately

This chapter has examined two additional predictions that follow from the general argument that any contextual level feature that increases the cognitive costs of voting will reduce participation, particularly among the poorly educated, and thus increase turnout inequality. The two selected features, coalition governments and media system, are quite different from each other and from ballot structure, the institutional feature selected in Chapter 3, and registration, discussed in Chapter 2. Finding the same pattern across a diverse range of contextual characteristics allows us to better assess the theoretical framework and suggest that the general argument has a wide range of applications. The three survey experiments and the studies with observational data, taken together, provide support for the core theoretical expectation of this first part of the book. Voter turnout seems to be more unequal in contexts in which voting is cognitively more challenging. Several features that increase the information and decision costs of voting depress the voter participation of the less educated, who have fewer resources to pay for these costs.

This research has started to provide a tentative answer to the question of what can be done to make participation more equal, which is that voting should be made as easy as possible. The findings are interesting and potentially useful. Because many contextual characteristics can affect how easy or difficult voting is, there is also a wide range of interventions that may perhaps make participation more equal across groups. Some contextual features that affect the cognitive costs of voting may be very difficult to change, or their change may be undesirable for other reasons. However, feasible and promising options may range from lowering the costs of learning about politics by providing more and better information, to choosing more user-friendly voting procedures.

5

Trade Unions in the Highly Educated Membership Era

Mobilization theories of unequal participation claim that turnout is more equal where political organizations mobilize many poorly educated citizens to vote (Verba, Kim, and Nie 1978; Rosenstone and Hansen 1993; Jusko 2011). Scholars consider trade unions as one of the most important organizations that can mobilize lower-status people to vote and reduce participatory gaps (Verba, Kim, and Nie 1978; Gray and Caul 2000; Radcliff and Davis 2000; Voos 2003; Leighley and Nagler 2007; Flavin and Radcliff 2011).[1] The literature on trade union mobilization notes that unions have historically organized socially disadvantaged groups and defended their interests. Where and when unions are strong, the argument goes, their activities increase the participation rates of lower-status citizens and reduce turnout inequality. Conversely, weak or weakening trade unions result in more unequal participation: "declines in labor organization mean a decline in the proportion of citizens contributing their preferences to the democratic process. To the extent that such demobilization

---

[1] The other main organizations that mobilize lower-status groups are of course left-wing political parties. However, in this chapter I will focus the discussion and the analysis on the equalizing impact of trade unions. I discuss alternative mobilization accounts that concentrate on the role of parties at the end of the chapter.

is likely to be concentrated among lower- and middle-status citizens, falling rates of organization mean that the electorate will increasingly over-represent higher-status individuals" (Radcliff and Davis 2000: 140).

Although the claim that turnout is more equal where trade unions are powerful has been tested in the American context (Leighley and Nagler 2007), previous analyses have not explicitly examined this claim in a comparative perspective. In this chapter, I argue that the willingness and ability of trade unions to equalize participation is currently more limited than is frequently supposed. As is well-known, trade union membership has declined substantially. In addition, the educational composition of union members has shifted in the last decades, such that today union members are on average better educated than nonmembers. Changes in the size and educational composition of membership have eroded the incentives of unions to focus their mobilization efforts on people with a low education level to vote.

The empirical section examines if stronger trade unions are associated with more equal participation using both individual and contextual data about union membership. The research strategy relies on observational data only and the results need to be interpreted cautiously. At the individual level, the results confirm that being a union member has a beneficial effect on turnout. Trade union members and their families vote at higher rates than nonmembers. In addition, contextual union density, that is, the percentage of workers who are union members, is associated with higher participation rates of nonunion members. In spite of this positive effect on turnout, the analyses reveal that a large union density reduces turnout inequality only slightly at the aggregate level.

The framework proposed in this book helps to explain why this is the case. At the individual level, the positive effect of union membership is similar in size for highly and poorly educated union members. At the contextual level, where union density is high, both highly and less educated people vote at higher rates. Union membership and union density seem to have approximately *homogeneous* positive consequences for voter participation across all education groups. The lack of heterogeneous effects implies that reductions in turnout inequality occur only where turnout is very high, due to ceiling effects. In fact, the United States and a few Scandinavian countries – where union density is very high – entirely drive the association between union density and turnout inequality. When these countries are excluded, union density is not associated with lower inequality in voter participation, presumably because unions do not focus their political mobilization efforts on the less educated but spread these efforts across the board.

The Classical Mobilization Account

Verba, Kim, and Nie (1978) asked a similar question to what the present author asks:[2] Why is political participation more unequal in some contexts than in others? They argued that cross-national variation in participatory inequality depends upon how politically organized lower-status groups are. This answer builds on previous work by Verba and Nie (1972) in the United States, and more generally on the idea that organization is the weapon of the weak (Michels 1915). The core argument runs as follows: Lower-status citizens have fewer resources and motivations to participate in politics than higher-status citizens. Therefore, they participate less in politics. Mobilization by organizations (a) subsidizes the costs of participation, which reduces the need for resources, and (b) increases the benefits of participation by enhancing the motivation to vote. When targeted at disadvantaged groups, mobilization can raise their participation rates and reduce participatory gaps. In the authors' words: "Lower-status groups (. . .) need a group-based process of political mobilization if they are to catch up to the upper-status groups in terms of political activity. They need a self-conscious ideology as motivation and need organization as a resource" (Verba, Kim, and Nie 1978: 14). Rosenstone and Hansen have succinctly summarized

---

[2] They also examined participation in activities other than voting.

a similar argument as "when political leaders offset the costs of political involvement – when they provide information, subsidize participation, occasion the provision of social rewards – they make it possible for people who have few resources of their own to participate" (1993: 242). In another example of this reasoning, several authors have argued that group mobilization causes African Americans to participate more in politics than their socioeconomic resources predict (Uhlaner, Cain, and Kiewiet 1989; Verba and Nie 1972; Verba, Schlozman, and Brady 1995).

While mobilization targeted to disadvantaged groups, who are more in need of help and motivation, can be a powerful force at creating equal participation, political mobilization can also exacerbate, rather than reduce it. The privileged are in many contexts better organized politically or otherwise than the disadvantaged and hence more likely to be in the kind of organizations where mobilization occurs (Morales 2009). Political parties also target higher-status individuals in their mobilization efforts (Rosenstone and Hansen 1993, but see Karp and Banducci 2008).

Political mobilization can both exacerbate and reduce biases in participation. The fact that organizations exist that could mobilize disadvantaged citizens does not imply that they will choose to do so. We need to understand the circumstances under which organizations will decide to target poorly educated people and to mobilize them politically.

This discussion, in particular, focuses on trade unions. Comparative mobilization theories identify unions as one of the most important organizations that may reduce participatory inequality. Trade unions are sometimes large (in the industrialized countries surveyed by Verba, Nie, and Kim, trade unions were the organizations with the largest number of members), thus they can have sizeable effects on aggregate participation. Trade unions often carry out actions specifically aimed at promoting voter participation and, crucially, they are often assumed to target, organize, and mobilize mainly lower-status groups. Mobilization accounts sustain that unions target lower-status people because of their historical mission, and where unions are strong, they are able to mobilize a sufficiently large number of lower-status people politically to make turnout more equal.

The proposition that trade unions can promote voter participation is uncontroversial and well established. First, the mechanisms that help trade unions increase the voter turnout rates of both their members and of nonmembers are manifold: They provide political information; actively encourage their members to vote; and teach civic skills (e.g., Norris 2002; Verba, Schlozman, and Brady 1995). Furthermore, high union density at the contextual level may result in higher participation rates of nonmembers for different reasons. Politically, strong trade unions can move the policy positions of left-wing parties to the left, and increase the motivation to vote of people who benefit from the kind of policies championed by these parties (Radcliff and Davis 2000; Leighley and Nagler 2007). Moreover, the increased participation of one union member can activate other family members and neighbors and nourish the social norm of participation in a community.

The evidence supports the claim that a high union density increases voter turnout. Using data from the European Social Survey for fifteen countries, Art and Turner (2007) find that union members are more likely to vote than are nonmembers by 7 percentage points. Using the International Social Survey Program for thirty-two countries, Flavin and Radcliff (2011) find that union members are 2 percentage points more likely to vote than nonmembers, even when controlling for other sociodemographic and attitudinal variables. Gray and Caul (2000) use longitudinal data and estimate that a 10 percentage points decline in union density led to a 1.4 percentage points decline in turnout. Radcliff and Davis (2000) examine data from nineteen industrial democracies and find that an increase of 5 percentage points in the share of union density increases voter turnout by 1 percentage point (for American estimates see Rosenfeld 2010; Freeman 2003; Radcliff 2001). Individual union membership and contextual union density are associated with moderate increases in the voter participation of both members and nonmembers.

In spite of the extensive evidence that trade unions have a positive effect on voter turnout, we do not know if unions affect or do not affect turnout inequality. Very little research has directly examined this question (the exception being Leighley and Nagler 2007 for the United States). Instead of directly assessing this claim, scholars *assume* that trade unions will want to mobilize lower-status individuals largely because of historical reasons:

"Trade unions have historically acted as facilitating organizations in unison with labor parties to achieve reforms and social justice through the potential electoral capital provided by the working class (. . .) the combined effect of strong unions and strong labor parties creates the greatest incentives and effectiveness of working class mobilization" (Gray and Caul 2000: 1103);

"Because unions typically have defined their political agendas in class terms, they are the most important political advocate for working people: They serve as the only truly important political 'voice' of lower- and middle-status people" (Radcliff and Davis 2000: 134);

"Labor unions, whose members traditionally are drawn from the working class, can potentially offset this socioeconomic bias [in voting] if they are successful in mobilizing workers with lower socioeconomic status" (Flavin and Radcliff 2011: 2).

In this line of argumentation, the hypothesis that strong trade unions reduce unequal participation seems to follow from the well-established observation that unions increase turnout along with the untested assumption that they mainly mobilize lower-status groups because of their historical legacy.

Do Trade Unions Enhance Turnout Equality?

Under which conditions can we expect trade unions to reduce unequal turnout? The framework proposed in the theoretical chapter can help illuminate this question. A factor can reduce turnout inequality if either:

(a) its effects are *homogeneous* across all population groups *and* so large that participation rates come close to the 100 percent *ceiling in participation,* so that almost everyone votes, or

(b) its effects are *heterogeneous* such that the factor *mainly*
fosters the participation of the less educated *and* the effects
are strong enough to affect aggregate turnout inequality.

For the first possibility to apply, unions should produce a substantial increase in the electoral participation of both highly and
less educated citizens. Highly educated people vote anyway at
high rates. Thus, ceiling effects constrain the positive impact
of trade unions on this group's turnout rates, which cannot be
larger than 100 percent. On the contrary, the turnout rates of
less educated citizens are lower and have more room to grow.

As previously reviewed, analyses have found that the effect
of union density on voter turnout is positive, but moderate in
magnitude. For example, take Gray and Caul's (2000) estimate
that a 10 percentage point decline in union density leads to a 1.4
percentage points decline in voter turnout. Perhaps very large
differences in union density (say a 50 percentage points increase)
would produce a noticeable increase in voter turnout (7 percentage points). If the increase is homogeneous across education
groups, and it takes place in a context where highly educated people vote at very high rates, we may then expect some moderate
reductions in turnout inequality due to ceiling effects.

The second possibility focuses on the question whether unions
can push the turnout rates of the less educated higher, without
increasing the participation of the highly educated to the same
degree. This of course, would equalize participation. Unions will
mainly mobilize the less educated if they (a) seek to organize this
specific group, that is, have the *willingness* to mobilize the less
educated; and (b) are strong enough to produce a visible effect
on their aggregate turnout inequality, that is, have the *capacity*
to mobilize large numbers of the less educated.

The two most important changes experienced by trade unions
since the mid-twentieth century have implications for unions'
willingness and capacity to mobilize lower-status people to vote.
Union membership has declined in most advanced industrial
democracies, and the class composition of unions has shifted

toward middle-class professions. These changes can be expected to undermine trade unions' capacity to mobilize the less educated to vote.

The thesis that declining membership erodes the influence of trade unions in electoral politics is straightforward. Even if unions wanted to mobilize the less educated to vote, as their membership dwindles, so does their power to affect electoral politics. In most countries, union density (the key indicator of union strength) has declined from its postwar peak (Norris 2002; Visser 2006; Western and Rosenfeld 2011; Bryson, Ebbinghaus, and Visser 2011). For example, Visser (2006) reports that between the 1970s and 2003 union density declined in nineteen out of twenty-four countries surveyed, and stagnated in one. It only increased in countries that use a Ghent system (Sweden, Finland, Denmark, Belgium), which links unemployment insurance to union membership. For instance, density declined by 33 percentage points in New Zealand (from 55 percent to 22 percent of unionized workers), by 27 percentage points in Australia and Austria, by 18 percentage points in Ireland, and by 15 percentage points in Japan. In relative terms, many of these declines are dramatic. In Hungary, the Czech Republic, Slovakia, Poland, the United States, Australia, New Zealand, and France, union density declined by more than half the level reached in their respective high points.[3] Between 1978 and 2008, union density declined from 44 to 23 percent in the European Union (Bryson, Ebbinghaus, and Visser 2011).

Trade unions need to have members for their actions to affect aggregate politics in general and turnout inequality in particular. As Margaret Levi summarizes, "The strength of labor lies in its numbers; the smaller its membership, the less effective its economic power, electoral and lobbying clout, and capacity to

---

[3] The causes of this decline are manifold, including deindustrialization, increases in labor force participation, cultural changes, and increased international competition, which intensified the opposition of employers to centralized wage bargaining (e.g., Allern, Aylott, and Christiansen 2007).

mobilize on behalf of social-justice issues" (2003: 49). For instance, if unions are very effective at bringing their members to the polls, but only a very small fraction of the population is unionized, their strong individual level impact is unlikely to shape aggregate turnout inequality. Low membership in the United States is the reason why Verba, Schlozman, and Brady (1995) discount the equalizing potential of unions in their study of participation and equality.

The important question remains of why unions would focus their efforts at the poorly educated. To examine the question of willingness, I assume, as others have done (Allern, Aylott, and Christiansen 2007), that trade unions are organizations that seek to foster the interests of their members and the size of their membership. One way to advance members' interests is to influence their voting behavior. Voting as a block pushes politicians into approving union-backed measures, or else risk losing political support. For example, teachers' unions seek to have more members and to advance the interests of teachers. They propose education policies that teachers like, tell teachers about the parties' positions, and encourage them to vote for teacher-friendly parties. The same applies to other occupations. This assumption implies that unions defend the interests of their members and mobilize them to vote. It is neutral on the class profile of those mobilized.

The class and educational composition of trade union members has changed in the last four decades. Trade unions were one of the instruments used by working class social movements to advance the interests of workers (Alford 1963; Burnham 1982; Bartolini 2000). Male, blue-collar industrial workers were the stronghold of trade unions until the 1970s (Ebbinghaus and Visser 1999). However, the decline in trade union membership has been concentrated precisely in blue-collar, private sector unions. By contrast, unionization has been stable or has increased among public sector employees, such as doctors, teachers, and nurses, who are typically better educated. Leighley and Nagler (2007) report that the proportion of blue-collar workers among union members declined from 50 to 38 percent between 1983 and 2000 in the United States, while the proportion of union members employed in the public sector increased from 17 to 46 percent between 1973 and 2003. Putnam (2000) reports that three-quarters of American blue-collar unions lost members from the postwar peak to 1997. The median decline was of nearly two-thirds of the membership. Similar changes occurred in a comparative perspective. Visser (2006) shows that in all twenty-four countries included in his study, union density in the early twenty-first century was larger in the public sector than in the private sector. In most European countries, workers with incomes above the median are better organized in unions than workers with incomes below the median and the income of the median union member exceeds the income of the median voter (Becher and Pontusson 2011).

In regard to education, some analyses using the European Social Survey find that union members are more educated than nonmembers (Art and Turner 2007), while others find that an intermediate level of education is associated with a larger likelihood to be a member (Ebbinghaus, Gobel, and Koos 2011; Fazekas 2011). In the United States, union workers were much less likely to have college education than nonunion workers between 1973 and 1984, but the difference was substantially smaller between 1996 and 2007 (Western and Rosenfeld 2011).

Among CSES respondents, people with low levels of education are in fact underrepresented among union members, whereas people with higher levels of education are overrepresented, as shown in Table 5–1. This holds true both among the whole population and among the smaller subset of the active population (i.e., the employed and the unemployed). About 42 percent of the respondents who belong to unions have postsecondary education or university education and thus are definitely not members of the working class. If we add to them those who have completed secondary education, it becomes clear that about two-thirds of all union members have relatively high levels of education. Even in the active population, just 32 percent of self-reported union members are low-skilled workers, who have not completed secondary

TABLE 5–1. *The Educational Composition of Union Members and Nonunion Members*

	Primary Education	Incomplete Secondary	Secondary Education	Postsecondary	University Education	N
Whole population						
Nonmember	24.2	20.9	23.8	16.6	14.5	95,234
Member	15.3	18.9	23.6	20.8	21.4	29,217
Both	22.1	20.4	23.8	17.6	16.2	124,451
N both	27,485	25,391	29,584	21,894	20,097	
Active population						
Nonmember	16.5	21.0	25.4	18.1	19.0	52,709
Member	12.6	19.3	25.4	19.5	23.2	22,072
Both	15.4	20.5	25.4	18.5	20.2	74,781
N both	11,496	15,328	18,991	13,839	15,127	

Source: CSES cumulative dataset. Data are not weighted. Entries are row percentages and frequencies.

education, while this figure is 38 percent among nonunionized active respondents.

These figures suggest that union members are on average just as educated, if not more, as the whole population in most countries. We can expect unions to mobilize and defend the interests of both highly and less educated people, not only or mostly of the latter. If the effect of union membership on voter participation is homogeneous across education groups, mobilization by unions may result in increases in voter turnout that are similar across education groups.

Admittedly, the positive effect of unions on voter turnout can be unintentionally heterogeneous. Even if unions lack the willingness to mobilize mainly the poorly educated, some of their actions may mostly increase this groups' propensity to vote. People with fewer resources are more in need of information and other subsidies that help them vote. Unions may supply information and otherwise mobilize all their members and some nonmembers equally. Because the less educated are more in need of this pull, the same mobilization effort may result in a comparatively larger boost in their turnout rates.

The only detailed study on heterogeneous union effects has thrown mixed conclusions on the American case (Leighley and Nagler 2007). The authors propose that the capacity of unions to close turnout gaps eroded over time as their membership and composition changed. They examined the changes in union strength and composition between 1964 and 2004 using data from the American National Election Studies and their impact on the voter participation of different social groups. Their estimates suggest that the decline of union membership produced somewhat lower voter turnout among all groups.[4] While they

---

[4] It is puzzling that the analysis does not explicitly examine whether the effects of unionization on voter participation changed over the period. The theory suggests that unions were better able to mobilize lower-status individuals in the 1960s than after 2000. The models include fixed effects for state and year, accounting for variation in the baseline probability of voting across space and time. However, the authors do not model the hypothesized differences in the ability of unions to mobilize lower-status individuals over time (for example, by introducing interactive terms for time periods). Thus, the estimates can be

find that union membership produces larger increases in voting at the middle and low ends of the income distribution, contextual union density mainly increases the probability of voting for middle- and high-income individuals.[5] Thus, the relatively larger effects of contextual density on the participation of the rich may offset the larger effects of individual membership on the participation of the poor.

In sum, the main argument of this chapter is that while trade unions increase voter participation, they may not affect turnout inequality much. I have examined several arguments why trade unions could equalize participation. If individual and contextual union membership have homogeneous effects on highly and less educated people, larger unions may reduce inequality in participation due to ceiling effects. Organizations that mobilize the less educated, but not the highly educated, to vote can offset turnout inequality. However, in light of the current educational composition of trade union membership, it is not obvious why unions should be the champions of the poor, and mainly mobilize them to vote.

Trade Unions and Their Composition

There are different ways of measuring the strength of trade unions across countries. The most accepted measure is union density, the percentage of wage and salary earners who are union members (Visser 2006: 38). Trade unions provide the numerator. This may compromise the validity of the figures, because unions have incentives to overreport their affiliates and, moreover, these incentives may vary across countries. In addition, the

interpreted only as the mean effect of individual membership or union density over the whole period.

[5] In the authors' words: "the effect of the decline of unions on class bias in the electorate is rather surprising in light of standard views of labor unions and voter mobilization. Labor unions may mobilize and therefore represent workers, but we show that they do not necessarily mobilize low- or middle-income individuals at the expense of high-income individuals. Moreover, the contextual effects of union strength are slightly greater for middle- and high-income individuals than they are for individuals in the bottom third of the income distribution" (Leighley and Nagler 2007: 439).

exclusion of unemployed and inactive people from the denominator is problematic, because many union members are currently unemployed or retired. For example, in Italy almost half of all union members are retired (Visser 2006). Another way of measuring union strength is by using self-reported membership in public opinion surveys. Self-reports are inaccurate in different ways. Some respondents answer the question erroneously. They may pay their membership dues, but forget about this, or they may have been union members in the past and forget that they no longer are. Thus, I use both union density and reported aggregate union membership in the analyses.

The CSES asks if other people living in the respondents' household are union members. As previously reviewed, trade unions boost turnout rates not only among their members, but also among nonmembers. We know little about which nonmembers unions activate. The most obvious possibility is that members spread the positive effect of union membership to people who live with them. Nickerson (2008) found that two-thirds of the increase in voter turnout caused by get-out-the-vote activities is passed on to household members who did not receive the mobilization appeal themselves. Other research shows that more than 80 percent of the variation in voter turnout in two-member households is attributable to the household level, rather than to the individual, postcode, or ward level (Cutts and Fieldhouse 2009), suggesting that the participation of other household members greatly influences one's propensity to vote.

Figure 5–1 plots the percentage of people who report being a union member in the CSES, the percentage of people who report living with a union member, and official union density figures.[6] There are very large differences in the strength of unions across countries. Less than one in ten people are union members or live

---

[6] Unfortunately, the questions on union membership are not available for Chile, Lithuania, and Peru, so the analyses exclude these countries. In addition, data on union density are not available for Croatia and Taiwan, and the information on whether the respondent is living with a union member is missing in Ireland and Denmark. These cases will be missing from some analyses. Union density data are from Visser (2006) supplemented with the Quality of Government dataset (2011).

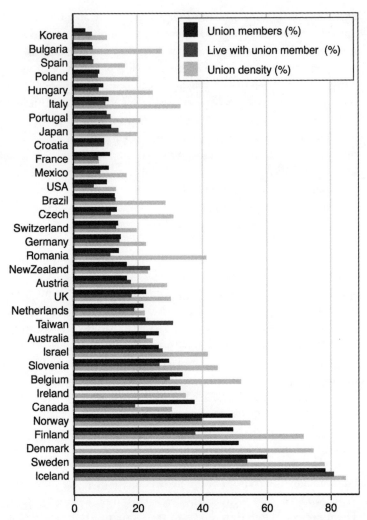

FIGURE 5–1. Strength of trade unions across country. *Source*: Self-reported union membership and living with a union member from the CSES, union density data from Visser (2006), and the Quality of Government dataset (2011). The survey data are weighted.

with a union member in South Korea, Bulgaria, Spain, Poland, and Hungary. Thus, membership is rare in some countries, and it seems unlikely that unions might have a large mobilization potential. In many countries, between approximately one in five and one in ten people are union members or live with a union member: Italy, Portugal, Japan, Croatia, France, Mexico, the United States, Brazil, the Czech Republic, Switzerland, Germany, Romania, Austria, New Zealand, the UK, and the Netherlands. In Scandinavian countries and Belgium, union membership is the norm rather than the exception. As stated earlier, in some countries (Sweden, Finland, Denmark, and Belgium) unions administer the payment of unemployment benefits, which provides a strong incentive for workers to join unions.

Unsurprisingly, union density figures are larger than self-reported membership in most countries. In spite of this, union density exceeds 40 percent in only eight countries. The *capacity* of unions to mobilize politically varies widely.

Are union members on average more or less educated than the population? Figure 5–2 plots the percentage of union and nonunion members who have a university degree for both the whole population and the active population (i.e., the employed and the unemployed).[7]

In most countries, union members are on average better educated than nonunion members. In some countries, the difference is rather large. For example, 24 percent of union members have a university degree in Portugal, compared to 10 percent among nonunion members in the population. In Mexico, Bulgaria, Japan, Poland, and Hungary, the difference in the percentage of university degree holders among the unionized and the nonunionized was 10 percentage points or more. By

---

[7] There is large variation across countries in the qualifications needed to work in industrial jobs. In spite of comparability objections, it is safe to say that people with university degrees do not fit the classical blue-collar union member stereotype. The "working class" label does not apply to them. I have also compared the average education of union members and nonunion members using five categories of education with very similar results.

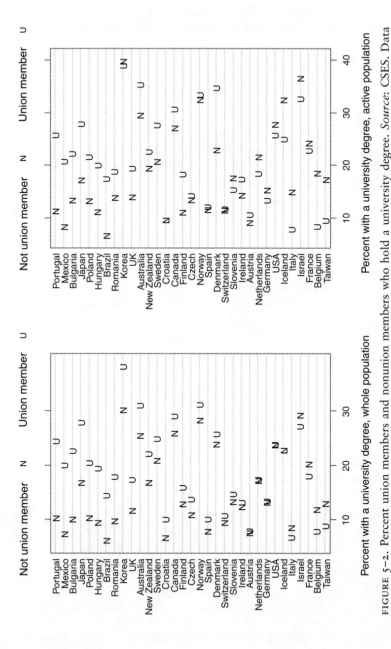

FIGURE 5-2. Percent union members and nonunion members who hold a university degree. *Source:* CSES. Data sorted by the size of the difference in the percentage of union and nonunion members who hold a university degree among the whole population, in descending order. The active population comprises the employed and the unemployed, aged twenty-five to sixty-four. The data are weighted.

contrast, union members are on average less educated than non-members in only five countries: Taiwan, Belgium, France, Israel, and Italy. The difference is largest in Taiwan, where 9 percent of union members hold university degrees compared to 13 percent of nonunion members. In the whole sample, 21 percent of union members have a university degree, compared to only 14 percent of nonunion members. Among the active population, these figures are 22 percent and 18 percent, respectively.

Union members nowadays are just as likely as or more likely than nonunion members to have a high education level. In this respect, there is not a large amount of variation across countries.[8] Accepting that unions represent the interests of their members, the findings of this section provide indirect evidence that the unions' willingness to mobilize mainly the less educated politically may be limited in general.

Trade Unions and Turnout Inequality

Can mobilization by trade unions reduce turnout inequality? The next analyses examine if the association between education and voting is smaller (a) among citizens who are union members and their families than among citizens who are not, and (b) in contexts where unions are powerful than in contexts where they are not.

The multilevel logistic regression models have elections as the higher-level unit. Unionization is measured at both the individual level (one's and/or a household member's union membership) and the contextual level (union density and percent of union members as reported in the CSES).

Individual membership has four categories: Nonunion members who do not live with a union member (70 percent of the sample); union members who do not live with a union member

---

[8] The differences in the education level of union members and the rest are not included as an independent variable in the analysis because the degree of variation is small and because there is no clear way of operationalizing differences in the educational composition of unions across countries.

(10 percent); nonunion members who live with a union member (10 percent); and union members who live with a union member (10 percent).

The models include individual-level controls for the respondent's employment situation. Employment is positively associated with voter turnout and union membership. Failing to control for the employment situation would result in an overestimation of the unionization effect. The reference category is people in employment. The dummy variables distinguish between being unemployed, retired, student, in domestic labor, or in other situations. As in previous chapters, the models control for age, age squared, and sex.[9]

I ask if contextual union density reduces the effect of education on turnout. The focus of interest is on aggregate turnout inequality, not individual voter participation. Thus, the interpretation of the interaction between individual education and union density is the main result of interest. A negative interaction would suggest that where unions are large, the association of education and voting is weaker, and thus turnout is more equal.

The first two models examine the interaction between contextual unionization and education using two alternative indicators: union density (first column) and percentage of union members as reported in the CSES (second column). As explained, both measures have validity problems and using both allows us to test the robustness of the results. In the third model, union density and individual measures of union membership are included simultaneously as predictors. These three first models are random intercepts, random coefficient models, which allow a separate slope for education across countries. In the fifth and sixth models, I break down the education variable into five dummies, interact them with union density (model 5), and include individual membership as controls (model 6), to rule out the possibility

[9] All the analyses have been replicated including compulsory voting countries and modeling their higher participation rates by both a compulsory voting variable and the interaction of compulsory voting and education. While the results are very similar, I display the results of the analyses excluding compulsory voting countries for simplicity.

that the linear specification of education is driving the results. The last three regressions are random intercepts, but fixed slopes models.[10] The forth model replicates the third to show that the results are stable across both random and fixed effects models.

Union density and the percentage of CSES respondents who report that they are union members are positively associated with voter turnout in all models. However, the coefficients are only statistically significant when the individual membership variable is not included. This suggests that a large part of the positive association between contextual union membership and voter turnout is because union members and their families vote more frequently, rather than because trade unions mobilize many non-members.

Union membership of the respondent, of another household member, and of both the respondent and another household member, is associated with a higher propensity to report voting in elections as seen in models 3, 4, and 6.

Importantly, contextual unionization does not reduce the strength of the association between education and voter turnout. A negative interaction coefficient would suggest that the relationship between education and participation is less steep in elections where union membership is large, but the coefficients are in fact positive. The same finding replicates when using the linear education variable or the set of dummy education variables.

On the contrary, the interactions of education and being a union member or living with a union member (at the individual level) are negative, even if not all coefficients reach conventional levels of statistical significance. It seems that living with a union member has a particularly beneficial consequence for the participation of poorly educated people. The negative correlations suggest that education is less important as a predictor of voter

---

[10] The reason for choosing this type of multilevel regression is that in models 5 and 6 I included each education category as a dummy variable and interacted each dummy with unionization measures. Doing so reduces the degrees of freedom and can cause random slopes, random intercepts models to fail to converge.

TABLE 5-2. *Multivariate Models of Voter Turnout: Trade Unions and Education*

	Random Education Slopes				Fixed Education Slopes	
	Contextual Union Density	Contextual in Unions from CSES	Individual Membersh. and Density	Individual Membersh. and Density	Density, Education as Dummies	Density, Indiv. Edu. as Dummies
Education in 5 categories (0 is primary or less, to 4)	0.28*** (0.04)	0.27*** (0.03)	0.28*** (0.05)	0.27*** (0.02)		
Union density in percent	0.015** (0.004)	0.012** (0.004)	0.008+ (0.005)	0.008+ (0.005)	0.015*** (0.004)	0.007 (0.005)
Union density*education	0.0003 (0.0009)	0.0006 (0.0009)	0.001 (0.001)	0.002* (0.0006)		
Union member (dummy) Ref. neither self nor other			0.39*** (0.07)	0.40*** (0.07)		0.34*** (0.04)
Lives with union member			0.41*** (0.07)	0.40*** (0.07)		0.29*** (0.04)
Union: self and other			0.71*** (0.10)	0.74*** (0.09)		0.51*** (0.05)
Union member*education Ref. neither self nor other			−0.03 (0.04)	−0.03 (0.04)		
Lives w. union m.*education			−0.06+ (0.03)	−0.07* (0.03)		
Union: self and other*education			−0.10* (0.04)	−0.13** (0.04)		
Incomplete secondary (dummy) Ref. is primary or less					0.19*** (0.002)	−0.02 (0.07)

Secondary					0.71***	0.58***
					(0.05)	(0.07)
Postsecondary					0.74***	0.55***
					(0.06)	(0.09)
University					1.16***	1.06***
					(0.06)	(0.08)
Union density*Incom. secondary					0.003*	0.008***
					(0.002)	(0.002)
Ref. is primary or less						
Union density*Secondary					-0.003+	-0.0001
					(0.001)	(0.002)
Union density*Postsecondary					0.003*	0.01***
					(0.002)	(0.003)
Union density*University					0.0007	0.003
					(0.002)	(0.002)
Constant	-2.18***	-2.05***	-2.07***	-2.08***	-2.23***	-1.98***
	(0.19)	(0.17)	(0.21)	(0.20)	(0.17)	(0.20)
Controls++	Yes	Yes	Yes	Yes	Yes	Yes
Std. deviation constant	0.77	0.79	0.71	0.66	0.68	0.66
	(0.07)	(0.07)	(0.08)	(0.07)	(0.06)	(0.07)
Std. deviation slope (education)	0.15	0.16	0.15			
	(0.015)	(0.016)	(0.02)			
Correlation education, constant	-0.49	-0.51	-0.38			
	(0.10)	(0.10)	(0.14)			
N (elections)	10546/68	108510/70	63094/49	63094/49	105446/68	78779/59

+ p < 0.1, * p < 0.05, ** p < 0.01, *** p < 0.001. Entries are multilevel logistic regression coefficients (standard errors) from multilevel models. ++Controls: age, age squared, sex, employment situation. Compulsory voting countries are excluded. No weights applied.

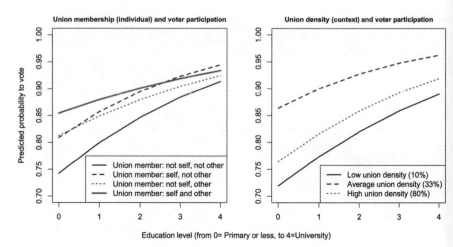

FIGURE 5–3. Predicted voter turnout by education, union membership, and union density. *Source*: Calculated from model 3, Table 5.4. The predicted probabilities plotted in the first figure are estimated for a forty-year-old woman in employment, holding union density constant at its average level (33 percent) in countries under voluntary voting.

turnout among people who live with union members, who are most probably their spouses and adult children.

Even more than in previous chapters, we need simulations to assess whether union membership is associated with reduced inequalities in voter participation. To do so, I draw on the estimates of model 3, which included both individual and contextual measures of unionization.[11]

The first set of simulations estimated the predicted probability of voting for a forty-year-old woman in employment, holding contextual union density constant at its mean level in the sample, which is 33 percent. I examine if individual union membership reduces the association between education and voting. The first panel in Figure 5–3 reports the predicted probabilities of voting for different types of citizens. Among people who are

---

[11] The results should not be interpreted as causal effects of unionization. Being observational data, the results are surely biased. The simulations provide a useful illustration of average expected differences in turnout rates.

union members and live with other union members (10 percent of the sample), the gradient of the education–voting relationship is clearly less steep than among other groups. The predicted probability that a union member who lives with another union member reports voting is 0.85 if she has primary education or less and 0.93 if she has a university degree. The size of the gap in participation by education level is small compared to the gap found among nonunion members, which is twice as large: The predicted probability of voting of a nonunion member who does not live with a union member is 0.74 if she has a low level of education and 0.91 if she has a university degree. The differences in the turnout gaps of highly and less educated people who are union members but do not live with other members, or who are not union members, but live with union members, are quite large at 0.14 and 0.11, respectively.

Thus, education seems to be less important as a predictor of participation among people who have some personal link with trade unions. However, the reductions in the turnout gaps are only large among the small subset of union members who live with other union members. This is intriguing, and it may indicate that education is much less relevant as a predictor of participation in some lower-status *social milieus* or certain working class families in which unionization is frequent. Besides, it is also clear that both highly educated and less educated union members vote at higher rates.

In any case, the central issue of interest is if union density reduces turnout inequality in the whole population. Do powerful unions equalize participation? To assess this question through simulations, individual union membership and contextual union density require simultaneous consideration because they are of course correlated ($r = 0.4$). There are more union members in contexts that have a high union density. The simulations have to take on plausible values of individual and contextual unionization.

To examine if unionization is associated with less turnout inequality, I calculated the predicted probability of voting for citizens in three scenarios with different values of (a) union density, and (b) the proportion of self-reported (own or other household member's) union membership that are jointly plausible.

For example, in the low-density scenario, union density is set at 10 percent. A plausible value of individual union membership in a low-density scenario is calculated looking at the average values in election studies that have low values of union density. I selected the election studies that had a union density of 20 percent or less. In this subset of cases, 83 percent of respondents report that neither they, nor anyone in the household, are union members; 7 percent report being a union member, but not living with one; 7 percent report not being a union member but living with one; 3 percent report being both a union member and living with one. Then, I calculated the predicted probability of voting using the estimates in model 3 for each of twenty groups (defined by education level and union membership status). The aggregate predicted probability of voting by education group is each group's predicted value, weighted by the plausible values of union members, not union members, and so on.[12]

Next, I repeated the same procedure for a scenario in which union density is average (33 percent) and a scenario in which

[12] To illustrate the calculations, the following table displays the predicted probability of voting (in percentages) by union membership and education in the low union density scenario. The aggregate predicted turnout rate is a weighted average: each groups' estimated turnout is weighted by the percentage of people who fall into this group in the population as estimated from studies in which union density is low (20 percent or less).

	Union Membership				Mean Turnout,
	Not Self, Nor Other	Self, Not Other	Not Self, But Other	Self and Other	Weighted by % in Population
Primary or less	70	76	81	85	89
Incomplete secondary	78	83	87	90	93
Secondary	78	82	85	88	90
Postsecondary	83	85	88	90	91
University degree	72	77	82	86	89
% in the population	70	76	81	85	89

union density is high (80 percent). Again, I plugged in plausible values of people in each of the union membership categories calculated from sample estimates.[13]

The second panel in Figure 5–3 displays the results of the simulations. Voter turnout is higher on average where union density is large. Turnout inequality, defined as the difference in the turnout rates of highly and less educated people, is very similar in the simulations with a low and average level of union density. In the low-density scenario, the estimated gap is 17 percentage points and in the average density case, the gap is 15 percentage points. In the high-density group, some reduction is visible. The estimated gap in the turnout rates by education level is just 10 percentage points, but this reduction is most likely due to ceiling effects. Average voter turnout in the high density scenario is 92 percent, a very large figure. Thus, the simulations suggest that union density is only associated with more equal participation once we reach very high unionization rates.

A final, different way of looking at this question is to examine the bivariate relationship between union density and gaps in the turnout rates of the highly and less educated as estimated from the OLS models described in Chapter 1. Figure 5–4 plots the summary measure of turnout inequality against union density in countries where voting is voluntary.

We can see in this graph that the gaps in the turnout rates of the highly and less educated are small in the subset of mostly Scandinavian countries where union density is very high. Among cases with low or average levels of union density, there is large variation in the measure of turnout inequality across elections. Scandinavian countries are different in many respects, not only union density, from other contexts. Thus, it is doubtful that union density, rather than a complex bundle of characteristics typical

---

[13] The plausible percentages of union members in the high-density situation were plugged in using the values of the subset of countries that have union densities of 50 percent or more. In the middle density situation, they are estimated using the subset of countries with union densities between 21 and 49 percent. For example, in the high-density group, the percentage of people who are both union members and live with a union member was 34 percent.

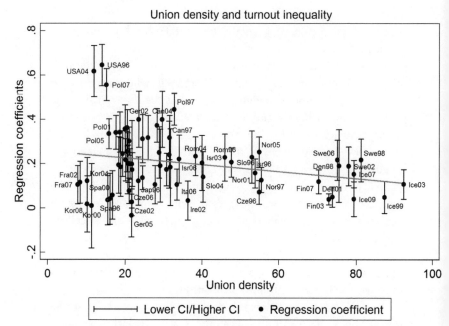

FIGURE 5–4. Turnout inequality and union density. *Source*: CSES, Visser (2006), and Quality of Government dataset. Union density is plotted against the regression coefficients of education on voting from OLS models. Elections held under compulsory voting are excluded.

of these countries, is causing low levels of turnout inequality.[14] Once Scandinavian countries are removed from the analysis, the bivariate relationship between turnout inequality and union density vanishes.

To summarize, this chapter has found mixed results. Having individual or familial ties to trade unions seems to be favorable to political participation, and less educated people who live with union members have much higher turnout rates than other people with a low education level. In this respect, it seems that less

---

[14] It is noteworthy, that in some of these high union density cases there is a gap of 20 percentage points in the turnout rates of highly and less educated people. This figure is quite large considering that turnout rates are 80 percent or higher.

educated people benefit from having sturdy ties with unions. In spite of this, aggregate union density is weakly associated with turnout inequality. I have shown that union members mainly are not poorly educated people and that both highly and less educated citizens benefit from individual union membership and contextual union density. The multilevel models suggest that, although high union density is associated with more voter participation, trade unions do not disproportionately mobilize poorly educated people to vote. The small reduction in turnout inequality at high union density rates (visible in both the simulations from the regression models and in the bivariate graphical analysis) is mainly driven by the fact that turnout rates are very high in Scandinavian countries. Thus, union density is associated with higher turnout rates but it seems to have a reduced potential to equalize turnout *in the aggregate*.

Mobilization by Political Parties

Mobilization theories of unequal participation claim that voter turnout is equal when and where organizations mobilize socially disadvantaged groups to vote. This chapter has focused on just one type of organization, trade unions, because scholars consider unions as one of the most important organizations that aim to represent the interests of the working class. As such, they have a central role in mobilization theories. A second reason is that focusing on just one type of agency allows us to analyze the case and the evidence in more depth. Other organizations that can under some circumstances mobilize disadvantaged groups and reduce turnout inequality include religious organizations, farmers' groups, social movements, housing associations, and especially political parties.

In previous work (Gallego 2008), and in explorations not shown here, I have examined if a larger share of people affiliated with any social and political organization or the cumulative power of the left during the second half of the twentieth century are associated with more equal participation. The intuition is that where many people are affiliated with any kind of association or where left-wing parties are powerful, the less educated vote at high rates and turnout inequality is reduced. I could not find clear evidence in support for this hypothesis and this is a third reason why I do not report the results here.

The bottom line is that broad propositions such as "trade unions reduce turnout inequality," "strong left-wing parties reduce turnout inequality," or "large associational membership reduces turnout inequality," have limited ability to predict cross-national variation in turnout inequality, at least as conceptualized in this book. This is not to say that mobilization accounts are invalid. No doubt, political organizations can mobilize lower-status people to vote and reduce turnout inequality. However, these null results suggest that we need a more nuanced theoretical approach and empirical examination to understand under which circumstances mobilization reduces turnout inequality. We need to ask when certain actors have incentives to mobilize socially disadvantaged citizens, and not just assume that they do so because of historical reasons, which may have changed.

Left-wing parties have undergone major transformations in their political aims, the composition of their electorate, and their links with their traditional constituencies, just as trade unions have. Furthermore, the relationship between left-wing parties and lower-status voters has been a core theme of the comparative political economy literature that focuses on a small set of industrial countries. We cannot take for granted that the linkages between lower-status voters and left-wing parties are similar today in new democracies.

The work by Karen Jusko (2011) is perhaps the only comparative example of a more detailed mobilization account of unequal participation. She examines under what circumstances political parties have strategic incentives to mobilize the poor electorally. Her argument is that unequal turnout depends on the legislators' and political parties' incentives to mobilize low-income voters politically, which in turn depend on electoral geography – the joint distribution of voters and seats across electoral districts. The more electoral power the poor have (i.e., the higher the percentage of seats they could secure if they all voted for the same party), the more parties have incentives to mobilize them, and the more they vote.

Previous research assumed that, for some vague reasons, some organizations (such as left-wing parties or trade unions) mobilize the poor, and predicted that where these organizations are strong, the disadvantaged vote more and turnout is more equal. Jusko's work specifies where there are more incentives for (any) parties to mobilize the poor electorally. Thus, it is an important step forward in mobilization accounts of participation. She tests the theory with both cross-national and U.S. subnational data. The dependent variable is the OLS coefficient of income (in quintiles) on reported voter turnout, controlling for age and education. The findings confirm that the differences in the turnout rates of members of different income groups are larger where the poor are pivotal in a low percentage of districts. At the same time, however, a large part of variation in unequal participation is unexplained by electoral geography. The association of the electoral power of low-income blocs and equal participation across income groups is positive, but moderate, once the influential cases of the United States and France are removed from the analysis. The variation in the electoral power of low-income blocs across countries is small. Thus, there is room for other versions of the mobilization account and for other theories of unequal participation.

In sum, this chapter qualifies the view that trade unions are equality-enhancing organizations. Given that union members are today as educated as nonmembers, it is unclear why unions should mainly mobilize socially disadvantaged groups to vote. The empirical results do not provide compelling support for the contention that union density is associated with more equal participation, particularly once the special case of Scandinavian countries is set apart. Traditional mobilization accounts require refinement to understand variation in unequal participation across elections, or else supplementation by other theories.

6

Income Inequality and the Participation of Lower-Status Groups

The rise of income inequality over recent decades in many advanced industrial democracies (Brandolini and Smeeding 2008; Neckerman and Torche 2007) has spurred worries about the likely consequences of this trend for democracy in general, and for political equality in particular. Scholars have claimed that income inequality depresses the participation of lower-status groups and that their low turnout rates make it possible to implement policies that increase income inequality even more. In turn, this further depresses the participation of lower-status groups, and so on (Lijphart 1997; Verba 2003; Birch 2009: 53–54). Concerns about the emergence of a vicious circle of income inequality and participatory inequality are at the heart of contemporary research about the political causes and consequences of rising income inequality (Bartels 2008: 286; APSA Task Force 2004; Jacobs and Skocpol 2005; Gilens 2005, 2011). These concerns extend well beyond the academic community. In 2011, social movements across the world protested the growing concentration of both wealth and political influence in the hands of "the 1 percent," partly on the grounds that it corrupts democracy.

Recent empirical work has provided some support for the claim that income inequality may increase turnout gaps, showing that higher levels of inequality are associated with lower levels of political engagement by low-income people, both cross-nationally and within the United States (Solt 2008, 2011). On closer inspection, however, the evidence supporting this claim is highly inconclusive. There is no clear consensus about whether income inequality depresses everyone's participation or mostly the participation of lower-status people. Several investigations have found that income inequality depresses participation across the board (Beramendi and Anderson 2009; Mankowska 2011; Steinbrecher and Seeber 2011). In fact, Solt's own results do not reject the hypothesis that reductions in participation are similar for all income groups.

Previous work has other shortcomings. It lacks a simple bivariate description of the relationship between turnout inequality and income inequality[1] and has not attempted to pin down possible mechanisms that link income inequality to unequal participation. In addition, previous studies have not distinguished between the consequences of gross income inequality before taxes and transfers and net income inequality after taxes and transfers. This distinction is consequential. Although gross income inequality shapes the incentives to demand or oppose redistribution in political economy approaches, relative differences in disposable resources (i.e., net inequality) mostly affect differences in the actual capacity of different groups to influence the political process in resource models of participation.

This chapter describes the relationship between income inequality and turnout inequality and advances this research agenda in several ways. Most importantly, I provide a transparent description of the bivariate relationship between turnout inequality and both gross and net income inequality across countries for both individual education levels and income. I also tentatively explore one mechanism through which income inequality may reduce the participation of lower-status people.

---

[1] To my knowledge, the exception is a study that plots a Gini index of voter turnout by income group against total government redistribution for nine countries (Mahler 2008).

The results of the analyses are surprising. I find that the turnout gaps due to both education and income are, on average, larger in countries where income inequality before taxes and transfers is high. On the contrary, income inequality after taxes and transfers is unrelated to turnout inequality in bivariate and multilevel analysis. In the conclusion, I discuss implications of these results for theories of the democratic consequences of income inequality.

Theories of Income Inequality and Participation

One set of theories claims that higher income inequality can be expected to sharpen turnout inequality because the rich use their resources to dominate the political process, ultimately causing the poor to drop out (Goodin and Dryzek 1980, Rueschemeyer 2005). In a pluralistic society, all groups can use their resources to defend their interests through the political process, but inequality shapes the *relative* amount of resources that different income groups can mobilize to pursue their goals. Increases in income inequality concentrate not only money but also power and influence in the hands of a few, resulting in a more uneven political playing field.

In very unequal contexts, the poor dispose of comparatively few resources to pursue their political goals, and higher-status groups can dominate the political agenda and exclude the interests of the poor from the political debate easily (Schattschneider 1960). Recurrent experiences of exclusion from public debate convince the poor that their attempts are hopeless, and they stop participating as a result. Inequality "eventually convinces poorer individuals who consistently find themselves unable to prevail in political contests or even to gain a hearing for their positions that their interests cannot be pursued through the political process" (Solt 2008: 49).

One central mechanism that leads the poor to stop participating under conditions of high income inequality in this account is the realization that participation is meaningless. The cause of lower participation is not the rich's domination of the agenda or their higher availability of resources per se, but rather the poor's recognition that the political system is not responsive to their demands and participation is worthless. When income inequality is high, the poor "rationally conclude that there is little point to being engaged in politics" (Solt, idem) because they cannot have an impact. In this account, abstention reflects a reduction in the perceived value of participation that follows from the suppression of meaningful alternatives. If this account is true, we should also observe that lower-status groups have much more negative attitudes toward politics than higher-status groups in highly unequal societies. A negative change in core attitudes toward politics should mediate the negative effect of income inequality on the participation of lower-status groups.

Note that in relative power theories posttax and transfers income inequality is the key independent variable of interest. Higher-status groups use the resources *at their disposal* to influence the political process and to exclude other voices. Resources available for actual use are those the groups control after the state collects taxes and provides services and transfers. In fact, net income inequality is the measure used in empirical analyses testing this theory.

An alternative influential approach focuses on how gross income inequality shapes the incentives to participate in the political conflict across contexts (Solt 2008: 49), yet the implications for turnout inequality are less clear. An increase in gross income inequality widens the difference between the income of the mean and the median earner and increases the stakes in the outcome of the political process for both the rich and the poor (Brady 2004). In workhorse models of redistribution, the median voter demands more redistribution as income inequality before taxes and transfers grows (Meltzer and Richard 1981). In a society with an extremely equal pretax income distribution there should be little conflict over redistribution and the stakes of the political process would be low, hence reducing the motives to participate. As income inequality grows, politics become more polarized: The poor have more to win from redistribution and the rich have more to lose. The higher stakes of the political process imply that the benefits of obtaining their most desired policy increases for all income groups.

Such models assume full participation, yet to the extent that participation depends on the benefits obtained from having one's party win the election, the higher stakes in the political process in unequal contexts may positively affect political participation. If all groups have more incentives to participate, then *all groups* should participate more. In these accounts, income inequality has a positive impact on voter turnout, but it may not necessarily affect turnout inequality.

From this perspective, the effects of gross income inequality on voter participation are perhaps direct, if, as assumed in political economy models, the actors realize what their interests are and, in particular, that the stakes of the political process increase as income inequality grows. If anything, some political attitudes such as political interest should be higher in economically unequal contexts for all citizens.

In sum, the two main theories about the link between income inequality and the political participation of different social groups cited in previous studies focus in fact on two different measures of inequality: pretax and posttax. Relative power theory predicts that in societies with high net inequality higher-status groups will use the resources at their disposal to dominate the political process and lower-status groups will fail to vote because they realize that their participation is worthless; conflict theories build on accounts that focus on pretax inequality and, although the claims are often unclear, seem to lead to the prediction that everyone participates more in unequal societies because the stakes of the political process are higher.

Such models may be too simple. Empirical research on income inequality and attitudes toward redistribution suggest the links between income inequality and voter participation are very complex, and may depend on institutional and cultural factors. An important critique to simple political economy models is that economic interests influence political attitudes and behavior much less than these assume. In addition to self-interest, institutions, culture, and individual characteristics also shape how individuals conceive of and react politically to economic inequality, leading to many different possible predictions about the effect of inequality on participation.[2]

We may add to the complexity that income inequality has been linked to a very wide variety of social and political outcomes that can indirectly affect political behavior through complex pathways. In fact, studying the effects of income inequality may be one of the most challenging areas of research, and here I step short of aiming to provide a full overview and a new account. Instead, this chapter simply attempts to critically review the results of previous empirical studies, to describe the relationship between both pretax and posttax income inequality and turnout inequality, and to assess one proposed mechanism that flows through political attitudes.

Review of Previous Empirical Studies

Does income inequality affect political attitudes and behaviors? If so, are the consequences heterogeneous for different types of citizens? Several political behavior and political economy studies have found that income inequality is associated with lower aggregate participation rates.[3] This result has also been replicated using instrumental variables (Anderson and Beramendi 2008; Franzese and Hays 2008). A meta-analysis of the voter turnout literature concludes that the evidence is mixed (Geys

---

[2] For instance, a study of lottery winners suggests that economic self-interest barely affects general beliefs about economic issues (Doherty, Gerber, and Green 2007). We also know that acceptance or critique of income inequality hinges on beliefs about how legitimate differences in individual income are and such beliefs have cultural origins (Alesina and Angeletos 2005; Alesina, Cozzi, and Mantovan 2009) and depend upon the conditions in which individuals were socialized (Alesina and Fuchs-Schundeln 2006; Dallinger 2010). Support for redistribution also varies with ideological affinities and levels of altruism, egoism (Scheve 2010; Klor and Shayo 2010), or ethnic fractionalization (Alesina and Glaeser 2005), to name a few factors. Also, the relative importance of self-interest as a predictor of demand for redistribution varies across contexts (Dion and Birchfield 2010).

[3] See Goodin and Dryzek 1980; Galbraith and Hale 2008; Solt 2004; Boix 2003; Oliver 2001; Mahler 2002.

2006), but overall there is considerable support for the statement that income inequality depresses participation.

The evidence on *whose* participation is lower in highly unequal contexts is much less compelling. Frederick Solt has presented the most visible results, showing that income inequality undermines political engagement among all but the most affluent. In one analysis (Solt 2008), he uses data for twenty-two countries and sixty-two country-years. In multilevel models, turnout inequality is associated with lower participation rates among all income groups. The models indicate that the interaction between income quintile and turnout inequality is negative but not statistically significant. It is unclear if the data do not fully support the interpretation that income inequality increases inequalities in voter participation. Similarly, in an analysis of differences across the United States between 1978 and 2000 (Solt 2011), he finds that income inequality is associated with lower participation, but the negative interaction between income quintile and income inequality is not statistically significant and the magnitude of the differences is small.

A larger set of studies, both published and unpublished, has failed to find heterogeneous effects of income inequality on voter turnout. Anderson and Beramendi (2008) use individual data from the World Values Survey and contextual data for eighteen countries and find that income inequality reduces the reported intention to vote. They split individuals in the sample between those who are below and above the median income. The negative effect of inequality is not concentrated in a segment of the population. On the contrary, it is almost identical in substantive terms for both rich and poor individuals. Income inequality reduces voter turnout whereas turnout inequality remains unchanged. In the United States, rising income inequality has not increased the class bias in turnout over time (Leighley and Nagler 2006).

Other unpublished studies obtain similar null findings. Mankowska (2011) examines the question of whether rising income inequality has depressed participation among the poor in Eastern Europe. The case selection is compelling, because inequality has risen dramatically and turnout has declined in many of these countries. Income inequality is associated with lower voter participation, political interest, and internal and external efficacy. However, she finds no interaction between income inequality and relative income, suggesting that income inequality reduces engagement for all voters, and such reduction is not concentrated among people at the lowest income quintile.

Another study using the fourth round of the European Social Survey examines the correlation between participatory inequality by income groups and income inequality. The results are opposite from those hypothesized; income inequality is negatively rather than positively associated with turnout inequality (Steinbrecher and Seeber 2011).

All these studies use net income inequality as the main independent variable of interest.[4] In summary, a review of past research suggests that the evidence is at best mixed, or even plainly rejects the correlation between income and turnout inequality.

A Graphical Bivariate Description

I offer here a comprehensive description of actual patterns in the association between income inequality and turnout inequality.[5] Figure 6–1 displays the bivariate relationship. The two left panels plot the gross Gini index of income inequality before taxes and

---

[4] In addition to the mixed results linking income inequality and voter turnout, income inequality may not produce heterogeneous effects on political attitudes. In a multilevel analysis of twenty European countries, Anderson and Singer (2008) find that income inequality is associated with lower satisfaction with democracy and lower trust in institutions, but the negative link is not moderated by income (the interaction term is not significant and has a contrary sign to that expected).

[5] This description is useful in other literatures and in particular for models of cross-national variation in redistribution. Several theories building on the Meltzer-Richard model claim that gross income inequality increases redistribution only when the poor participate in elections (Franzese 2002; Kenworthy and Pontusson 2005; Mahler 2008; Pontusson and Rueda 2010). Most studies, however, introduce voter turnout as a proxy of income skew in voter participation instead of estimating turnout skew directly. As reported in Chapter 1 the assumption that it is a good proxy is questionable once compulsory voting countries are excluded.

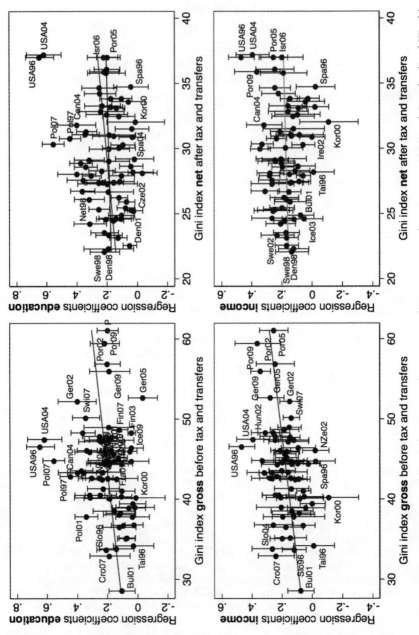

FIGURE 6–1. Turnout inequality (education and income) and income inequality. *Source:* CSES and Standardized World Income Inequality Database (Solt 2009a, 2009b). Income inequality is plotted against the regression coefficients of

152

transfers in the x-axis. The data come from the Standardized World Income Inequality Database, as provided by Solt (2011). The two right panels plot the Gini index of income inequality after taxes and transfers. While the rest of the book has examined differences in voter participation across education groups, here I also calculated the summary measure of turnout inequality across income quintiles. The correlation between turnout due to income and that due to educational inequality is quite large at 0.65. The two upper graphs plot turnout inequality due to education in the y-axis, and the two lower graphs plot turnout inequality due to income. The graphs exclude compulsory voting countries.

Gaps in voter turnout rates due to both education and income are on average larger in elections where income inequality before taxes and transfers is higher. On the contrary, the bivariate relationship between turnout inequality and income inequality after taxes and transfers is weak or nonexistent. This is especially true after excluding the case of the United States, which is a clear outlier.[6]

This exploration suggests that income inequality before taxes and transfers is associated with lower participation rates of the poor and the poorly educated. On the contrary, income inequality after taxes and transfers bears no association with increases in the inequality of participation. This is not what relative power theory predicts. Net income inequality should be more consequential than gross income inequality, because it is the difference in the disposable resources of higher- and lower-status groups that makes political competition uneven. Higher-status groups can use the resources at their disposal in the public arena to dominate the political agenda and preclude lower-status groups from

---

[6] To examine the robustness of the bivariate relationship, I also excluded all countries with majoritarian electoral systems. Turnout rates and government redistribution are lower in majoritarian systems (Iversen and Soskice 2006). The inclusion of these cases should overestimate, not underestimate, the relationship between turnout inequality and income after taxes and transfers. Finding the same pattern in a smaller and more homogeneous set of countries should add confidence to the results. The relationship in fact remained extremely similar after excluding countries with majoritarian electoral systems.

having their voices heard. The relevant resources to influence politics are those available after taxes and transfers. Higher-status groups cannot use resources that the state takes away from them.

Multivariate Analyses and Political Attitudes as a Mechanism

This section uses a multivariate framework to assess whether gross and net income inequality are associated with lower participation rates of lower-status groups. In addition, I explore the role of basic political attitudes as possible mechanisms linking income inequality to lower participation by lower-status groups.

As has been reviewed, relative power theory claims that very unequal societies exclude the views of lower-status groups from the political process. These groups come to realize that the political system is not responsive to their demands, and that participation does not change outcomes, rendering it meaningless, which causes them to vote at lower rates. The CSES has no abundance of attitudinal variables, but some survey items allow us to glimpse at the mediating role of political attitudes. The first is political efficacy or the "feeling that individual political action does have, or can have, an impact upon the political process, that is, that it is worthwhile to perform one's civic duties" (Campbell, Gurin, and Miller 1954: 187). If lower-status groups rationally realize that they cannot affect the political process in more unequal contexts, this knowledge should result in lower political efficacy. Second, satisfaction with democracy should be lower for disadvantaged groups. Third, if there is political capture of the elites, the available political options in unequal contexts will fail to address the concerns of lower-status people. If this is true, they may be less likely to feel close to any of the main political parties.

The CSES asks respondents if they agree that "who is in power can make a difference"[7] and about respondents' degree of

---

[7] The five response options range from agree strongly to disagree strongly. Disagreement is a sign of low external political efficacy.

satisfaction with the way democracy works.[8] Respondents are also asked if they usually think of themselves as close to any particular political party. If they respond "no" they are further questioned if they feel a little bit closer to one of the parties than to the others.[9] The three variables are recoded to range from 0, which is the most negative attitude, to 1, which is the most positive one.

The analysis of mediation mechanisms is challenging. An unbiased estimation would not only require manipulating both cause and mechanism experimentally, but also make a set of additional assumptions (Bullock and Ha 2011; Imai et al. 2011). This is well beyond the possibilities of this study, and I rely instead on the classical approach proposed by Baron and Kenny (1986). While this approach is surely problematic, a cautious exploration can provide valuable insights. The analysis is even more challenging because the focus of interest here is the interaction between income inequality and socioeconomic status in predicting voter participation.

In Baron and Kenny–style mediation analysis, it is first necessary to show that the initial variable (income inequality) correlates with the outcome (reported voter participation). In the sample, voter turnout correlates with net income inequality at −0.35, while the correlation with gross income inequality is lower at −0.10. However, the real estimate of interest is the interaction between individual education or income and income inequality as a predictor of voter participation.

Table 6–1 reports the results of multilevel logistic analyses that examine whether income inequality moderates the correlation between individual socioeconomic position and voting likelihood. The models include both household income operationalized in income quintiles and education in five categories. The first three columns introduce gross income inequality before

---

[8] Respondents can report being very satisfied, fairly satisfied, neither satisfied nor dissatisfied, not very satisfied, or not at all satisfied.

[9] Responses to this question are coded in three categories: feeling close to a party, feeling closer to one party than to others, and not feeling close to any party.

TABLE 6–1. Multivariate Models of Voter Turnout: Net and Gross Income Inequality and Education

	Gross Income Inequality			Net Income Inequality		
	Education	Income	Edu. and Income	Education	Income	Edu. and Income
Education in five categories (0 primary or less, to 4)	0.07 (0.05)		0.04 (0.06)	0.41*** (0.06)		0.29*** (0.07)
Income quintiles		−0.05 (0.05)	−0.08 (0.06)		0.27*** (0.06)	0.27*** (0.06)
Income inequality	−0.004 (0.02)	−0.02 (0.02)	−0.02 (0.02)	−0.04+ (0.02)	−0.05+ (0.02)	−0.04 (0.02)
Education * inequality	0.005*** (0.001)		0.006*** (0.001)	−0.004* (0.002)		−0.001 (0.002)
Income * inequality		0.006*** (0.001)	0.006*** (0.001)		−0.001 (0.002)	−0.004+ (0.002)
Constant	−1.28+ (0.68)	−0.51 (0.72)	−0.67 (0.71)	−0.29 (0.67)	−0.08 (0.71)	−0.56 (0.70)
Controls++	Yes	Yes	Yes	Yes	Yes	Yes
Std. deviation constant	0.76 (0.06)	0.79 (0.07)	0.78 (0.07)	0.73 (0.06)	0.77 (0.07)	0.75 (0.06)
N elections	71	71	71	71	71	71
N respondents	113,029	95,307	95,307	113,029	95,307	95,307

+ p < 0.1, * p < 0.05, ** p < 0.01, *** p < 0.001. Entries are multilevel logistic regression coefficients (standard errors). ++ Controls: age, age squared, sex, electoral system with PR as the reference category, and majoritarian and mixed as dummies. No weights applied.

taxes and transfers, and the last three columns introduce net income inequality after taxes and transfers. I look first at the interaction between education and inequality, then at the interaction between household income and inequality, and then at both interactions jointly.[10] The analyses include one dummy for majoritarian systems and another one for mixed member systems. The reference category is PR systems. Voter participation is on average lower in majoritarian systems, at least in advanced industrial democracies (Geys 2006; Blais 2006). Majoritarian systems also redistribute less because they are more likely to be dominated by right-wing parties (Iversen and Soskice 2006) and should have lower values of net income inequality.

The results confirm the findings of the bivariate analysis. The interaction coefficients of education and income with gross income inequality are all positive and statistically significant, suggesting that in highly unequal contexts there is a stronger association between education or income and reported voter participation.

Net income inequality, by contrast, is unrelated to gaps in turnout rates between education and income groups. In the three models that include net income inequality as a predictor, education and relative income are quite strongly associated with the propensity to vote. The coefficients of net income inequality are again negative, and some approach conventional levels of statistical significance. This suggests that voter turnout is lower in

---

[10] Besides age, age squared, and sex, these analyses also include the electoral system as a control because it may be a confounding variable. Voter participation is on average lower in majoritarian systems, at least in advanced industrial democracies (Geys 2006; Blais 2006). Majoritarian systems also redistribute less because they are more likely to be dominated by right-wing parties (Iversen and Soskice 2006) and thus should have lower values of net income inequality. The reference category is PR systems, and the analyses include one dummy for majoritarian systems and another one for mixed member systems. In addition, I have replicated all the analyses including each education category as a dummy variable instead of including education as a continuous variable (see also Chapter 5). The results have the same overall pattern and are not reported in the interest of space.

highly unequal contexts, as most of the literature has found. Yet the interaction coefficients of net income inequality and education or income are all negative instead of positive. Thus, while these results confirm that net income inequality is associated with lower participation, the decline does not seem to be concentrated among lower-status groups. Rather, net inequality may reduce the participation of all groups to a similar extent.

The next analysis focuses on only gross income inequality because the first step did not confirm that net income inequality is associated with lower voter participation of lower-status groups. There is little point in examining mediation if the main variables of interest are not related as expected. While political attitudes are more central to relative power theory, which emphasizes the role of net income inequality, it is worthwhile to explore the possibility that gross income inequality depresses the participation of lower-status groups because it creates more negative political attitudes.

In Table 6–2, I examine if gross income inequality, education, and income predict political efficacy, satisfaction with democracy, and closeness to a party. The multilevel models also test if income inequality moderates the association of education and income with these outcome variables. This would suggest that there are larger attitudinal differences between lower- and higher-status people in very unequal contexts.

The results of this analysis are mixed. Education and income predict political efficacy. Gross income inequality is negatively associated with efficacy, though the coefficient is not statistically significant. However, the two interaction coefficients are negative rather than positive. The association between individual resources and political efficacy is weaker, instead of stronger, in very unequal societies, which is certainly not what we would expect.

In the case of satisfaction with democracy, the results conform more closely to the expectations. The interactions between income and education and gross income inequality are positive and significant. In very unequal societies, higher-status people are

TABLE 6–2. *Multivariate Models of Political Attitudes: Gross Income Inequality and Education*

	Political Efficacy	Satisfaction Democracy	Closeness to Party
Education in five categories	0.02***	−0.01*	0.007
(0 primary or less to 4)	(0.006)	(0.005)	(0.007)
Income quintiles	0.03***	0.002	0.01
	(0.006)	(0.005)	(0.01)
Gross income inequality	−0.004	−0.0008	−0.0001
	(0.004)	(0.002)	(0.003)
Education * inequality	−0.0002	0.0004***	0.0003+
	(0.0001)	(0.0001)	(0.0002)
Income * inequality	−0.0006*	0.0003**	0.0001
	(0.0003)	(0.0001)	(0.0002)
Constant	0.77***	0.57***	0. 32***
	(0.17)	(0.09)	(0.14)
Controls++	Yes	Yes	Yes
Std. deviation constant	0.19	0.10	0.16
	(0.02)	(0.01)	(0.013)
Std. deviation residual	0.31	0.25	0.41
	(0.001)	(0.001)	(0.001)
N elections	69	71	71
N respondents	89,385	91,113	91,824

+ $p < 0.1$, * $p < 0.05$, ** $p < 0.01$, *** $p < 0.001$. Entries are multilevel linear regression coefficients (standard errors). ++ Controls: age, age squared, sex, electoral system with PR as the reference category, and majoritarian and mixed as dummies. No weights applied.

more likely to be satisfied with democracy than are lower-status people. By contrast, satisfaction with democracy is similar across groups in equal societies.[11]

---

[11] Because these are linear models, it is straightforward to calculate the predicted differences in satisfaction with democracy across groups in different contexts. For example, in an egalitarian society with a Gini index of 20 and a PR system, the predicted value of satisfaction with democracy of a forty-year-old woman is similar at any value of income and education, about 0.47 (the scale ranges from 0 to 1). On the contrary, there are large differences in satisfaction in a highly unequal society. A woman with the minimum level of income and

Higher-status people are more likely than lower-status people to identify with parties in very unequal contexts, but they are not much more likely to identify with parties in equal contexts. The interaction of education and gross income inequality is positive as hypothesized, and almost reaches statistical significance.[12]

From the three main attitudes examined, satisfaction with democracy and closeness to a party show the expected patterns. In unequal societies, there are larger differences in satisfaction and identification between lower- and higher-status groups than in equal societies. Thus, I keep only these two variables.

The next step examines if the mediators are also associated with the outcome variable. The correlation between satisfaction with democracy and voter participation is 0.11 in the sample. The correlation between closeness to a party and voter participation is higher at 0.2. Both variables thus fulfill the condition of association with the outcome variable.

The final step assesses if the relationship between the initial variable and the outcome of interest declines when we introduce the mediators in a regression framework. In this case, my interest lies in determining whether the impact of socioeconomic predictors of voting is larger in unequal contexts than in equal contexts. The hypothesis is that one of the reasons that lower-status people vote less often in unequal contexts is that they are more dissatisfied with democracy, and are less likely to feel close to political parties than higher-status people. To attempt to address this question, I divided the sample into equal and unequal contexts. This allows us to assess separately if the decline in the association among education, income, and participation is

education has a predicted value of satisfaction with democracy of 0.41; if she has the maximum education and income, the predicted score is 0.55.

[12] In an equal context (Gini equals 20), a person with the minimum education and income has an expected value of closeness to a party of 0.46 (on a scale from 0 to 1). If she has the maximum education and income, the expected value is 0.56. In a very unequal context, a person with the minimum education and income has only a somewhat lower expected value of closeness of 0.44. The difference in the political attitudes of higher- and lower-status people is larger in unequal contexts; people with high education and income are more likely to feel close to parties, with an expected value of 0.61.

sharper in unequal contexts once we introduce the mediators. The mean value of gross income inequality in the sample is 43, which is used to divide equal from unequal societies. Table 6–3 reports the results of multilevel models, which first introduce only education and income, and then control for political attitudes.

The coefficients of education and income are larger in highly unequal societies than in relatively equal societies, suggesting that the gaps in the turnout rates across education groups are larger in the former than in the latter. The values decline, but only slightly, once the models include the hypothesized mediators. This holds both in equal and unequal contexts.

To interpret the results in substantive terms, Table 6–4 displays the predicted gap in the turnout rates for people who have the minimum and the maximum level of education and income. The marginal effects have been estimated holding all other variables at their means and modifying the value of education from primary or less to university, and the value of income from the first to the fifth quintile.

Introducing the mediators somewhat reduces the marginal effects of both education and income. The size of the reduction is similar in contexts with high and low levels of income inequality. For example, in unequal contexts university-educated citizens report voting at rates that are on average higher than those reported by citizens who have at most primary education by 15 percentage points. After controlling for differences in political attitudes, the marginal effect of education is somewhat lower at 13 percentage points.

The results suggest that differences in political attitudes across education groups are indeed part of the reason why the less educated vote at lower rates than the highly educated. My interpretation, however, is that this evidence does not support the claim that lower-status people vote less often in unequal contexts because they are more dissatisfied with democracy, and less likely to feel close to political parties than are higher-status people. If that were true, I would expect a larger reduction in the marginal effect of education and income in highly unequal societies than in more equal societies. Contrary to this

TABLE 6-3. *Multivariate Models of Voter Turnout: Gross Income Inequality, Political Attitudes, and Education*

	High Inequality (gross gini>43)		Low Inequality (gross gini<43)	
	Education and Income	Education, Income, and Attitudes	Education and Income	Education, Income, and Attitudes
Education in five categories (0 is primary or less, to 4)	0.31*** (0.01)	0.28*** (0.01)	0.20*** (0.01)	0.18*** (0.01)
Income in quintiles	0.20*** (0.01)	0.18*** (0.01)	0.13*** (0.01)	0.10*** (0.01)
Satisfaction with democracy		0.86*** (0.05)		0.68*** (0.06)
Closeness to a party		1.17*** (0.03)		1.31*** (0.04)
Constant	-1.42*** (0.17)	-2.25*** (0.19)	-1.92*** (0.21)	-2.58*** (0.23)
Controls[++]	Yes	Yes	Yes	Yes
Std. deviation constant	0.76 (0.09)	0.81 (0.09)	0.77 (0.10)	0.84 (0.11)
N elections	41	41	32	32
N respondents	55,365	52,768	42,012	37,338

+ $p < 0.1$, * $p < 0.05$, ** $p < 0.01$, *** $p < 0.001$. Entries are logistic regression coefficients (standard errors). [++] Controls: age, age squared, sex, electoral system with PR as the reference category, and majoritarian and mixed as dummies. No weights applied.

TABLE 6–4. *Marginal Effects of Education and Income with and Without Mediators*

		Without Mediators	With Mediators
High inequality	Education	0.15	0.13
Gross gini>43	Income	0.12	0.10
Low inequality	Education	0.12	0.10
Gross gini<43	Income	0.07	0.05

Source: CSES. The entries are the difference in the predicted probability of voting for people with the minimum and maximum level of education and income. All variables are held constant at their means.

expectation, the reduction in the estimated effect of education and income is similar in equal and unequal contexts.

Notwithstanding all the admittedly large shortcomings of this analysis, the tentative conclusion is this: More negative political attitudes held by lower-status citizens are probably not the main mechanism that explains why they vote at lower rates than higher-status citizens in contexts characterized by unequal distribution of income (before taxes and transfers).

Income Inequality and Political Behavior

The results presented in this chapter are puzzling. On the one hand, pretax and transfers income inequality correlates with turnout inequality. This is perhaps one of the clearest findings of this book. The fact that this finding emerges across different methods, specifications, and selections of cases underscores its robustness. On the other hand, posttax and transfers inequality is unrelated to turnout inequality. This holds true when we look at gaps in the turnout rates across both education and income groups. Thus, this study supports the growing volume of literature that claims that net income inequality depresses voter participation among all voters rather than mostly among lower-status groups. In other words, net inequality reduces voter turnout but not turnout inequality.

Two questions deserve discussion. What do these results imply for existing theories about the democratic consequences of income inequality? Also, why is only gross income inequality rather than net income inequality associated with unequal participation?

The findings of this chapter do not fit well with the assumptions of relative power theory, nor do they fit conflict perspectives. Higher-status groups are able to use their *available* resources to capture the political process and dominate the agenda. Hence, net income inequality should be more important as a predictor of turnout inequality than gross income inequality. Conflict theory claims that the stakes of the political process grow as income inequality increases. This should make participation more, rather than less, attractive for everyone in unequal contexts.

The relationship between objective economic parameters and political behavior is surely more complex than these models allow. Many factors, including institutions, culture, and individual dispositions, shape how people think about inequality and redistribution. Beyond the well-developed literature on economic voting, we still know relatively little about how economic fundamentals affect political behavior in a comparative perspective. The observation made by the APSA Task Force on Inequality and American Democracy that "we know little about the connections between changing economic inequality and changes in political behavior" (2004: 661) remains true today.

Some economic outcomes are relatively straightforward. It is hard not to realize that unemployment has climbed to 20 percent, or that the economy has entered a recession. Income inequality may not be one of these self-evident economic outcomes. It only changes slowly over time, and citizens may have blurry ideas about what the actual income distribution is. Their beliefs about the ideal income distribution may be inconsequential in predicting their behavior. For example, recent work by economists Michael Norton and Dan Ariely shows that Americans consistently underestimate how unequal income is. When given a choice between hypothetic income distributions, more than 90 percent prefer one that resembles Sweden. In spite of this, many Americans do not favor more redistributive policies in elections (for more inconsistencies in opinions on inequality see McCall and Kenworthy 2009).

Of course, there are explanations available to account for net income inequality's depression of participation in all social groups. Generalized trust is lower in unequal societies (Rothstein and Uslaner 2005). If income inequality undermines social capital and prosocial behavior, the social norm of voting may be less widespread in unequal societies. One plausible possibility, which I admittedly cannot test,[13] is that income inequality makes for less cohesive societies and reduces the propensity of all citizens, be they high- or low-status, to think that they should comply with the civic duty of voting. An erosion of prosocial behavior would explain why the participation rates of all income and education groups are lower in unequal contexts.[14]

This still does not account for the connection between unequal participation and gross income inequality uncovered in this chapter. One wild speculation is that the data may be capturing

---

[13] The CSES does not ask respondents if they think that voting is a civic duty. In fact, not even the American National Election Study has included questions on duty for a long time (Achen 2010).

[14] Beramendi and Anderson (2008) make sense of similar findings by arguing that "the mechanism by which inequality affects participation differs between high- and low-income individuals: Although inequality at the lower end reduces participation among low-income individuals because it deprives them of resources, higher inequalities at the upper end reduce participation by creating disincentives to get involved [. . .] there are too many ways for individuals in the highest income categories to avoid the consequences of policies to care sufficiently to be involved in the electoral process" (303–304). I find this explanation unconvincing. First, inequality does not necessarily deprive lower-status people of resources: In an unequal but rich society they may have more resources than lower-status people in a more equal but poorer society (do poor Americans have fewer resources than poor Bulgarians?) and certainly enough resources to vote. Second, it is unclear why higher-status people have fewer incentives to participate in unequal societies. People at the very top may have many means through which to avoid the consequences of policies, but mid- or high-income citizens are affected by taxes and mostly lack very direct access to political power, hence voting is a way to defend their interests and preferences.

a static picture in the midst of a dynamic long-term process. Gross income inequality has risen in many contexts because of a diverse set of factors such as technological change (Neckerman and Torche 2007). Redistribution by the state is strongly path-dependent and does not shift overnight because it operates through a large set of entrenched policies. Elites have mounting interest in reducing redistribution in contexts in which gross inequality has recently increased. The lower-status electorate must be demobilized to make changes in entitlement programs politically feasible and to reduce programs that cut redistributive spending by the state. Trade unions, one of the main historical instruments of political mobilization representing lower-status groups (see Chapter 5), have come under severe attack in recent decades, undermining their capacity to oppose economic reforms (for a discussion of the British case see Daniels and McIlroy 2009). A story along these lines could be consistent with the absence of a relationship between net income inequality and turnout inequality, if the incentives to reduce redistribution have initiated efforts to demobilize lower-status groups to ultimately cut down on redistribution, but the result of this agenda has not yet been accomplished.[15] Of course, even if this speculation held some truth, we still do not know exactly how some sectors of the electorate are being demobilized.

Importantly, the results also have implications for theories of redistribution that draw on the Richard-Meltzer model. In these theories, the median voter will demand more redistribution as gross income inequality increases. However, this theoretical result is undermined in the presence of unequal participation. If, as suggested by the results of this chapter, gross income inequality is correlated with higher turnout inequality (for reasons as yet unknown), increases in income inequality may not lead to a higher demand for redistribution because the median

---

[15] Turnout decline has been concentrated among young, poorly educated citizens in countries as different as Canada, Sweden, Norway, and Germany (Blais et al. 2004; Gallego 2009). However, there are alternative explanations for these declines.

voter becomes richer and more likely to oppose redistribution as inequality grows.

This chapter leaves many questions unanswered, but it has shed some new findings on the important relationship between income inequality and turnout inequality. First, it has shown that net income inequality is associated with lower participation but that the decline is not concentrated among lower-status groups. Gross income inequality, on the contrary, is associated with turnout inequality. Existing theories are ill-equipped to account for these combined findings. Further work needs to clarify the mechanisms through which income inequality affects political behavior and the democratic process.

7

Consequences of Unequal Participation for Representation

Unequal participation worries scholars because of its consequences. Specifically, some authors have argued that unequal participation produces unequal representation, that is, it privileges the interests, preferences, and needs of some citizens over those of others (Lijphart 1997; Verba 2003), thus corrupting the democratic process. This chapter presents the argument that unequal participation distorts representation, discusses relevant findings from previous studies, and adds new comparative evidence that speaks to this claim.

A democratic government should be continuously responsive "to the preferences of its citizens, considered as political equals" (Dahl 1971: 1). Elections are a virtuous – if imperfect – procedure because they provide incentives for politicians to respond to the electorate's demands (Przeworski and Stokes 1999). In mandate conceptions of representation, voters vote for the electoral programs they think will best suit their interests and views. Parties thus have incentives to present programs that voters like. In accountability conceptions of representation, incumbents seek to maintain or to increase the share of the vote they receive in the next election. Popular policies increase support for incumbent governments, while unpopular policies reduce it. Therefore, governments are incentivized to approve policies backed by the public, or at least by large fractions of it.

However, there is an important mismatch. Although politicians should normatively give equal weight to the views of the *people*, they have incentives to be responsive only to *voters*. Unless participation is universal, voters are only a subset of the adult population. To the extent that participation is unequal, voters are a socially privileged subset of the population. Unfortunately, there is no compelling reason why politicians should represent people who self-select out of the electorate: "if you don't vote, you don't count" (Burnham 1987: 99). Thus, unequal voter participation may tilt the representation process toward the interests of the privileged. This constitutes a deviation from the ideal that governments should be responsive to all citizens as political equals.

The relationship between participation and representation is a broad and important question, yet the proposition that "unequal participation generates unequal representation" is difficult to test. Instead, researchers examine a number of more specific aspects of the representation process. The three most important sets of questions are:

1. Do the political preferences of voters and nonvoters differ? What about the preferences of lower- and higher-status people? Whose preferences do politicians represent? If the preferences of different population subgroups differ, and politicians are more responsive to high-turnout groups, the policies implemented by the government will be biased toward the preferences of high-turnout groups when participation is unequal.

2. Would the results of elections be different if everybody voted? If nonvoters voted, they might vote for different candidates and parties than those preferred by actual voters, and their participation could modify election outcomes. Thus, unequal participation may affect who is elected.

3. Do governments strategically target public resources to voters? Even if election results were identical if everybody

voted, and the preferences of voters and nonvoters were similar, unequal turnout could still produce unequal representation. This would happen if politicians targeted some benefits or public resources at high-turnout populations. Resource-allocation decisions would respond to the interests of voters to a larger degree than they should.

Clearly, the research spurred by this concern is extremely broad. This chapter starts by reviewing the main findings of the literature. One important point to keep in mind throughout is that, as usual, a large share of the research focuses on the American case. We know much less about the relationship between unequal participation and representation in other countries. Moreover, to the best of my knowledge the literature has not related differences in political preferences to cross-national variation in the levels of unequal participation and thus has not explicitly connected unequal participation to unequal representation.

The second section of the chapter contributes to the comparative literature by examining if there are differences in political preferences across population groups and if these differences are larger in countries where participation is more unequal. First, I show that in most countries, highly and less educated people hold differing views on both economic and cultural issues. Poorly educated citizens are more left wing on redistributive issues, but more right wing on cultural issues than are highly educated citizens. Voters and nonvoters have similar preferences on most issues at first sight. However, digging further, a different picture emerges. The opinions of voters and nonvoters are only similar in countries where participation is equal. In countries where inequalities in voter participation are large, on the other hand, there are substantial gaps in political preferences: Voters are less likely to demand redistribution and more likely to have liberal cultural opinions than nonvoters. This finding suggests that unequal participation can have harmful consequences for representation outcomes.

Heterogeneous Preferences Among Populations

A first stream of research compares the political preferences of different population groups, such as voters and nonvoters, or the socially advantaged and the disadvantaged. If all the groups had the same preferences over policies (say if everyone opposed taxes on the rich), then unequal participation would perhaps be irrelevant. Being responsive to one subset of the population would produce the same outcome as being responsive to the whole set. On the contrary, if opinions differ across groups, it is not possible to please everyone. For instance, in many distributive situations, interests are antagonistic; if one group obtains its preferred outcome, another group does not. Moreover, resources are limited and politicians face choices about whom they choose to satisfy. Politicians have incentives to be more responsive to high-turnout groups than their demographic weight grants, with the result that the political process does not treat the preferences of all citizens equally.

A first step, however, is to ask if politicians are responsive to the political preferences of voters at all. If governments do not react to public opinion, the distribution of this opinion is beside the point. Extensive research has demonstrated that politicians do largely respond to the public's demands. In a review of the literature, Gilens (2005: 779–780) distinguishes among three types of empirical work. First, research has found a correlation between public preferences and legislators' voting behavior. Second, public opinion favorable to an issue generally precedes, rather than follows, policy change. This is especially true for salient issues. We also know that the influence of public opinion is smaller in areas better insulated from public scrutiny such as foreign policy. The comparative literature is less well developed, but it tilts toward the same optimistic conclusion (see, for example, Luna and Zechmeister 2005; Kang and Powell 2010; Wlezien and Soroka 2008; Roberts and Kim 2011; Warwick 2011).

If the government is responsive to public opinion, and different groups have similar opinions on political issues, the governments' decisions will be, in general, equally congruent with the opinions of all groups. Representation can in principle work well even if some groups fail to vote. On the contrary, if preferences differ across groups, government officials face choices about whose opinion to prioritize. Two research questions follow from this observation: Do differences of opinion exist between different groups? Whose opinions are represented in policy decisions? This chapter focuses on the first question, as differences in opinion are a precondition for the second question to be pertinent.

Issue-specific differences in opinion arise when comparing political preferences across socioeconomic groups. American research has documented that low income and low education citizens are more in favor of welfare spending and redistributive policies, whereas in other policy areas there are no remarkable differences in the opinions of different population groups (Soroka and Wlezien 2008; Gilens 2005, 2009; Page and Jacobs 2009; Enns and Wlezien 2011) and for the most part the preferences of different subconstituencies move simultaneously over time (Ura and Ellis 2008). Sure enough, education and income are consistent predictors of political attitudes in comparative public opinion studies with data from the World Values Survey, the International Social Survey Program, the Eurobarometer, or the European Social Survey. They predict opinions on a wide range of issues such as preferences on income equality and redistribution (Amat and Wibbels 2009; Alesina and Giuliano 2009), voting for left-wing parties (de la O and Rodden 2008), welfare policies (Svallfors 1997), or immigration attitudes (Ceobanu and Escandell 2009). This research proves the existence of robust differences in opinions across socioeconomic groups. However, the sizes of the opinion gaps are not often discussed, making it hard to establish how consequential the differences in opinion are, or to determine whether the gaps are larger in some issues than in others.

Voters and nonvoters have also been found to have remarkably similar views on most, but not all, political issues. In the United States, a number of well-known studies show that nonvoters hold attitudes quite similar to those of the general population, despite the demographic differences that characterize nonvoters

(Wolfinger and Rosenstone 1980; Teixeira 1992). Other studies find that nonvoters are more liberal than voters on a number of issues such as redistribution, the role of government in the economy, and welfare policies (Bennett and Resnick 1990; Leighley and Nagler 2007). In Canada, voters and nonvoters differ little in their preferences, and in contradictory ways. On some issues, voters are more liberal than nonvoters, while on other issues they are more conservative (Rubenson et al. 2007). The opinions of voters and nonvoters in Britain differ in only less than a third of the issues examined, leading scholars to conclude that nonvoters do not have a different attitudinal structure than voters do (Studlar and Welch 1986). On the contrary, in Belarus, Russia, and Ukraine there are substantial differences. Voters are less likely to favor market policies, more likely to support the Soviet Union, and less pro–European Union than nonvoters (White and McAllister 2007).

There is very little comparative research that brings together the issue positions of political elites, voters, and nonvoters. In one of the most interesting comparative studies to date, Kissau, Lutz, and Rosset (2011) use data from the European parliamentary election in 2009. In twelve out of fourteen countries, nonvoters agree more than both voters and elites with the statement that governments should redistribute income toward poorer people. Similarly, nonvoters take stronger anti-immigration positions than voters and elites in eleven out of fourteen countries. A multivariate analysis shows that the issue positions of political elites are closer to the positions of voters than to the positions of nonvoters. The difference persists after controlling for sociodemographic and attitudinal variables. This suggests not only that voters and nonvoters in European countries hold different views, but that these differences are consequential. Political elites are closer in opinion to voters than to nonvoters. Along the same lines, Griffin and Newman (2005) find in the United States that voter ideology predicts senator roll-call voting whereas nonvoter ideology does not predict it, concluding that "those segments of the public that do not vote appear, as a group, to have little influence on legislators' roll-call voting, opening the path to biases in legislator behavior and ultimately public policy" (p. 122).[1]

A final concern is that politicians may always be more responsive to the preferences of the rich, independent of voter preferences. Rich people can influence politicians by means other than voting, such as directly interacting with them and persuading them with arguments, donating money, influencing public opinion and cultural discourse through the media, or threatening to use their economic power in specific ways (Rueschemeyer 2005). In his landmark study, Bartels (2008) uncovered heavy distortions in the representation process. Partisanship and the political preferences of affluent people influence the roll-call votes cast by U.S. senators but the preferences of low-income people have no effect on the votes. This holds true even when controlling for differences in turnout levels.

This presents an important conundrum. Politicians may not be responsive to socially disadvantaged voters *even if they vote*. This nonresponsiveness could be a cause, rather than a consequence, of unequal participation. If the political decision process dismisses the opinion of disadvantaged voters, why bother casting a vote? There is no obvious equivalent of roll-call votes or legislators' ideal points in comparative analyses, and to my knowledge, no research in other countries has specifically examined this question. This area surely deserves further attention.

Full Turnout and Electoral Results

A different strand of literature asks if turnout levels affect electoral outcomes. In many contexts, poor and poorly educated people are more likely to vote for the left than are rich and educated people, and the disadvantaged are less likely to participate in elections. Connecting the two ideas, we arrive at the popular suspicion that low turnout rates harm left-wing parties and favor

---

[1] However, in Eastern European countries, policies do not seem to follow the opinion of the highly educated to a larger degree than the opinion of the poorly educated (Roberts and Kim 2011).

right-wing parties. In close elections, this bias may even alter the election results. Yet, as Grofman, Owen, and Collet (1999) have argued, this logic is not as smooth as it seems. Ultimately, what researchers care about is the counter-factual question: Would electoral results change if everybody voted? If true, this would reveal the existence of a very serious flaw in the representation process, because elected representatives and governments would be different from those elected if all citizens manifested their preferences.

Because nonvoters don't vote, it is very hard to know what they would choose if they voted. Thus, any analysis needs to make a number of assumptions about the likely, but nonobserved, behavior of nonvoters in a full turnout world. Researchers using a variety of strategies, designs, and assumptions have arrived at different conclusions. Despite this variability, a relatively coherent picture arises from the literature.

First, some studies find that left-wing parties fare better when turnout is high, and interpret this as support for the proposition that electoral results would change if everybody voted. Voter turnout rates are associated with success for left-wing parties in industrial democracies (Pacek and Radcliff 1995) and in European Parliamentary elections (Pacek and Radcliff 2003). Voter turnout is higher and the share of the vote captured by left-wing parties is larger when there are economic downturns in elections in developing countries (Aguilar and Pacek 2000) as well as Eastern European countries (Bohrer, Pacek, and Radcliff 2000). Hansford and Gomez (2010) examine the consequences of voter turnout in American presidential elections between 1948 and 2000 using rainfall on Election Day as an instrument of voter turnout, and find that high turnout benefits the Democratic Party. Similarly, the introduction of compulsory voting in Australia benefited the Labor Party (Fowler 2011). These results suggest that lower turnout does indeed affect parties' vote share and sometimes even electoral outcomes at the county and national levels.

Other research is much less supportive of the argument that low turnout affects election results. For example, Highton and Wolfinger (2001) argue that the party preferences of voters and nonvoters are too similar to generate any substantial effects on electoral outcomes in the United States, even if everybody voted. Bernhagen and Marsh (2007) use data from the CSES in twenty-eight elections. They treat nonvoters as a missing data problem and impute their preferences using information on characteristics that are associated with vote choice. The results suggest that there are no systematic gains from increased voter turnout for the left, whereas under some circumstances, small parties and nonincumbents can benefit from high turnout. Other studies find similarly tiny differences both in one-country case studies and in cross-national comparisons (e.g., Toka 2002, Rubenson et al. 2007; Van der Eijk and van Egmond 2007). While high turnout sometimes benefits left-wing parties, the effects are so small that authors judge it unlikely that overall results could possibly change if all potential voters participated. The editors of a special journal issue on the electoral consequences of voter turnout claim that participation rates have no impact on election outcomes across countries and over time, and that this result is robust when using a variety of methods (Lutz and Marsh 2007).

This conclusion may be overly blunt. The very existence of small differences in the actual and simulated electoral results of elections in which everyone votes suggests that full turnout may cause the electoral outcome to change *in very close elections*. For example, Bernhagen and Marsh (2007) report that in a few elections the difference between actual and contrafactual results was substantial enough that it may have been consequential for the results. Along the same lines, U.S. nonvoters are somewhat more Democratic than voters are, and simulations of electoral results under universal turnout in Senate elections suggest that these differences could have an impact in close races (Citrin, Shickler, and Sides 2003).

Seen globally, the literature yields some support for the proposition that voters and nonvoters have slightly different party preferences, and that left-wing parties do better when turnout is high in some contexts. The differences are admittedly small. Nonetheless, small differences can be consequential for election results in close elections. Thus, while in the majority of elections electoral outcomes would be identical if everybody voted, in some cases, the electoral participation of nonvoters would change the election results.

Policy Outcomes and Resource Targeting

A final line of research looks at policy outcomes and asks if expenditure in redistributive and welfare policies is predicted by unequal turnout and if resources are targeted at high-turnout areas within constituencies. An affirmative answer to both questions provides direct evidence that unequal participation biases the outcomes of the representation process. The logic here is that politicians target certain resources strategically at groups whose votes they need as well as at high-turnout populations. Targeted spending can occur even if the issue opinions of all groups are similar and even if election results would not change if everybody voted.

Hill and Leighley (1992) examine if an electorate disproportionately composed of higher-status citizens is rewarded with public policies congruent with their interests (whatever their preferences are). They look at variation in policies across the United States and find a negative relationship between the degree of class bias and four measures of the generosity of welfare spending. This suggests that parties and governments reward poor voters with beneficial policies when they vote at high rates. The findings reported by Hill, Leighley, and Hinton-Anderson (1995) are similar in spirit, though they show that the relationship holds mainly in Democratic states. Using a different strategy, Martin (2003) arrives at a similar conclusion. He shows that counties with higher participation rates receive more federal grants, suggesting that members of the U.S. congress strategically use the limited resources at their disposal to target high-participation areas, while neglecting low-turnout areas.

Although research is rather scarce, the findings reviewed support the idea that unequal participation biases the representation process. Redistributive policies and poverty relief efforts are smaller in contexts where voter turnout is more unequal and the interests of high-turnout groups guide spending to a larger degree than the interests of low turnout groups do.

To my knowledge, there are few similar studies in other countries. The literature on the relationship between voter turnout, social inequality, and redistributive policies, reviewed in Chapter 6, has generally found a positive correlation between turnout and social spending. Jusko (2008, 2011, see discussion in Chapter 5) has examined the relationship between the electoral power of low-income people and turnout inequality, and between the former and poverty relief policies separately, but her work has not directly linked turnout inequality to poverty relief. Thus, a direct assessment of the implications of unequal turnout for the strategic targeting of policies to high turnout groups is, to date, lacking.

Issue Opinions by Education and Voter Participation Across Countries

This section examines differences in issue opinions between voters and nonvoters and between the highly and the less educated across countries. Issue opinions are more suitable measures than left-right positions for the assessment of topics on which population groups have different views. In Europe, political competition is multidimensional (for a recent discussion see Kissau, Lutz, and Rosset 2011) and the left-right scale conflates preferences that do not always go hand in hand in the electorate's mind.

A bivariate analysis aims to establish the existence and magnitude of opinion gaps, and a multivariate analysis estimates average differences in opinion, holding the age, sex, and country of the respondent constant. I also examine if differences in the political preferences of voters and nonvoters are larger in countries where participation is unequal than in countries where participation is equal. The analysis uses data from the fourth round of the European Social Survey (ESS), because the CSES has very little information on respondents' opinions about political issues.

I use data from twenty-six countries, gathered between 2008 and 2010.[2]

The ESS asks respondents about their agreement with the statement that "the government should take measures to reduce differences in income levels." The five response categories ranged from agree strongly to disagree strongly, and they are recoded so that 1 stands for agreement with this statement and 0 stands for disagreement. Table 7–1 reports the percentage of people who agree or agree strongly with this statement by education level and reported voter participation. Education is recoded in three groups: lower secondary or less; upper secondary education; and postsecondary or tertiary education. Column 4 reports the differences in the percentage of highly and less educated people who agree with this statement, and column 7 reports the differences in the percentage of voters and nonvoters agreeing with it.

The countries are sorted by decreasing order of unequal participation. I estimated the extent to which turnout is unequal by using the OLS procedure discussed in Chapter 1 (see Figure 1–4). Countries in which the differences in the reported voter participation of highly and less educated people are large appear at the top of the table. High inequality countries include Poland, the Czech Republic, and Germany. At the bottom are Belgium, Greece, Bulgaria, and Romania. Though the education classification used is different, the order is reassuringly similar to the previous results using CSES data.

The opinions of highly and less educated people diverge. On average, 80 percent of people with a low level of education agree that the government should take measures to reduce income inequality, compared to 65 percent of the highly educated. A difference of 15 percentage points is large in magnitude and highly statistically significant.

---

[2] The universe of the ESS is all people aged 15 and older in the participating countries, but I do not include people under 18 years. To maintain consistency with the selection criteria used throughout the book, the countries that did not achieve a Freedom House rating of less than 3 in 2008 (Turkey and the Russian Federation) were excluded from the database, as was Cyprus because of missing information.

TABLE 7-1. Percent Agreeing That Government Should Reduce Differences in Income Levels

	Low Educ.	Mid Educ.	High Educ.	Diff. High-Low Education	Nonvoters	Voters	Diff. Voters – Nonvoters
Poland	84.8	78.1	58.1	−26.7***	80.4	71.9	−8.4***
Czech Rep.	72.0	57.3	35.4	−36.5***	62.6	52.8	−9.8***
Germany	74.6	73.0	60.0	−14.6***	75.4	67.1	−8.3***
Switzerland	82.3	68.5	54.5	−27.8***	71.3	63.9	−7.5**
Finland	79.7	78.7	67.2	−12.6***	80.0	76.1	−3.9
France	81.6	83.7	68.3	−13.3***	79.4	77.7	−1.7
Estonia	76.9	70.7	62.6	−14.2***	73.1	64.8	−8.3**
Latvia	88.9	81.8	76.5	−12.4***	83.3	81.8	−1.5
Slovakia	77.8	70.8	51.5	−26.3***	66.9	70.1	3.2
Croatia	83.4	81.0	73.7	−9.7**	79.7	80.4	0.7
Hungary	87.7	82.5	77.0	−10.7	87.9	83.3	−4.5*
Norway	72.2	63.4	55.1	−17.1***	58.4	61.2	2.8
Netherlands	64.6	54.9	48.2	−16.4***	59.7	55.5	−4.3
Slovenia	92.1	89.8	74.4	−17.7***	88.2	86.4	−1.8
Portugal	90.7	91.2	85.3	−5.4*	86.8	91.5	4.7**

UK	65.4	60.9	52.7	-12.6^{***}	61.8	58.2	-3.5
Ukraine	82.4	78.3	73.8	-8.6^{**}	70.6	77.6	7.0^{**}
Sweden	73.9	62.8	54.8	-19.1^{***}	63.4	64.5	1.1
Spain	83.0	76.9	74.5	-8.4^{***}	81.3	78.9	-2.4
Israel	83.7	76.7	72.6	-11.1^{***}	78.5	75.6	-2.9
Denmark	45.9	41.0	40.6	-5.3	31.9	42.7	10.8^{+}
Ireland	80.3	78.0	64.8	-15.5^{***}	70.2	74.4	4.2
Belgium	76.9	73.2	61.9	-15.0^{***}	73.8	70.6	-3.2
Greece	93.8	92.8	88.7	-5.0^{**}	92.1	92.0	-0.1
Bulgaria	88.1	77.5	67.7	-20.4^{***}	74.1	80.1	6.0^{**}
Romania	83.0	79.8	71.0	-12.0^{***}	76.7	80.5	3.8^{+}
Mean of means	79.6	74.2	64.6	-15.1^{***}	73.5	72.6	-1.0

$+$ $p < 0.1$, $*$ $p < 0.05$, $**$ $p < 0.01$, $***$ $p < 0.001$. *Source*: fourth wave of the ESS. The entries are the percentage of people in each country who agree or agree strongly with the statement that the government should reduce differences in income levels. The question had five answer categories, which were recoded into two: agree or agree strongly are coded as 1, and neither agree nor disagree, disagree, and disagree strongly are coded as 0. Column 4 reports the difference in the mean response of people with lower secondary education or less and people with vocational postsecondary or university education. Column 7 reports the differences in the mean response of voters and nonvoters. Countries are ordered by decreasing level of turnout inequality, estimated as described in Chapter 1.

By contrast, voters and nonvoters in most countries hold similar opinions on average. Ordering countries by level of unequal participation, however, reveals an important pattern. In countries with large inequalities in voter participation, there are differences in the opinions of voters and nonvoters. This is of course a consequence of the combined presence of different opinions across education groups and the electorate's composition in countries with higher inequality of turnout. Conversely, the absence of differences in the opinions of voters and nonvoters follows from the fact that the level of education of voters and nonvoters is very similar in countries where participation is more equal. This finding speaks to the proposition that unequal participation may bias representation. The opinions of voters and nonvoters are similar in general, as the literature has suggested. In spite of this, in some contexts, their preferences can be quite different. Voters and nonvoters have different opinions on the role of the state in reducing income inequality only when voter turnout is unequal.

The next analysis assesses differences in opinion on other political issues. Gender attitudes are a relevant cultural issue in most countries. Asking respondents if they agree that men should have more rights to a job than women when jobs are scarce captures attitudes toward gender equality in the labor market. Agreement with this statement indicates that the respondent is in favor of labor market discrimination against women.

Age is a confounded variable. For example, older people should be more likely to agree with this statement, more likely to be poorly educated, and more likely to vote. Thus, a bivariate comparison may exaggerate differences in gender attitudes across education groups, but mask differences between voters and nonvoters.

Table 7–2 shows that highly educated people are more likely to disagree with the statement "men should have more right to a job than women when jobs are scarce." Only 12 percent of the highly educated agree with this statement, while the less educated are almost three times as likely to agree with it. The difference is large in magnitude in almost all countries. The exceptions are

TABLE 7–2. *Percent Agreeing That Men Should Have More Right to a Job Than Women*

	Low Educ.	Mid Educ.	High Educ.	Diff. High-Low Education	Nonvoters	Voters	Diff. Voters – Nonvoters
Poland	48.6	27.4	9.2	−39.4***	32.6	24.7	−7.9**
Czech Rep.	40.7	25.6	18.1	−22.6***	31.0	22.9	−8.2***
Germany	26.5	18.2	6.9	−19.6***	25.6	12.9	−12.7***
Switzerland	35.1	20.5	8.7	−26.4***	22.4	18.8	−3.6+
Finland	12.4	4.0	2.1	−10.3***	7.2	5.9	−1.3
France	28.5	11.3	4.1	−24.5***	14.1	15.0	0.9
Estonia	30.0	17.7	10.5	−19.6***	21.1	16.7	−4.4+
Latvia	24.7	19.4	15.2	−9.5***	23.4	16.0	−7.4***
Slovakia	42.9	29.0	16.8	−26.1***	28.6	29.7	1.0
Croatia	42.4	19.8	14.8	−27.7***	27.5	23.0	−4.5
Hungary	46.8	26.0	24.9	−21.9***	43.4	36.7	−6.7*
Norway	10.0	3.4	2.2	−7.8***	3.6	3.8	0.2
Netherlands	21.0	8.7	4.4	−16.6***	15.1	11.5	−3.5
Slovenia	35.7	13.5	3.7	−32.0***	16.6	17.4	0.8

(*continued*)

TABLE 7-2 (continued)

	Low Educ.	Mid Educ.	High Educ.	Diff. High-Low Education	Nonvoters	Voters	Diff. Voters – Nonvoters
Portugal	28.4	14.2	10.9	−17.6***	26.8	23.6	−3.2
UK	23.4	7.2	7.3	−16.1***	11.6	15.7	4.1*
Ukraine	51.2	48.5	39.5	−11.7***	41.8	43.5	1.7
Sweden	6.1	1.4	1.2	−4.8***	4.2	3.0	−1.2
Spain	25.6	6.5	4.9	−20.7***	22.6	14.3	−8.3***
Israel	55.0	32.5	21.4	−33.6***	38.6	28.4	−10.2***
Denmark	5.5	3.0	1.6	−3.9**	10.7	2.5	−8.1*
Ireland	22.4	10.5	4.4	−17.9***	12.3	11.9	−0.4
Belgium	33.1	17.3	8.9	−24.2***	30.1	18.0	−12.1**
Greece	60.8	40.2	29.8	−30.9***	37.6	45.4	7.8*
Bulgaria	46.6	30.6	20.5	−26.0***	32.3	33.5	1.3
Romania	43.9	36.6	21.9	−22.0***	34.5	37.6	3.1
Mean of means	33.59	19.66	12.47	−21.1***	24.36	21.16	−3.2

+ p < 0.1, * p < 0.05, ** p < 0.01, *** p < 0.001. *Source:* fourth wave of the ESS. The entries are the percentage of people in each country who agree or agree strongly with the statement that men should have more right to a job than women when jobs are scarce. The question had five answer categories, which were recoded into two: agree or agree strongly are coded as 1, and neither agree nor disagree, disagree, and disagree strongly are coded as 0. Column 4 reports the difference in the mean response of people with lower seconcary education or less and people with vocational postsecondary or university education. Column 7 reports the differences in the mean response of voters and nonvoters. Countries are ordered by decreasing level of turnout inequality, estimated as described in Chapter 1.

Scandinavian countries where very small percentages of the poorly educated disagree with this statement, and thus floor effects bar large differences in opinion.

In the majority of countries, voters and nonvoters have similar opinions about this gender issue. However, it is noteworthy that in countries with high levels of turnout inequality, gaps in opinion between voters and nonvoters exist. In contexts with unequal turnout (as well as in a handful of other countries including Israel, Spain, Denmark, and Belgium) voters are less likely to report conservative gender views than are nonvoters.

Bivariate country-by-country analyses suggest that preferences vary depending on education levels, and that the opinions of voters and nonvoters differ only where turnout is unequal. These results are to some extent confounded by the fact that young people have different issue opinions than older people, and they also vote at lower rates. Moreover, we would like to know if there are differences in opinions about a larger number of issues, to see how consistent these differences are across topics.

A multivariate analysis complements the previous examination. Column 1 in Table 7–3 reports the expected difference in the proportions of highly and less educated people who agree with eight issue opinions, conditional on their age, sex, and country of origin. Column 2 reports the conditional difference in the proportions of voters and nonvoters who agree with the statements. Each coefficient has been estimated from a different linear regression model.[3] The dependent variable is agreement with the statements, coded as in the previous analyses. Education (in three categories ranging from 0 to 1), in the models of the first column, and voting, in the models of the second column, are included as predictors along with age, sex, and country. The coefficients are the expected differences in the proportions of highly and less educated people, or voters and nonvoters, who agree with the statements, conditional on the values of the covariates. They are

---

[3] Even though the dependent variable is binary, using OLS allows the coefficients to have a direct and more intuitive interpretation as the expected difference in proportions, conditional on the values of the covariates.

TABLE 7–3. *Differences in Issue Opinion by Education Level and Voter Participation*

	Education	Vote
Redistribution and social spending		
Government should reduce	−0.136***	−0.039**
differences in income levels	(0.018)	(0.014)
Large income differences are	0.061***	0.025*
acceptable to reward talent	(0.013)	(0.016)
Fair society, differences in living	−0.095**	−0.005
standard should be small	(0.027)	(0.013)
Insufficient benefits in country to	−0.094***	−0.053**
help people in real need	(0.020)	(0.017)
Cultural values		
Gays and lesbians should be free	0.092***	0.040*
to live life as they wish	(0.013)	(0.017)
Schools should teach children to	−0.080***	−0.012
obey authority	(0.015)	(0.021)
People who break the law should	−0.162***	−0.033
get harsher sentences	(0.029)	(0.022)
Men should have more right to a	−0.164***	−0.053**
job when jobs are scarce	(0.020)	(0.019)

$^{+}$ $p < 0.1$, * $p < 0.05$, ** $p < 0.01$, *** $p < 0.001$, standard errors clustered by country in parenthesis. *Source*: fourth wave of the ESS. The entries are OLS regression coefficients of sixteen separate regressions, including education (column 1) and voter participation (column 2) as predictors of opinion on issues, which are the dependent variable in the models. All responses were recoded as 1 if the person agrees or agrees strongly with the statement and 0 otherwise. Education, in three groups, and voting range from 0 to 1. All models include controls for age, age squared, and gender, and country fixed effects. The design and population weights provided by the ESS were applied.

The coefficients of the first column can be interpreted as "the expected difference in the proportion of highly and less educated citizens who agree with each statement, conditional on the value of the covariates":

$$\text{Expected difference in proportions by education:}$$
$$E\left(\text{Opinion}_{\text{high\_edu}} - \text{Opinion}_{\text{low\_edu}} \mid \text{Controls}\right)$$

In the second column, they are "the expected difference in the proportion of voters and nonvoters who agree with each statement, conditional on the value of the covariates":

$$\text{Expected difference in proportions by voter participation}$$
$$= E\left(\text{Opinion}_{\text{voter}} - \text{Opinion}_{\text{nonvoter}} \mid \text{Controls}\right)$$

thus analogous to the values in columns 4 and 7 in Table 7–1 and Table 7–4, conditional on a vector of covariates.

Highly educated people declare, on average, more conservative economic opinions than do less educated people. The results confirm that they are less likely to agree that the government should reduce income differences. According to this estimation, there is a 14 points percentage difference in agreement between highly and less educated people.[4] The average estimate of the bivariate analysis (in Table 7–1) was 15 percentage points. Thus, the estimated difference in opinions is very similar whether or not we hold age, sex, or country of origin constant.

Highly educated people are also more likely to agree that income differences are acceptable as means to reward talent than less educated people. Highly educated respondents are more likely to think that, in a fair society, differences in the standard of living should be small, but less likely to respond that benefits to help people in real need are insufficient, conditional on age, sex, and country.

On the other hand, highly educated people are more liberal than less educated people on cultural issues. They are more likely to agree that gays and lesbians should be free to live their lives as they wish, and they are less likely to agree that schools should teach children to obey authority, that people who break the law should get harsher sentences, or that men should have more job opportunities than women.

The estimated differences in the proportion of highly and less educated people agreeing with these statements ranges from 0.06 to 0.16. Although they are not dramatic, these differences are quite substantial. Differences of this size are not consequential if there is a consensus in public opinion about an issue (for example, if 90 percent of the population thinks alike). However, the opinion on many relevant issues splits more evenly. In the absence of a societal consensus, differences in opinion of 10 percentage

---

[4] For example, if 65 percent of the poorly educated agree with the statement, and 79 percent of the highly educated agree, this results in a 14 percentage points difference or a 0.14 difference in proportions.

points can mean that although a majority of highly educated people agrees with one issue position, a majority of less educated people disagrees with it, or vice versa.

Gaps in opinion between voters and nonvoters are smaller in magnitude and not as pervasive. When they are statistically significant, the differences in proportions range from 0.03 to 0.05. Gaps this small are unlikely to make much difference. Voters are less likely to support policies that redistribute income and reduce income inequality than are nonvoters. On the other hand, voters are slightly more liberal on some cultural issues than are nonvoters. For example, voters are more likely to agree that gays and lesbians should be free to live life as they wish and less likely to think that men should have more right to jobs than women when jobs are scarce. In this case, the magnitude of the opinion difference is somewhat larger than in the bivariate analysis. The expected difference in proportions conditional on the covariates is 0.05, and it is statistically significant at conventional levels. However, the small magnitude of the gaps suggests that, on average, voters and nonvoters in European countries have similar issue opinions.

The conclusion of this examination is that highly educated people in European countries are more conservative than less educated people on economic issues but more liberal on cultural issues. On the other hand, when pooling over countries, voters and nonvoters stand remarkably close on economic and cultural issues on average.

Opinion Gaps Between Voters and Nonvoters When Participation Is Unequal

The previous analysis blends countries in which there is no turnout inequality and countries in which inequalities in voter participation are large. If voters and nonvoters are similar in their socioeconomic circumstances in many of these countries, it is not particularly surprising that their issue opinions do not differ. However, this aggregate result does not preclude the presence of differences in opinion in countries where turnout is unequal.

To address the question of whether unequal participation leads to unequal representation, we need to examine if the opinions of voters and nonvoters do indeed differ in countries where participation is unequal.

Table 7–4 highlights the differences in the opinions of voters and nonvoters in four countries where participation is highly unequal. Replicating the procedure used to estimate the gaps in the turnout rates of highly and less educated people in Chapter 1, these data suggest that voter participation is very unequal in Poland, the Czech Republic, Germany, and Switzerland. The estimated differences in the turnout rates of highly and less educated people range from 41 to 48 percentage points. Although a large majority of highly educated citizens reports voting in elections, a minority of less educated citizens reports voting. The countries with the next largest turnout gaps in this dataset are Finland and France, but at 32 percentage points turnout gaps in these countries are considerably smaller. Thus, the first four countries listed are clearly the cases in the ESS dataset that exhibit more unequal turnout.

Table 7–4 reports the conditional difference in the proportion of highly and less educated respondents agreeing on each of the cultural and economic issues. To estimate the coefficients, I ran the models for each country separately. Issue opinions are again the dependent variables and voter participation is the main independent variable of interest, along with age and sex as controls.

In countries with high levels of turnout inequality, in general, voters are more conservative than nonvoters on economic issues, but voters are more liberal on cultural issues. In some cases, there are no significant differences in the estimated proportion of voters and nonvoters agreeing with the statements. Yet in most cases, the differences are significant and, though not dramatic, they are often large in magnitude. For example, in Germany the percentage of voters agreeing that government should reduce differences in income levels is 9 points lower than the percentage of nonvoters agreeing with this statement. The estimated difference in the percentage of voters and nonvoters agreeing that there are insufficient benefits in the country to help people in real need

TABLE 7-4. *Difference in Issue Opinion by Voter Participation in High Turnout-Inequality Countries*

	Poland	Czech Rep.	Germany	Switzerland
Redistribution and social spending				
Government should reduce differences in income levels	-0.083*** (0.024)	-0.124*** (0.027)	-0.089*** (0.027)	-0.064* (0.029)
Large income differences are acceptable to reward talent	0.116*** (0.029)	0.057* (0.025)	0.070* (0.029)	-0.013 (0.031)
Fair society, differences in living standard should be small	-0.074** (0.028)	-0.099* (0.027)	-0.014 (0.029)	0.016 (0.030)
Insufficient benefits in country to help people in real small	0.003 (0.021)	-0.031 (0.028)	-0.158*** (0.029)	-0.101*** (0.031)
Cultural values				
Gays and lesbians should be free to live life as they wish	0.084** (0.030)	0.015 (0.026)	0.114*** (0.024)	0.054* (0.023)
Schools should teach children to obey authority	0.019 (0.014)	0.001 (0.021)	-0.125*** (0.028)	-0.022 (0.030)
People who break the law should get harsher sentences	0.004 (0.024)	0.020 (0.021)	-0.152*** (0.027)	-0.091** (0.030)
Men should have more right to a job when jobs are scarce	-0.077** (0.028)	-0.061* (0.024)	-0.143*** (0.024)	-0.092*** (0.023)

+ p < 0.1, * p < 0.05, ** p < 0.01, *** p < 0.001, standard errors in parenthesis. Source: fourth wave of the ESS. The entries are OLS regression coefficients of thirty-two models. The dependent variable of the models is agreeing or strongly agreeing with each of the issues (coded as 1). The entries are the regression coefficients of the variable voter participation (1 for voters, o for nonvoters). The models control for age, age squared, and sex.

The coefficients can be interpreted as "the expected difference in the proportion of voters and nonvoters who agree with each statement, conditional on the value of the covariates":

Expected difference in proportions by voter participation = E(Opinion$_{voter}$ − Opinion$_{nonvoter}$ | Controls) is 16 percentage points. Thus, nonvoters are significantly more likely than voters to think that benefits are insufficient.

Continuing with the German case, the percentage of voters agreeing that gays and lesbians should be free to live life as they wish is higher than the percentage of nonvoters by 11 percentage points on average. Agreement that schools should teach children to obey authority is 13 percentage points lower among voters than among nonvoters. The gap is 15 percentage points regarding support for harsher sentences for offenders, and 14 percentage points regarding labor market discrimination against women.

However, the differences are not pervasive. For example, in the Czech Republic voters and nonvoters have similar positions on cultural issues. In spite of this, it is clear from these analyses that voters and nonvoters often think differently on cultural and economic issues in these four countries with high levels of turnout inequality.

Unequal Participation and Unequal Representation

This chapter has reviewed one of the main reasons why unequal participation is problematic, which is that unequal participation produces unequal representation. I have started by dividing this broad concern into a more tractable set of questions. The literature review has made clear that we know much more about the American case than about other countries. Furthermore, previous research has not reached clear consensuses. Although scholars agree that education underlies differences in opinion, their findings on whether or not voters and nonvoters have similar preferences are mixed. Most simulations suggest that election results would be unlikely to differ dramatically if everybody voted. While many scholars interpret this finding as evidence that turnout levels and turnout inequality are irrelevant, others argue that small differences are consequential when elections are very competitive. Finally, there is little direct evidence on the consequences of unequal participation for policy outcomes; a recent American debate about what groups politicians are responsive to has no clear analogues yet in the comparative literature.

The empirical section of this chapter has shown that in most European countries' opinions on policy issues differ across education groups. Highly educated people are more conservative than less educated people on economic issues but more liberal on cultural issues. Next, the analyses have shown that on average the opinions of voters and nonvoters on political issues are very similar. However, I have added a qualification that I think is new and important: The opinions of voters and nonvoters are different when participation is unequal.

To understand the implications of these findings for unequal representation, recall the (very reasonable) assumption that politicians have incentives to be responsive to the distribution of preferences in the electorate, not in the population. The findings suggest that where participation is equal the preferences of voters and nonvoters are undistinguishable. By being responsive to the part, politicians are responsive to the whole. This is not the case in countries where turnout is unequal, because in these countries voters and nonvoters have different opinions. Policies responsive to the electorate's mean issue position are likely to follow, but these may not correspond to the society's mean position.

The analyses presented in this chapter of course stop short of exploring the whole argument. I have not provided evidence on policy outputs. In the four countries examined where turnout is unequal, it can be said only that there are differences in the opinions of voters and nonvoters. If we accept the premise that politicians are responsive to voters, this finding suggests that there may be a bias in the public opinion-policy link. In these countries politicians have incentives to adopt more conservative economic policies but also more liberal cultural policies than their societies as a whole would prefer demand. Whether or not these different incentives produce different policies surely deserves further empirical investigation. That said, the findings of this chapter are overall consistent with the claim that unequal participation can bias the representation process.

Conclusions

This book has studied differences in the levels of unequal participation across countries and reasons that can help explain these differences. That less educated people in the United States vote less frequently than highly educated people is among the better-established empirical regularities in political science research. From a broad comparative perspective, this book shows that there is a great deal of variation in the extent to which a high level of education is positively associated with having a larger propensity to vote. There are no differences in the turnout rates of highly and less educated citizens in elections in countries such as Spain, Denmark, or South Korea. One of the most important contributions of this book is that it provides an accurate description of unequal turnout across countries and shows that educated people are more likely to vote than less educated people in some contexts, but not in others. As reviewed in Chapter 1, political scientists frequently assume that socioeconomic status is correlated with voter participation everywhere. Although it is natural to generalize from the local and well-known finding (education is correlated with voting in the United States) to the universal pattern (education is correlated with voting), such a generalization is inaccurate, and I hope that the detailed assessment offered here helps establish a new known fact: Voter turnout is unequal in some contexts but not in others.

The finding that there is variation in the extent to which participation is unequal has important implications. If unequal participation – defined by highly and less educated people having different turnout rates – was universal, we could infer that this inequality is concomitant with democratic politics. We could conclude that some underprivileged groups are simply less motivated or able to vote and nothing short of compulsion may bring them to the polls *en masse*.

The fact that unequal participation is not universal suggests that whether voter turnout is equal depends on specific characteristics of the context of elections. Modify some features of the context and you may be able to equalize participation. In other words, the finding that there is variation in the degree to which participation is unequal suggests that there is scope for political action. If policy makers or the public opinion decide – at some point and for whatever reason – that large inequalities in voter participation are unacceptable or undesirable, then a public debate can emerge on how to make participation more equal. Academics may have something important to add to this debate in the form of prescriptions. If there is enough political will, governments can implement policies aimed at equalizing participation.

This book, along with an important body of literature, shows that the context in which elections are held has profound implications for who participates in politics. As Franklin (2004) states, voting is both an individual decision and a product of the context in which individuals make political decisions. Voting is simultaneously about people and about elections. Individuals live in contexts that profoundly shape politically relevant choices. However, the effects of micro and macro features are not additive. Rather, individual and contextual characteristics interact to affect the decision to participate in politics: The exact same individual characteristic, such as education, can hinder or promote participation in some environments, but may be irrelevant (or even have the contrary effect) in others. This book has shown that education can be a strong predictor of voting or it can be largely irrelevant. This finding joins a growing stream of research on comparative political behavior that claims that we need to *jointly* assess micro and macro determinants of political participation.

Going one step beyond description, the book has proposed a theory about where and why participation should be more or less equal and has applied an innovative strategy to investigate the interaction of individual and contextual characteristics as predictors of political behavior by testing predictions through both experimental and observational data.

I argue that to understand unequal participation we should think about which characteristics of the context can affect highly and less educated people in heterogeneous ways. Contextual characteristics that affect the cognitive costs of voting should affect the propensity to vote of members of different groups heterogeneously. Hence, I claimed that anything that makes voting more cognitively challenging will reduce the participation of less educated people disproportionately and will result in sharper turnout inequalities.

In formulating the predictions, I spelled out specific contextual characteristics that should affect highly and less educated people in heterogeneous ways and shape turnout inequality: registration, the voting procedure, the existence of coalitions, and the structure of the media system. I have also studies other characteristics, such as the number of parties or the number of items in a ballot, in previous work (Gallego 2008, 2010). Taken together, the results strongly suggest that making voting as cognitively easy as possible helps reduce inequalities in participation.

Before turning to the specific findings, their implications, and their limitations, I would like to stress that one relevant contribution of this book is methodological. No proof of a theory is fully convincing, but by *combining* experimental and observational tests in Chapters 3 and 4, this book has gone one step further than the current standard practice in comparative political research.

The current standard when studying the interaction of individual and contextual characteristics uses multi-level analyses of observational survey data. In the last decade high-quality comparable survey data for a broad number of countries, such as the CSES or the ESS, have become broadly available. The usual research designs, however, provide little leverage to learn what it is exactly about the environment that causes individuals to act in different ways across contexts. Elections, countries, regions, and other geographic units differ in many aspects and social, institutional, and political features tend to be bundled together. This bundling is central to typological descriptions of the varieties of welfare states or capitalistic regimes (Esping-Andersen 1990; Hall and Soskice 2001). For example, Scandinavian countries tend to have a comprehensive and universalistic welfare state, powerful trade unions, effective redistribution, low income inequality, a high-quality education system, a large proportion of Protestants, PR, low levels of corruption, and high social trust, to name only a few characteristics. If we discover that citizens in these countries are more likely than citizens in Mediterranean countries to participate in politics, we will suspect that there is something about the Scandinavian context that motivates or facilitates their participation. To tackle which specific characteristic of the context is important, researchers usually employ a regression framework in which the behavior of interest is regressed against the preferred contextual feature. But because the differences are so many, the number of potential omitted variables is enormous. What it is exactly about the context that affects participation? Most of the time we cannot know.

Although the assertion that human behavior is context-dependent is hardly controversial, our knowledge about exactly what context affects political participation and who participates is still quite limited due in large part to these identification challenges. In addition to using observational data, this book innovates by also using experiments to address the same questions about the heterogeneous effects of contexts. The experiments attempted to manipulate, in a survey context, some theoretically relevant features of contexts to make voting more cognitively difficult. I believe that we can learn a great deal from experiments similar to the ones presented in this book. In every instance, increasing the cognitive difficulty of voting, either by making the procedure less user friendly (giving people more votes or an open ballot) or by increasing the number of partners in a government reduced less educated respondents' willingness to participate, as expected. Highly educated respondents, on the contrary, were unaffected by modifications in the difficulty of voting. Their average reported willingness to vote was identical in the experimental contexts in which voting was rather easy or rather difficult. That less educated people are more sensitive to increases in the cognitive costs of voting than are highly educated people is exactly what the theory predicted. Finding this pattern using an experimental strategy provides a different type of support for the theory that has a strong internal validity.

A possible critique to the experimental strategy is that it did not change the difficulty of voting but as doing something else. A related problem is that education may only be a proxy for the real characteristic of interest. Because the cognitive costs of voting and the ability to pay for them cannot be directly observed, the validity of conclusions crucially depends on agreeing that the treatments made voting more cognitively taxing, and increases in cognitive costs are relatively more difficult to bear for less educated citizens. I have attempted to discuss these issues at length, but ultimately the conclusions hinge on accepting these two basic assumptions.[1]

A different question is how certain we can be that differences in voting difficulty are associated with differences in unequal participation in the real world. Experimental internal validity does not amount to convincing external validity.

To address this, I turned to observational studies. Even if criticism toward observational methods grows, the quest for external validity makes the use of survey data irreplaceable. It was striking

---

[1] Furthermore, it can be argued that more tests of the theory are needed to see if different features that modify the cognitive difficulty of voting have similar detrimental effects on the participation of less educated people. The small number of features examined here are insufficient to be certain that the theory applies to a wide range of situations. I expect that future work will replicate similar findings while examining alternative contextual characteristics that modify cognitive costs.

that, in all cases, the results of the experiments were supported by the observational results. The analyses with CSES data suggest that voter turnout is more unequal in contexts that use open ballots, in countries that have multiparty coalition governments, and also in countries that have public service-oriented media systems.

I expect that it is the *coincidence* of the experimental and observational results found in Chapters 3 and 4 that mostly speaks to the merits of the theory. Testing theory with both quantitative and qualitative evidence, that is, triangulation, is not unusual in political science research. Testing theory with experimental and observational evidence is perhaps less usual. This work is among the first investigations in comparative political behavior that do this.

The main theoretical contribution of this work is that it found support for a simple but general theory about why voter turnout is more unequal in some contexts than in others: Increasing the information and decision costs of voting results in lower turnout rates among less educated citizens, ultimately leading to larger differences in the turnout rates of the highly and the less educated.

This finding, if true, leads to specific advice for policy makers and advocates of equal participation. Make voting simple and there may well be fewer differences in the turnout rates of highly and less educated people. Not all features that affect the costs of voting can be conceivably changed, nor is this necessarily desirable. Electoral systems design is a craft characterized by trade-offs among equally important but mutually exclusive aims. Majoritarian formulae enhance governability, but they also make election results less proportional. Institutions of direct democracy allow citizens more say in politics, but they also make participation more socially biased. And so on. That said, the idea that anything that makes the voting experience less cognitively challenging can help diminish inequalities in participation is useful because it can inform decisions on electoral reform.

This usefulness becomes obvious when contrasted with another prominent prescription: Make voting compulsory. Arendt Lijphart (1997), Martin Wattenberg (2006), and others have offered this prescription to equalize participation and there can be little doubt that this is correct advice. Elections that employ compulsory voting witness extraordinarily high participation rates and very small differences in the turnout rates of highly and less educated people. In spite of this, a massive adoption of compulsory voting in advanced industrial democracies is hardly conceivable. Contemporary societies value individual freedom, and although the moral case for compulsory voting is solid, the adoption of this rule would probably be politically unrealistic in most contexts. By contrast, minor reforms that make voting more user-friendly can be easily imagined. Although the design of new electoral systems is a rare event, minor changes are much more frequent (Renwick 2010). Every instance of reform provides an opportunity to come closer to the ideal of equal participation if options that minimize the cognitive costs of voting are prioritized over other options. All else being equal, it may be preferable to choose features that make voting easy over others that make voting difficult, because adopting the former can help equalize participation.

Of course, this prescription is not new. American political scientists as well as progressive activists and reformers have long noted that barriers to voting reduce the participation of the poor. Yet, recent studies have tended to downplay the consequences of reducing registration costs for turnout inequality hence cooling off the advocates of reforming electoral administration in ways that lower barriers to participation.[2] This investigation not only clearly supports the position of reform advocates, but it is also one of a few studies that look at the effect of raising the cognitive costs of voting in a comparative perspective.

---

[2] Authors such as Ansolabehere and Konisky (2006) argue that early studies overstated the negative consequences of registration barriers on the participation of the poor in the United States. However, by failing to account for lagged effects in turnout, it may be that recent research is underestimating the effects of registration barriers. There is an inertial component in voting, such that older people tend to continue voting or not voting independently of changes in the context. Young people are much more reactive. Therefore, it may take more than forty years for a change to unveil its full effects. This is because it takes a long time for young generations, who learn to vote or to abstain under the new institutional setting, to replace older generations in the electorate.

One important unaddressed question, of course, is why do some countries have electoral environments that make voting more cognitively costly than others. I have stopped short of going one step further in the causality chain and endogeneizing the choice of contextual features that affect the difficulty of voting. Although the main explanation provided in this book is institutional – that is, focuses on the rules of the game in which elections take place – the question of the institutional choice and design is necessarily a political one. Political actors decide over the creation of institutions taking into account which arrangements favor their interests most. The configuration of specific institutions reflects the calculations and power of relevant actors at the time of adoption. Political actors cannot anticipate all the consequences of their choices, but indisputably there are strategic calculations when defending some alternatives over others. One element in the calculations made by political parties is surely how to suppress or mobilize turnout among the poor, a central question in partisan politics. One limitation of the book is that it does not provide a theory of when and why are some arrangements chosen that lead to more political inequality. This question provides a further avenue of research.

The more ambiguous findings presented in Chapters 5 and 6 are also worth noting. A well-established theory of unequal participation claims that the less educated vote at high rates where and when certain political organizations mobilize them to vote. This links to the former point about the interests of political actors. Chief among the organizations that are expected to mobilize the poor are trade unions, along with left-wing political parties. In Chapter 5, I used the theoretical framework outlined in the book to discuss under which conditions we can expect political organizations to mobilize lower-status groups. Only organizations that are willing and able to mobilize these groups should make participation more equal. While trade unions are assumed to target lower-status groups, I have shown that there are reasons to cast doubt on the validity of this assumption. Today, trade union members in most countries are just as educated or even more educated than the general population. Abundant research shows that unionization has declined among blue-collar workers from the private sector while it has been stable or has increased among white-collar, public sector workers. Many union members today are teachers and nurses, not factory workers. If unions mobilize their members, but members are not less educated than the average citizen, the mobilization efforts of trade unions may not result in more equal participation.

In fact, and contrary to the common view, there is scant evidence that trade union density is associated with smaller gaps in the turnout rates of highly and less educated people. The results suggest that where trade unions are strong they seem to mobilize both highly and less educated people to vote. Although a large union density seems to be associated with higher voter turnout rates, the relationship with turnout inequality is at best weak.

Again, one important caveat is that the analyses in Chapter 5 should be taken with caution as they draw on observational data not supplemented by other methods. Yet the findings are broadly consistent with the idea that unions mobilize their members, whatever their educational profile. If their members are similar to the population in socioeconomic terms, they will activate all types of citizens to vote instead of only mobilizing lower-status people. This view is consistent with the idea that trade unions may have been a very relevant equalizing force in the past, even if their current role seems limited today.

Chapter 6 presented a puzzling result and stopped short of solving it. Income inequality is rising in many countries, which has ignited fears that this evolution may have negative consequences for political equality. Recent work has claimed that high levels of income inequality may reduce the political involvement and participation of the poor. Yet, a rather large body of studies fails to replicate this result. My own analyses do not find a link between posttax income inequality and turnout inequality. These results cast doubts on the proposition that income inequality makes participation more unequal. Surprisingly, pretax income inequality seems to correlate with unequal participation. As discussed in Chapter 6, these combined findings are unexpected and current theories cannot accommodate them easily. I have considered some tentative ways to make sense of these results, but solving this puzzle is certainly an avenue for further research.

The finding that turnout inequality is higher in contexts with higher pretax income inequality is substantively important even if the mechanisms that lead to this association are unclear. In particular, it has implications for standard theories of redistribution based on the Richard-Meltzer model. The basic version of the theory assumes full participation and claims that as gross income inequality grows, the median voter will demand more redistribution. This central claim breaks down if gross income inequality correlates with turnout inequality. As income inequality grows, the median voter becomes richer. The richer median voter in unequal contexts may not demand more redistribution than the poorer median voter in equal contexts.

The bottom line is that we currently have a very shaky understanding about how and why income inequality may affect voter participation and turnout inequality. Both theory and evidence are inconclusive. Since the financial crisis, income inequality has continued to rise within many advanced industrial democracies, along with worries that the increased concentration of wealth produces a concentration of political power and makes the political process disproportionately responsive to the interests of the rich. Social movements have put the problem of income inequality and its political consequences in the public agenda. In the United States, important research efforts have examined the connections between income inequality and political equality over the past ten years, but in a comparative perspective we still know relatively little. This is an important subject, and the inconclusive findings suggest that this area calls for additional research.

To conclude, let me return to why we should care about unequal turnout. If socially disadvantaged groups do not participate at rates that match those of other groups, then policy makers do not have incentives to be equally responsive to their interests, preferences, and needs. Unequal participation can bias the representation process and result in policies that neglect the interests of lower-status groups and exacerbate their standing in society. Such a situation violates the democratic ideal that governments should be responsive to all citizens considered as political equals. This general formulation of the problem of unequal participation for democratic politics has more specific implications.

First, unequal participation may affect who is elected. If participation is unequal and the party preferences of voters and nonvoters differ systematically, actual election results may be unlike those of a hypothetical election in which everybody voted. Previous research suggests that although equal participation would leave election results unchanged most of the time, different results may happen in competitive, close elections.

Second, unequal participation may bias the policies implemented by governments. If lower-status groups vote less frequently and they prefer different policies than higher-status groups, the distribution of the preferences of voters will differ from the distribution of preferences of the adult population. Assuming that politicians are responsive to public opinion, but take into account only the preferences of voters, then the noncoincidence of the ideal points of voters and the whole public will move public policy away from the population's ideal point. Public policy will be tilted toward the preferences of higher-status groups. The evidence presented in Chapter 7 supports the claim that the more unequal participation, the more the preferences of voters and nonvoters differ. In particular, voters are more socially left-wing and economically right-wing than nonvoters in countries with high levels of unequal participation. In these countries, politicians have incentives to adopt policies that deviate from the ideal point of the eligible population in specific ways: They can be expected to adopt more socially liberal and more economically conservative policies than if participation were equal. Whether these differences in opinion between voters and the population actually bias the adoption of public policies is one topic about which there is little comparative evidence. Here is yet another area that deserves more attention.

There is some evidence that governments target public resources strategically at high-turnout communities while they neglect low-turnout communities. This finding suggests that who votes in elections determines who benefits from transfers, targeted programs, services, and other excludable goods, or geographically located public goods. Importantly, the strategic targeting of resources can benefit high-turnout groups relative to low-turnout groups, even if the party choices and political preferences of high- and low-turnout populations are identical. Again, we know much more about the strategic allocation of resources to voters in the United States than in other parts of the world.

In sum, turnout inequality can affect who gets elected, which public policies governments adopt, and how governments allocate public resources in ways that deviate from what would happen if everybody voted and governments were responsive to all citizens as political equals. Unequal turnout can taint the representation process and undermine the ideal of political equality.

This book has attempted to advance our understanding of the levels, reasons, and consequences of unequal participation in a broad comparative perspective. I have defended that making participation in the political process less cognitively costly can help equalize participation. Although voting is an easy political activity, it is not costless. Increases in costs may seem negligible for some citizens, but may dissuade others from participating, hence shrinking and biasing the size of the political community and leading to the political exclusion of vulnerable groups. This claim has policy implications. Along with other criteria, when evaluating alternatives in areas such as the electoral procedures or media regulation, we should consider how reforms may affect the cognitive ease of voting. Efforts to facilitate voter participation are, in principle, desirable.

Appendix

TABLE 1. *List of Elections and Contextual Variables*

	Year	Election	Turnout	CV
Australia	1996	Parliament	95.8	No
Australia	2004	Parliament	94.3	Yes
Australia	2007	Parliament	95.2	Yes
Austria	2008	Parliament	81.7	No
Belgium	1999	Parliament	90.6	Yes
Belgium	2003	Parliament	96.3	Yes
Brazil	2002	President	79.5	Yes
Brazil	2006	President	83.2	Yes
Bulgaria	2001	Parliament	66.6	No
Canada	1997	Parliament	67	No
Canada	2004	Parliament	60.9	No
Chile	2005	Parliament	87.67	Yes
Croatia	2007	Parliament	59.6	No
Czech R.	1996	Parliament	76.3	No
Czech R.	2002	Parliament	57.9	No
Czech R.	2006	Parliament	64.5	No
Denmark	1998	Parliament	85.9	No
Denmark	2001	Parliament	87.1	No
Finland	2003	Parliament	66.7	No
Finland	2007	Parliament	65	No
France	2002	President	79.7	No
France	2007	Parliament	84	No

(*continued*)

TABLE i (*continued*)

	Year	Election	Turnout	CV
Germany	1998	Parliament	82.2	No
Germany	2002	Parliament	79.1	No
Germany	2005	Parliament	77.7	No
Germany	2009	Parliament	70.8	No
Hungary	1998	Parliament	57	No
Hungary	2002	Parliament	73.5	No
Iceland	1999	Parliament	84.1	No
Iceland	2003	Parliament	87.7	No
Iceland	2007	Parliament	83.6	No
Iceland	2009	Parliament	85.1	No
Ireland	2002	Parliament	62.6	No
Ireland	2007	Parliament	67	No
Israel	1996	Parliament	79.3	No
Israel	2003	Parliament	67.8	No
Israel	2006	Parliament	63.6	No
Italy	2006	Parliament	83.6	No
Japan	1996	Parliament	59.6	No
Japan	2004	Parliament	56.4	No
Japan	2007	Parliament	58.6	No
Korea	2000	Parliament	57.2	No
Korea	2004	Parliament	60	No
Korea	2008	Parliament	46	No
Lithuania	1997	President	73.7	No
Mexico	2003	Parliament	41.7	Yes[+] enf.
Mexico	2006	President	58.9	Yes[+] enf.
Mexico	2009	Parliament	44.6	Yes[+] enf.
Netherlands	1998	Parliament	73.2	No
Netherlands	2002	Parliament	79.1	No
Netherlands	2006	Parliament	80.4	No
New Zeal.	1996	Parliament	88.3	No
New Zeal.	2002	Parliament	77	No
New Zeal.	2008	Parliament	79.5	No
Norway	1997	Parliament	78.3	No
Norway	2001	Parliament	75.5	No
Norway	2005	Parliament	77.4	No
Peru	2006	Parliament	88.7	Yes
Poland	1997	Parliament	47.9	No
Poland	2001	Parliament	46.2	No
Poland	2005	Parliament	40.6	No
Poland	2007	Parliament	53.9	No

	Year	Election	Turnout	CV
Portugal	2002	Parliament	62.8	No
Portugal	2005	Parliament	64.3	No
Portugal	2009	Parliament	59.7	No
Romania	1996	Parliament	76	No
Romania	2004	Parliament	58.6	No
Slovenia	1996	Parliament	73.7	No
Slovenia	2004	Parliament	60.6	No
Spain	1996	Parliament	78.1	No
Spain	2000	Parliament	68.7	No
Spain	2004	Parliament	76.7	No
Sweden	1998	Parliament	81.4	No
Sweden	2002	Parliament	80.1	No
Sweden	2006	Parliament	82	No
Switzerland	1999	Parliament	43.2	No
Switzerland	2003	Parliament	45.4	No
Switzerland	2007	Parliament	48.3	No
Taiwan	1996	Parliament	76.2	No
Taiwan	2001	Parliament	66.2	No
Taiwan	2004	President	80.28	No
UK	1997	Parliament	71.5	No
UK	2005	Parliament	61.4	No
USA	1996	Parliament	49.1	No
USA	2004	President	56.7	No

Notes: CV stands for compulsory voting. [+]Compulsory voting not enforced.

TABLE ii. *Absolute and Relative Education Effects in Three Countries*

	Absolute Model	Relative Education Effect Models	
Norway (N = 1,542)			
Education in years	0.17**	0.17**	
Edu. environment		0.90*	
Relative education			2.24**
Age	0.15**	0.19**	0.15**
Age squared	−0.001**	−0.001*	−0.001**
Constant	−4.64**	−18.82**	−4.11**
Pseudo R2	0.08	0.08	0.08
Spain (N = 1,404)			
Education in years	0.06**	0.06**	
Edu. environment		−0.43*	
Relative education			0.57**
Age	0.12**	0.01	0.10**
Age squared	−0.001**	−0.001*	−0.001**
Constant	−1.66**	6.34*	−1.17*
Pseudo R2	0.03	0.03	0.03
UK (N = 1,669)			
Education in years	0.12**	0.12**	
Edu. environment		−0.30	
Relative education			1.52**
Age	0.08**	0.06	0.07**
Age squared	0.00	0.00	0.00
Constant	−3.69**	1.02	−3.28**
Pseudo R2	0.09	0.09	0.09

* $p > 0.05$; ** $p > 0.005$.
Source: First Wave of the ESS.

On Relative and Absolute Education Models

Nie, Junn, and Stehlik-Barry[1] propose two alternative operationalizations of relative education. The first measure of relative education (re_i) is the ratio between an individual's years of education (e_i) and the educational environment (E_c)[2]: $re_i = \frac{e_i}{E_c}$, where the educational environment (E_c) for individuals from a birth year or cohort (c) is the ratio between the sum of years of education (e_i) for all individuals of the same cohort, or any of the preceding twenty-five birth cohorts, and the total number of individuals (n) in the twenty-six birth cohorts (c-25 to c): $E_c = \frac{\sum_{i=1}^{n} e_i}{n}$. The authors propose, as an alternative strategy, that both E_c and e_i be included as separate regressors in multivariate regression analyses.

Unfortunately, the CSES, which is the main dataset used in this book because of its global scope, does not contain data on the years of education held by each respondent. Here, I use data from the ESS to assess if relative education is more strongly associated with voting than education measured in years. Table ii displays the results of logistic regression models using the three operationalizations of education in three countries.[3]

The results do not provide convincing evidence in support of the need to use the relative education model. The three alternatives produce (in simulations not reported here) estimates of the gradient of the education effect that are similar in magnitude. The R-squared of the relative education models is very similar in the absolute education effects and the relative education effects models. Taken together, it is not clear that the relative education effects model fits the data so substantially better that it justifies the choice of this most complicated operationalization.

---

[1] The complete explanation about the operationalization of the measures is offered in the Appendix F (Jenkins 1996: 227–230).

[2] It is unclear why a ratio is preferable to the difference between the two components. A ratio creates a scale that can range from 0 to 1 for individuals that have less education than their educational environment, but the possible values for those with more education than their educational environment can range from 1 to any higher value.

[3] Similar results were found in the other countries.

Bibliography

Aarts, K., and H. A. Semetko. 2003. "The divided electorate: Media use and political involvement." *Journal of Politics* 65(3): 759–784.

Abrams, S., T. Iversen, and D. Soskice. 2010. "Informal social networks and rational voting." *British Journal of Political Science* 41(2): 229–257.

Abramson, P. R., and J. H. Aldrich. 1982. "The decline of electoral participation in America." *The American Political Science Review* 76(3): 502–521.

Achen, C. H. 2010. "Report on the performance of the new question about civic duty in the 2010 ANES." *Unpublished manuscript.*

Aguilar, E. E., and A. C. Pacek. 2000. "Macroeconomic conditions, voter turnout, and the working-class/economically disadvantaged party vote in developing countries." *Comparative Political Studies* 33(8): 995–1017.

Aldrich, J. H. 1997. "When is it rational to vote?" In D. Mueller (Ed.), *Perspectives on public choice: A handbook.* Cambridge: Cambridge University Press, 373–390.

Aldrich, J. H., J. M. Montgomery, and W. Wood. 2011. "Turnout as a Habit." *Political Behavior* 33(4): 535–563.

Alesina, A. F, and P. Giuliano. 2009. "Preferences for redistribution." *National Bureau of Economic Research working paper.*

Alesina, A. F., G. Cozzi, and N. Mantovan. 2009. "The evolution of ideology, fairness and redistribution." *National Bureau of Economic Research working paper.*

Alesina, A. F., and E. L. Glaeser. 2005. *Fighting poverty in the US and Europe: A world of difference*. Oxford: Oxford University Press.

Alesina, A. F., and N. Fuchs-Schündeln. 2006. "Good bye Lenin (or not?): The effect of Communism on people's preferences." *Working paper*.

Alesina, A. F., and G. M. Angeletos. 2005. "Fairness and redistribution." *The American Economic Review* 95(4): 960–980.

Alesina, A. F., N. Roubini, and G. D. Cohen. 1997. *Political cycles and the macroeconomy*. Cambridge: MIT Press.

Alford, R. R. 1963. *Party and society: The Anglo-American democracies*. Chicago: Rand McNally.

Allern, E. H., N. Aylott, and F. J. Christiansen. 2007. "Social Democrats and trade unions in Scandinavia: The decline and persistence of institutional relationships." *European Journal of Political Research* 46(5): 607–635.

Amat, F., and E. Wibbels. 2009. "Electoral incentives, group identity and preferences for redistribution." *Estudios/Working Papers (Centro de Estudios Avanzados en Ciencias Sociales)* 246.

Andersen, R., and T. Fetner. 2008. "Economic inequality and intolerance: attitudes toward homosexuality in 35 democracies." *American Journal of Political Science* 52(4): 942–958.

Anderson, C. J., and P. Beramendi. 2008. "Income, inequality and electoral participation." In P. Beramendi and C. J. Anderson (Eds.), *Democracy, inequality and representation*. New York: Russell Sage Foundation.

Anderson, C. J., and M. M. Singer. 2008. "The sensitive left and the impervious right." *Comparative Political Studies* 41(4–5): 564–599.

Anderson, J. 2009. *Cognitive psychology and its implications*. NY: Worth Publishers Inc.

Anduiza, E. 1999. 166 *¿Individuos o sistemas? Las razones de la abstención en Europa Occidental*. Madrid: Centro de Investigaciones Sociológicas. Siglo Veintiuno de España Editores.

———. 2002. "Individual characteristics, institutional incentives and electoral abstention in Western Europe." *European Journal of Political Research* 41(5): 643–673.

Angrist, J. D., and J. S. Pischke. 2008. *Mostly harmless econometrics: An empiricist's companion*. Princeton: Princeton University Press.

Ansolabehere, S., and D. M. Konisky. 2006. "The introduction of voter registration and its effect on turnout." *Political Analysis* 14(1): 83–100.

APSA Task Force on Inequality and American Democracy. 2004. "American Democracy in an Age of Rising Inequality." *Report to the American Political Science Association*.

Armstrong, D. A., and R. M. Duch. 2010. "Why can voters anticipate post-election coalition formation likelihoods?" *Electoral Studies*
29(3): 308–315.

Art, D., and T. Turner. 2007. "Trade unions and political participation
in the European Union: Still providing a democratic dividend?" *British
Journal of Industrial Relations* 45(1): 103–126.

Baek, M. 2009. "A comparative analysis of political communication
systems and voter turnout." *American Journal of Political Science*
53(2): 376–393.

Baldini, G. 2011. "The Different Trajectories of Italian Electoral
Reforms." *West European Politics* 34(3): 644–663.

Banerjee, A. V., and E. Duflo. 2003. "Inequality and growth: What can
the data say?" *Journal of Economic Growth* 8(3): 267–299.

Bargsted, M. A., and O. Kedar. 2009. "Coalition-targeted Duverg-
erian voting: How expectations affect voter choice under proportional representation." *American Journal of Political Science* 53(2):
307–323.

Baron, R. M., and D. A. Kenny. 1986. "The moderator–mediator variable distinction in social psychological research: Conceptual, strategic, and statistical considerations." *Journal of Personality and Social
Psychology* 51(6): 1173–1182.

Bartels, L. M. et al. 2004. "Inequality and American democracy: What
we know and what we need to learn." *Report to the American Political
Science Association.*

Bartels, L. M. 2008. *Unequal democracy: The political economy of the
New Gilded Age.* Princeton: Princeton University Press.

Bartle, J. 2005. "Homogeneous models and heterogeneous voters."
Political Studies 53(4): 653–675.

Bartolini, S. 2000. *The political mobilization of the European left,
1860–1980.* New York, Cambridge, Eng.: Cambridge University
Press.

Becher, M., and J. Pontusson. 2011. "Whose interests do unions represent? Unionization by income in Western Europe." *Research in the
Sociology of Work* 22: 181–211.

Beitz, C. R. 1989. *Political equality: An essay in democratic theory.*
Princeton: Princeton University Press.

Benabou, R. 2000. "Unequal societies: Income distribution and the
social contract." *American Economic Review* 90(1): 96–129.

Bendor, J. et al. 2011. *A behavioral theory of elections.* Princeton:
Princeton University Press.

Bennett, S. E., and D. Resnick. 1990. "The implications of nonvoting
for democracy in the United States." *American Journal of Political
Science* 34(3): 771–802.

Beramendi, P., and C. Anderson. 2008. *Democracy, inequality, and representation: A comparative perspective.* Russell Sage Foundation Publications.

Berinsky, A. J., and G. S Lenz. 2011. "Education and political participation: Exploring the causal link." *Political Behavior* 33(3): 1–17.

Bernhagen, P., and M. Marsh. 2007. "The partisan effects of low turnout: Analyzing vote abstention as a missing data problem." *Electoral Studies* 26(3): 548–560.

Bernstein, R., A. Chadha, and R. Montjoy. 2001. "Overreporting voting: Why it happens and why it matters." *Public Opinion Quarterly* 65(1): 22–44.

Birch, S. 2009. *Full participation.* New York: United Nations University Press.

Blais, A. 1988. "The classification of electoral systems." *European Journal of Political Research* 16(1): 99–110.

———. 2000. *To vote or not to vote?: The merits and limits of rational choice theory.* Pittsburgh: University of Pittsburgh Press.

———. 2006. "What affects voter turnout?" *Annual Review of Political Science* 9: 111–125.

Blais, A., and A. Dobrzynska. 1998. "Turnout in electoral democracies." *European Journal of Political Research* 33(2): 239–262.

Blais, A., and C. H Achen. 2010. "Taking civic duty seriously: Political theory and voter turnout." *Unpublished Paper. Princeton, NJ.*

Blais, A., and K. Aarts. 2006. "Electoral systems and turnout." *Acta politica* 41(2): 180–196.

Blais, A., and S. Labbé-St-Vincent. 2011. "Personality traits, political attitudes and the propensity to vote." *European Journal of Political Research* 50(3): 395–417.

Blais, A., et al. 2004. "Where does turnout decline come from?" *European Journal of Political Research* 43(2): 221–236.

Blais, A., et al. 2006. "Do voters vote for government coalitions?" *Party Politics* 12(6): 691–705.

Blaydes, L. 2011. *Elections and distributive politics in Mubarak's Egypt.* Cambridge: Cambridge University Press.

Bohrer II, R. E., A. C. Pacek, and B. Radcliff. 2000. "Electoral participation, ideology, and party politics in post-communist Europe." *Journal of Politics* 62(4): 1161–1172.

Bowler, S., and D. M. Farrell. 1993. "Legislator shirking and voter monitoring: Impacts of European Parliament electoral systems upon legislator voter relationships." *Journal of Common Market Studies* 31(1): 45–70.

Brady, H. E., and J. E. McNulty. 2011. "Turning out to vote: The costs of finding and getting to the polling place." *American Political Science Review* 105(1): 115–134.

Brady, H. E. 2004. "An analytical perspective on participatory inequality and income inequality." In K. Neckerman (Ed.), *Social Inequality*. New York: Russell Sage Foundation, 667–702.

Brandolini, A., and T. M. Smeeding. 2008. "Inequality patterns in Western democracies: Cross-country differences and changes over time." *American Journal of Political Science* 43(3): 649–80.

Brians, C. L., and B. Grofman. 1999. "When registration barriers fall, who votes?: An empirical test of a rational choice model." *Public Choice* 99(1): 161–176.

———. 2001. "Election Day Registration's effect on U. S. voter turnout." *Social Science Quarterly* 82(1): 170–183.

Brockington, D. 2004. "The paradox of proportional representation: The effect of party systems and coalitions on individuals' electoral participation." *Political Studies* 52(3): 469–490.

Bryson, A., B. Ebbinghaus, and J. Visser. 2011. "Introduction: Causes, consequences, and cures of union decline." *European Journal of Industrial Relations* 17(2): 97–105.

Bühlmann, M., and M. Freitag. 2006. "Individual and contextual determinants of electoral participation." *Swiss Political Science Review* 12(4): 13–47.

Bullock III, C. S., and M. V. Hood III. 2002. "One person – no vote; one vote; two votes: Voting methods, ballot types, and undervote frequency in the 2000 presidential election." *Social Science Quarterly* 83(4): 981–993.

Bullock, J. G., and S. E. Ha. 2011. "Mediation analysis is harder than it looks." In J. N. Druckman et al. (Eds.), *Cambridge Handbook of Experimental Political Science*. New York: Cambridge University Press.

Burnham, W. D. 1982. *The current crisis in American politics*. Oxford: Oxford University Press.

———. 1987. "The turnout problem." In A. J. Reichley (Ed.), *Elections American Style*. Washington, DC: Brookings Institution.

Burstein, P. 1972. "Social structure and individual political participation in five countries." *The American Journal of Sociology* 77(6): 1087–1110.

Calvo, E., M. Escolar, and J. Pomares. 2009. "Ballot design and split ticket voting in multiparty systems: Experimental evidence on information effects and vote choice." *Electoral Studies* 28(2): 218–231.

Campbell, A., et al. 1960. *The American voter*. New York: Wiley.

Campbell, D. E. 2006. *Why we vote: How schools and communities shape our civic life.* Princeton: Princeton University Press.

Campbell, A., G. Gurin, and W. E. Miller. 1954. *The voter decides.* Evanston: Row Peterson.

Carey, J. M., and M. S. Shugart. 1995. "Incentives to cultivate a personal vote: a rank ordering of electoral formulas." *Electoral Studies* 14: 417–440.

Ceobanu, A. M., and X. Escandell. 2010. "Comparative analyses of public attitudes toward immigrants and immigration using multinational survey data: A review of theories and research." *Annual Review of Sociology* 36: 309–328.

Chen, C. F. 2006. "The legislative election in Taiwan, December 2004." *Electoral Studies* 25(4): 820–825.

Chong, A., and M. Olivera. 2008. "Does compulsory voting help equalize incomes?" *Economics & Politics* 20(3): 391–415.

Citrin, J., E. Schickler, and J. Sides. 2003. "What if everyone voted? Simulating the impact of increased turnout in senate elections." *American Journal of Political Science* 47(1): 75–90.

Clark, W. R., M. Golder, and S. N. Golder. 2009. *Principles of comparative politics.* Washington: CQ Press.

Clarke, H. D. et al. 2004. *Political choice in Britain.* Oxford: Oxford University Press.

Colomer, J. M. 2004. *Handbook of electoral system choice.* London: Palgrave-Macmillan, 2004.

Converse, P. E. 1972. "Change in the American electorate." In A. Campbell and P. E. Converse (Eds.), *The Human Meaning of Social Change.* New York: Russell Sage Foundation, 263–337.

Cox, G. W., and M. C. Munger. 1989. "Closeness, expenditures, and turnout in the 1982 US House elections." *The American Political Science Review* 83(1): 217–231.

Cox, G. W. 1990. "Centripetal and centrifugal incentives in electoral systems." *American Journal of Political Science* 34(4): 903–935.

Curran, J. et al. 2009. "Media system, public knowledge, and democracy." *European Journal of Communication* 24(1): 5.

Cutts, D., and E. Fieldhouse. 2009. "What small spatial scales are relevant as electoral contexts for individual voters? The importance of the household on turnout at the 2001 General Election." *American Journal of Political Science* 53(3): 726–739.

Dahl, R. A. 1971. *Polyarchy: Participation and opposition.* New Haven: Yale University Press.

―――. 2008. *On Political Equality.* New Haven: Yale University Press.

Dallinger, U. 2010. "Public support for redistribution: What explains cross-national differences?" *Journal of European Social Policy* 20(4): 333.

Dalton, R. J. 2006. *Citizen politics: Public opinion and political parties in advanced industrial democracies.* Washington: CQ Press.

————. 2008. "Citizenship norms and the expansion of political participation." *Political Studies* 56(1): 76–98.

Dalton, R. J., and M. P. Wattenberg. 2000. *Parties without partisans: Political change in advanced industrial democracies.* Oxford; New York: Oxford University Press.

Daly, M., M. Wilson, and S. Vasdev. 2001. "Income inequality and homicide rates in Canada and the United States." *Canadian Journal of Criminology* 43(2): 219–236.

Daniels, G., and J. McIlroy. 2009. *Trade unions in a neoliberal world.* New York: Routledge.

De La O., A. L., and J. A. Rodden. 2008. "Does religion distract the poor?" *Comparative Political Studies* 41(4–5): 437–476.

Delli-Carpini, M. X., and S. Keeter. 1996. *What Americans know about politics and why it matters.* New Haven: Yale University Press.

Dee, T. S. 2004. "Are there civic returns to education?" *Journal of Public Economics* 88(9–10): 1697–1720.

Dimock, M. and S. Popkin. 1997 "Political knowledge in comparative perspective." In S. Iyengar and R. Reeves (Eds.), *Do the media govern?* Thousand Oaks, CA: Sage.

Dion, M. L., and V. Birchfield. 2010. "Economic development, income inequality, and preferences for redistribution." *International Studies Quarterly* 54(2): 315–334.

Doherty, D. J., A. S. Gerber, and D. P. Green. 2006. "Personal income and attitudes toward redistribution: A study of lottery winners." *Political Psychology* 27(3): 441–458.

Downs, A. 1957. *An economic theory of democracy.* New York: Harper & Row.

Druckman, J. N., and C. D. Kam. 2011. "Students as experimental participants." In J. N. Druckman et al. (Eds.), *Cambridge handbook of experimental political science.* New York: Cambridge University Press.

Duffy, J., and M. Tavits. 2008. "Beliefs and voting decisions: A test of the pivotal voter model." *American Journal of Political Science* 52(3): 603–618.

Dyck, J. J., and J. G. Gimpel. 2005. "Distance, turnout, and the convenience of voting." *Social Science Quarterly* 86(3): 531–548.

Ebbinghaus, B., and J. Visser. 1999. *Trade unions in Western Europe since 1945.* New York: Grove's Dictionaries.

Ebbinghaus, B., C. Göbel, and S. Koos. 2011. "Social capital, 'Ghent' and workplace contexts matter: Comparing union membership in Europe." *European Journal of Industrial Relations* 17(2): 107.

Elklit, J. 2011. "Preferential voting in Denmark: How, why, and to what effect?" *Paper presented at the Annual Meeting of the American Political Science Association.*

Emler, N., and E. Fraser. 1999. "Politics: the education effect." *Oxford Review of Education* 25(1–2): 251–72.

Enns, P. K, and C. Wlezien. 2011. *Who gets represented?* NY: Russell Sage Foundation.

Esping-Andersen, G. 1990. *The three worlds of welfare capitalism.* London: Polity Press.

European Social Survey Round 3 Data. 2006. *Data file edition 3.3.* Norwegian Social Science Data Services, Norway – Data Archive and distributor of ESS data (downloaded in July 2011).

European Social Survey Round 4 Data. 2008. *Data file edition 4.0.* Norwegian Social Science Data Services, Norway – Data Archive and distributor of ESS data (downloaded in July 2011).

Fazekas, Z. 2011. "Institutional effects on the presence of trade unions at the workplace: Moderation in a multilevel setting." *European Journal of Industrial Relations* 17(2): 153.

Fisher, S. D. et al. 2008. "Disengaging voters: Do plurality systems discourage the less knowledgeable from voting?" *Electoral Studies* 27(1): 89–104.

Fiske, S. T., R. R. Lau, and R. A. Smith. 1990. "On the varieties and utilities of political expertise." *Social Cognition* 8(1): 31–48.

Flavin, P., and B. Radcliff. 2011. "Labor union membership and voting across nations." *Electoral Studies.* 20(4): 633–641.

Fowler, A. 2001. "Turnout matters: Evidence from compulsory voting in Australia." *SSRN Working paper.*

Fowler, J. H. 2006. "Habitual voting and behavioral turnout." *The Journal of Politics* 68(2): 335–344.

———. 2008. "Altruism and turnout." *The Journal of Politics* 68(3): 674–683.

Fowler, J. H., L. A. Baker, and C. T. Dawes. 2008. "Genetic variation in political participation." *American Political Science Review* 102(2): 233–248.

Franklin, M. N. 2004. *Voter turnout and the dynamics of electoral competition in established democracies since 1945.* Cambridge: Cambridge University Press.

Franklin, M. N., C. van der Eijk, and E. Oppenhuis. 1996. "The institutional context: Turnout." In Van der Eijk and M. N. Franklin

(Eds.), *Choosing Europe?: The European electorate and national politics in the face of union*. Ann Arbor: University of Michigan Press, 306–331.

Franzese Jr., R. J. 2002. "Electoral and partisan cycles in economic policies and outcomes." *Annual Review of Political Science* 5(1): 369–421.

Franzese, R., and J. Hays. 2008. "Inequality and unemployment, redistribution and insurance, and participation: A theoretical model and an empirical system of endogenous equations." In P. Beramendi and C. Anderson (Eds.), *Democracy, inequality, and representation*, NY: Russell Sage.

Freeman, R. B. 2003. "What do unions do . . . to voting?" *National Bureau of Economic Research working paper.*

Gallagher, M. 2001. "The Japanese House of Councillors election 1998 in comparative perspective." *Electoral Studies* 20(4): 603–625.

Gallagher, M., and P. Mitchell. 2005. *The politics of electoral systems.* Oxford: Oxford University Press.

Gallego, Aina. 2008. *One person, one vote? Unequal participation in comparative perspective.* Doctoral dissertation, Universitat Autonoma de Barcelona.

———. 2009. "Where else does turnout decline come from? Education, age, generation and period effects in three European countries." *Scandinavian Political Studies* 32(1): 23–44.

———. 2010. "Understanding unequal turnout: Education and voting in comparative perspective." *Electoral Studies* 29(2): 239–247.

Gallego, A., G. Rico, and E. Anduiza. 2012. "Disproportionality and voter turnout in new and old democracies." *Electoral Studies*, 31(1): 159–169.

Gelman, A., and J. Hill. 2007. *Data analysis using regression and multilevel/hierarchical models.* New York: Cambridge University Press.

Gerber, A. S., D. P. Green, and R. Shachar. 2003. "Voting may be habit-forming: Evidence from a randomized field experiment." *American Journal of Political Science* 47(3): 540–550.

Gerber, A. S., D. P. Green, and C. W. Larimer. 2008. "Social pressure and voter turnout: Evidence from a large-scale field experiment." *American Political Science Review* 102(1): 33–48.

Geys, Benny. 2006. "Explaining voter turnout: A review of aggregate-level research." *Electoral Studies* 25(4): 637–663.

Gilens, M. 2005. "Inequality and democratic responsiveness." *Public Opinion Quarterly* 69(5): 778–796.

———. 2009. "Preference gaps and inequality in representation." *PS: Political Science and Politics* 42(2): 335–41.

————. 2011. "The benevolent baker: Altruism and political attitudes in the United States." *Unpublished paper.*

Golder, S. N. 2005. "Pre-electoral coalitions in comparative perspective: A test of existing hypotheses." *Electoral Studies* 24(4): 643–663.

Gomez, B. T., T. G. Hansford, and G. A. Krause. 2007. "The Republicans should pray for rain: Weather, turnout, and voting in US presidential elections." *Journal of Politics* 69(3): 649–663.

Goodin, R., and Dryzek, J. 1980. "Rational participation: The politics of relative power." *British Journal of Political Science* 10(3): 273–292.

Gratschew, M. 2004. "Compulsory voting." In R. López-Pintor and M. Gratschew (Eds.), *Voter turnout in Western Europe since 1945.* Sweden: Stockholm: International Institute for Democracy and Electoral Assistance.

Gray, M., and M. Caul. 2000. "Declining voter turnout in advanced industrial democracies, 1950 to 1997: The effects of declining group mobilization." *Comparative Political Studies* 33(9): 1091–1122.

Griffin, J. D., and B. Newman. 2005. "Are voters better represented?" *Journal of Politics* 67(4): 1206–1227.

Grofman, B. 1993. "Is turnout the paradox that ate rational choice theory?" In B. Grofman (Ed.), *Information, participation, and choice: An economic theory of democracy in perspective.* Ann Arbor: University of Michigan Press.

Grofman, B., G. Owen, and C. Collet. 1999. "Rethinking the partisan effects of higher turnout: So what's the question?" *Public Choice* 99(3): 357–376.

Gschwend, T. 2007. "Ticket-splitting and strategic voting under mixed electoral rules: Evidence from Germany." *European Journal of Political Research* 46(1): 1–23.

Gschwend, T., and M. Hooghe. 2008. "Should I stay or should I go? An experimental study on voter responses to pre-electoral coalitions." *European Journal of Political Research* 47(5): 556–577.

Hall, P. and D. Soskice. 2001. *Varieties of capitalism: The institutional foundations of comparative advantage.* New York: Oxford University Press.

Hallin, D. C., and P. Mancini. 2004. *Comparing media systems: Three models of media and politics.* Cambridge: Cambridge University Press.

Han, H. 2009. *Moved to action: Motivation, participation, and inequality in American politics.* Stanford: Stanford University Press.

Hanmer, M. J. 2009. *Discount voting: Voter registration reforms and their effects.* Cambridge and New York: Cambridge University Press.

Hansford, T. G., and B. T. Gomez. 2010. "Estimating the electoral effects of voter turnout." *American Political Science Review* 104(2): 268–288.

Hardarson, O. 2002. "The Icelandic Electoral System, 1844–1999." In B. Grofman and A. Lijphart (Eds.), *The evolution of electoral and party systems in the Nordic countries.* New York: Agathon Press.

Haspel, M., and H. G. Knotts. 2005. "Location, location, location: Precinct placement and the costs of voting." *Journal of Politics* 67(2): 560–573.

Henderson, J., and S. Chatfield. 2011. "Who matches? Propensity scores and bias in the causal effects of education on participation." *The Journal of Politics* 73(3): 646–658.

Herron, M. C., and J. S. Sekhon. 2003. "Overvoting and Representation: An examination of overvoted presidential ballots in Broward and Miami-Dade counties." *Electoral Studies* 22(1): 21–47.

Hershey, M. R. 2009. "What we know about voter-ID laws, registration, and turnout." *PS: Political Science & Politics* 42(1): 87–91.

Heston, A., R. Summers, and B. Aten. 2011. *Penn World Table Version 7.0*, Center for International Comparisons of Production, Income and Prices at the University of Pennsylvania (downloaded in May 2011).

Highton, B. and R. E. Wolfinger. 1998. "Estimating the effects of the National Voter Registration Act of 1993." *Political Behavior* 20 (2): 79–104.

————. 2001. "The political implications of higher turnout." *British Journal of Political Science* 31(1): 179–192.

Hill, K. Q., and J. E. Leighley. 1992. "The policy consequences of class bias in State electorates." *American Journal of Political Science* 36(2): 351–365.

Hill, K. Q., J. E. Leighley, and A. Hinton-Andersson. 1995. "Lower-class mobilization and policy linkage in the US States." *American Journal of Political Science* 39(1): 75–86.

Hillygus, S. 2005. "The missing link: Exploring the relationship between higher education and political engagement." *Political Behavior* 27(1): 25–47.

Hobolt, S. B., and J. A. Karp. 2010. "Voters and coalition governments." *Electoral Studies* 29(3): 299–307.

Holtz-Bacha, C. and P. Norris. 2001. "To entertain, inform, and educate: Still the role of public television." *Political Communication* 18: 123–140.

Hooghe, M., and K. Pelleriaux. 1998. "Compulsory voting in Belgium: An application of the Lijphart thesis." *Electoral studies* 17: 419–424.

Imai, K. et al. 2011. "Unpacking the black box of causality: Learning about causal mechanisms from experimental and observational studies." *American Political Science Review* 105(4): 765–789.

Irwin, G. 1974. "Compulsory voting legislation." *Comparative Political Studies* 7(3): 292–315.

Iversen, T., and D. Soskice. 2006. "Electoral institutions and the politics of coalitions: Why some democracies redistribute more than others." *American Political Science Review* 100(2): 165–181.

Iyengar, S. et al. 2010. "Cross-national versus individual-level differences in political information: A media systems perspective." *Journal of Elections, Public Opinion and Parties* 20(3): 291–309.

Jackman, R. W. 1987. "Political institutions and voter turnout in the industrial democracies." *The American Political Science Review* 81(2): 405–424.

Jackman, R. W., and R. A. Miller. 1995. "Voter turnout in the industrial democracies during the 1980s." *Comparative Political Studies* 27(4): 467–492.

Jackman, S. 2001. "Compulsory voting." In N. J. Smelser and P. B. Baltes (Eds.), *International Encyclopaedia of the Social & Behavioural Sciences*. Amsterdam: Elsevier.

Jacobs, L. R., and T. Skocpol. 2005. *Inequality and American democracy: What we know and what we need to learn.* New York: Russell Sage.

Johnson, J. W., and J. S. Wallack. 2011. *Electoral systems and the personal vote.* http://polisci2.ucsd.edu/jwjohnson/espv.htm (downloaded in July 2011).

Jusko, K. 2008. *The political representation of the poor.* Doctoral dissertation, University of Michigan.

———. 2011. "Partisan Representation of the Poor: Electoral Geography, Strategic Mobilization, and Implications for Voter Turnout." *Unpublished manuscript.*

Jusko, K. L., and W. P. Shively. 2005. "Applying a two-step strategy to the analysis of cross-national public opinion data." *Political Analysis* 13(4): 327.

Kahneman, D. 2011. *Thinking, fast and slow.* Farrar Straus & Giroux.

Kam, C. D., and C. L. Palmer. 2008. "Reconsidering the effects of education on political participation." *Journal of Politics* 70(3): 612–631.

Kang, S. G., and G. B. Powell Jr. 2010. "Representation and policy responsiveness: The median voter, election rules, and redistributive welfare spending." *The Journal of Politics* 72(4): 1014–1028.

Karp, J. A., and D. Brockington. 2005. "Social desirability and response validity: A comparative analysis of overreporting voter turnout in five countries." *Journal of Politics* 67(3): 825–840.

Karp, J. A., and S. A. Banducci. 2008. "Political efficacy and participation in twenty-seven democracies: how electoral systems shape political behaviour." *British Journal of Political Science* 38(2): 311–334.

Karvonen, L. 2004. "Preferential voting: incidence and effects." *International Political Science Review* 25(2): 203–226.

Katz, R. S. 1997. *Democracy and elections.* Oxford: Oxford University Press.

Kedar, O. 2005. "When moderate voters prefer extreme parties: Policy balancing in parliamentary elections." *American Political Science Review* 99(2): 185–199.

Keefer, P. 2010. *Database of political institutions: Changes and variable definitions.* Development Research Group, World Bank (downloaded in July 2011).

Kenworthy, L., and J. Pontusson. 2005. "Rising inequality and the politics of redistribution in affluent countries." *Perspectives on Politics* 3(3): 449–471.

Kim, J., J. R. Petrocik, and S. N. Enokson. 1975. "Voter turnout among the American States: Systemic and individual components." *The American Political Science Review* 69(1): 107–123.

Kimball, D. C., and M. Kropf. 2005. "Ballot design and unrecorded votes on paper-based ballots." *Public Opinion Quarterly* 69(4): 508.

Kissau, K. G. Lutz, and J. Rosset. 2011. "The political preferences of political elites, voters and non-voters in Europe." *Unpublished paper.*

Kittilson, M. C., and L. Schwindt-Bayer. 2010. "Engaging citizens: The role of power-sharing institutions." *Journal of Politics* 72(4): 990–1002.

Klingemann, H. D. 2009. *The comparative study of electoral systems.* Oxford: Oxford University Press.

Klor, E. F., and M. Shayo. 2010. "Social identity and preferences over redistribution." *Journal of Public Economics* 94(3–4): 269–278.

Knack, S. 2001. "Election-day Registration." *American Politics Research* 29(1): 65.

Krosnick, J. A., P. S. Visser, and J. Harder. 2011. "The psychological underpinnings of political behavior." In S. T. Fiske, D. T. Gilbert, and G. Lindzey (Eds.), *Handbook of social psychology* (5th ed., Vol. 2). Hoboken, NJ: Wiley & Sons, 1288–1342.

Laakso, M., and R. Taagepera. 1979. "Effective number of parties: A measure with application to West Europe." *Comparative Political Studies* 12(1): 3–27.

Lassen, D. D. 2005. "The effect of information on voter turnout: Evidence from a natural experiment." *American Journal of Political Science* 49(1): 103–118.

Leighley, J. E., and J. Nagler. 2007. "Unions, voter turnout, and class bias in the US electorate, 1964–2004." *The Journal of Politics* 69(2): 430–441.

Levine, D. K., and T. R. Palfrey. 2007. "The paradox of voter participation? A laboratory study." *American Political Science Review* 101(1): 143.

Lijphart, A. 1990. "The political consequences of electoral laws, 1945–85." *The American Political Science Review* 84(2): 481–496.

———. 1994. *Electoral systems and party systems: A study of twenty-seven democracies, 1945–1990.* Oxford: Oxford University Press.

———. 1997. "Unequal participation: Democracy's unresolved dilemma." *The American Political Science Review* 91(1): 1–14.

———. 1999. *Patterns of democracy: Government forms and performance in thirty-six countries.* New Haven: Yale University Press.

Lopez-Pintor, R., and M. Gratschew. 2002. "Voter registration." In R. Lopez-Pintor and M. Gratschew (Eds.), *Voter turnout since 1945: A global report.* Stockholm: International Institute for Democracy and Electoral Assistance.

Luna, J. P., and E. J. Zechmeister. 2005. "Political representation in Latin America." *Comparative Political Studies* 38(4): 388–416.

Lupia, A., M. D. McCubbins, and S. L. Popkin. 2000. *Elements of reason: Cognition, choice, and the bounds of rationality.* Cambridge: Cambridge University Press.

Lutz, G., and M. Marsh. 2007. "Introduction: Consequences of low turnout." *Electoral Studies* 26(3): 539–547.

Lyons, W., and R. Alexander. 2000. "A tale of two electorates: Generational replacement and the decline of voting in presidential elections." *Journal of Politics* 62(4): 1014–1034.

Mahler, V. A. 2008. "Electoral turnout and income redistribution by the state: A cross-national analysis of the developed democracies." *European Journal of Political Research* 47(2): 161–183.

Mankowska, K. 2011. "Income inequality and political engagement in Eastern Europe." *Unpublished manuscript.*

Marcus, G. 2009. *Kluge: The haphazard evolution of the human mind.* Mariner Books.

Marian, C. G., and R. F. King. 2010. "Plus ça change: Electoral law reform and the 2008 Romanian parliamentary elections." *Communist and Post-Communist Studies* 43(1): 7–18.

Martin, P. S. 2003. "Voting's rewards: Voter turnout, attentive publics, and congressional allocation of federal money." *American Journal of Political Science* 47(1): 110–127.

Mayer, A. K. 2011. "Does education increase political participation?" *The Journal of Politics* 73(3): 633–645.

McCall, L., and L. Kenworthy. 2009. "Americans' social policy preferences in the era of rising inequality." *Perspectives on Politics* 7(3): 459–484.

McCuen, B., and R. B. Morton. 2010. "Tactical coalition voting and information in the laboratory." *Electoral Studies* 29(3): 316–328.

Meffert, M. F., and T. Gschwend. 2011. "Polls, coalition signals and strategic voting: An experimental investigation of perceptions and effects." *European Journal of Political Research* 50(5): 636–667.

Meltzer, A. H., and S. F. Richard. 1981. "A rational theory of the size of government." *The Journal of Political Economy* 889(5): 914–927.

Merriam, C. E., and H. F. Gosnell. 1924. *Non-voting: Causes and methods of control.* Chicago: The University of Chicago Press.

Michels, R. 1915. *Political parties: A sociological study of the oligarchical tendencies of modern democracy.* Free Press.

Miller, W. E, and J. M. Shanks. 1996. *The new American voter.* Cambridge, MA: Harvard University Press.

Milligan, K., E. Moretti, and P. Oreopoulos. 2004. "Does education improve citizenship? Evidence from the United States and the United Kingdom." *Journal of Public Economics* 88(9–10): 1667–1695.

Milner, H. 2002. *Civic literacy: How informed citizens make democracy work.* Tufts University.

Mitchell, G. E., and C. Wlezien. 1995. "The impact of legal constraints on voter registration, turnout, and the composition of the American electorate." *Political Behavior* 17(2): 179–202.

Montero, J. R. 1986. "La vuelta a las urnas: participación, movilización y abstención." In J. Linz and J. R. Montero (Eds.), *Crisis y cambio: Electores y partidos en la España de los años ochenta.* Madrid: Centro de Estudios Constitucionales.

Morales, Laura. 2009. *Joining political organizations: Instituitions, mobilization and participation in Western Democracies.* Colchester: European Consortium for Political Research.

Mueller, D. C. 2003. *Public choice III.* Cambridge: Cambridge University Press.

Narud, H. M. and H. Valen. 2008. "Coalition membership and electoral performance in Western Europe." In K. Strøm, W. C. Müller and T. Bergmann (Eds.), *Cabinets and coalition bargaining. The democratic life cycle in Western Europe.* Oxford: Oxford University Press.

Neckerman, K. M., and F. Torche. 2007. "Inequality: causes and consequences." *Annual Review of Sociology.* 33: 335–357.

Nevitte, N., Blais, A., Gidengil, E., and Nadeau, R. 2009. "Socioeconomic status and non-voting." In H. D. Klingemann (Ed.), *The Comparative Study of Electoral Systems.* Oxford: Oxford University Press, 85–108.

Nie, N. H., G. B. Powell, and K. Prewitt. 1969. "Social structure and political participation: developmental relationships, Part I." *The American Political Science Review* 63(2): 361–378.

Nie, N. H., J. Junn, and K. Stehlik-Barry. 1996. *Education and democratic citizenship in America.* Chicago: University of Chicago Press.

Nikolenyi, C. 2011. "When electoral reform fails: The stability of proportional representation in post-communist democracies." *West European Politics* 34(3): 607–625.

Norris, P. 2000. *A virtuous circle: Political communications in postindustrial societies.* Cambridge: Cambridge University Press.

———. 2002. *Democratic phoenix: Reinventing political activism.* Cambridge: Cambridge University Press.

———. 2004. *Electoral engineering: Voting rules and political behavior.* Cambridge: Cambridge University Press.

Pacek, A., and B. Radcliff. 1995. "Turnout and the vote for left-of-centre parties: A cross-national analysis." *British Journal of Political Science* 25(1): 137–43.

Page, B. I., and L. R. Jacobs. 2009. *Class war?: What Americans really think about economic inequality.* Chicago: University of Chicago Press.

PARLINE database. 2011. Parliaments on-line. Geneva, Switzerland: Inter-Parliamentary Union, http://www.columbia.edu/cgi-bin/cul/resolve?ANC0061 (downloaded in June 2011).

Parry, G., G. Moyser, and N. Day. 1992. *Political participation and democracy in Britain.* Cambridge: Cambridge University Press.

Pereira, P. T., and J. Silva. 2009. "Citizens' freedom to choose representatives: Ballot structure, proportionality and." *Electoral Studies* 28(1): 101–110.

Persson, M. 2011. "An Empirical Test of the Relative Education Model in Sweden." *Political Behavior* 33(3): 455–478.

Pierce, R., 1995. *Choosing the chief: Presidential elections in France and the United States.* Ann Arbor, MI: University of Michigan Press.

Piven, F. F., and R. A. Cloward. 1988. *Why Americans don't vote.* New York: Pantheon Books.

Plutzer, E. 2002. "Becoming a habitual voter: Inertia, resources, and growth in young adulthood." *American Political Science Review* 96(1): 41–56.

Pontusson, J., and D. Rueda. 2010. "The politics of inequality: Voter mobilization and left parties in advanced industrial states." *Comparative Political Studies* 43(6): 675–705.

Popkin, S. L. and Dimock, M. 1999. "Political knowledge and citizen competence." In S. Elkin and K. Soltan (Eds.), *Citizen competence and democratic institutions.* University Park: Pennsylvania State University Press, 117–146.

Popkin, S. L. 1991. *The reasoning voter: Communication and persuasion in presidential campaigns.* Chicago: University of Chicago Press.

Powell, G. B. 1986. "American voter turnout in comparative perspective." *The American Political Science Review* 80(1): 17–43.

———. 2000. *Elections as instruments of democracy: Majoritarian and proportional visions.* New Haven: Yale University Press.

Power, T. J., and J. C. Garand. 2007. "Determinants of invalid voting in Latin America." *Electoral Studies* 26(2): 432–444.

Power, T. J., and J. T. Roberts. 1995. "Compulsory voting, invalid ballots, and abstention in Brazil." *Political Research Quarterly* 48(4): 795–826.

Prior, M. 2005. "News vs. entertainment: How increasing media choice widens gaps in political knowledge and turnout." *American Journal of Political Science* 49(3): 577–592.

———. 2007. *Post-broadcast democracy: How media choice increases inequality in political involvement and polarizes elections.* New York: Cambridge University Press.

Przeworski, A. 2003. "Freedom to choose and democracy." *Economics and Philosophy* 19(2): 265–279.

———. 2007. "Is the science of comparative politics possible?" In C. Boix and S. Stokes (Eds.), *Oxford Handbook of Comparative Politics.* Oxford: Oxford University Press.

———. 2010. *Democracy and the limits of self-government.* Cambridge: Cambridge University Press.

Przeworski, A., and S. C. Stokes. 1999. *Democracy, accountability, and representation.* Cambridge: Cambridge University Press.

Putnam, R. D. 2002. *Bowling alone: The collapse and revival of American community.* Simon and Schuster.

Quintelier, E., M. Hooghe, and S. Marien. 2011. "The effect of compulsory voting on turnout stratification patterns: A cross-national analysis." *International Political Science Review* 32: 396–416.

Rabe-Hesketh, S., and A. Skrondal. 2008. *Multilevel and longitudinal modeling using Stata.* Stata Corp.

Radcliff, B. 2001. "Organized labor and electoral participation in American national elections." *Journal of Labor Research* 22(2): 405–414.

Radcliff, B., and P. Davis. 2000. "Labor organization and electoral participation in industrial democracies." *American Journal of Political Science* 44(1): 132–141.

Rae, D. 1967. *The political consequences of election laws.* New Haven: Yale University Press.

Renwick, A. 2010. *The politics of electoral reform: Changing the rules of democracy.* Cambridge: Cambridge University Press.

Renwick, A. and J.-B. Pilet. 2010. "Is there a trend towards the personalization of electoral systems?" *Paper presented at the EPOP Annual Conference*, University of Essex, 10–12 September 2010.

Reynolds, A., and M. Steenbergen. 2006. "How the world votes: The political consequences of ballot design, innovation and manipulation." *Electoral Studies* 25(3): 570–598.

Roberts, A., and B. Y. Kim. 2011. "Policy Responsiveness in Post-communist Europe: Public Preferences and Economic Reforms." *British Journal of Political Science* 1(1): 1–21.

Rose, R. 1978. "Citizen participation in the presidential process." *Society* 16(1): 43–48.

Rosenberg, J. S., and M. Chen. 2009. *Expanding democracy: Voter registration around the world.* Brennan Center for Justice.

Rosenfeld, J. 2010. "Economic determinants of voting in an era of union decline." *Social Science Quarterly* 91(2): 379–395.

Rosenstone, S. J., and R. E. Wolfinger. 1978. "The effect of registration laws on voter turnout." *The American Political Science Review* 72(1): 22–45.

Rosenstone, S. J., and J. M. Hansen. 1993. *Mobilization, participation, and democracy in America.* New York: Macmillan Pub Co.

Rothstein, B., and E. M. Uslaner. 2005. "All for all: Equality, corruption, and social trust." *World Politics* 58(1): 41–72.

Rubenson, D. et al. 2007. "Does low turnout matter? Evidence from the 2000 Canadian federal election." *Electoral Studies* 26(3): 589–597.

Rueschemeyer, D. 2005. "Addressing Inequality." In L. Diamond and L. Morlino (Eds.), *Assessing the Quality of Democracy.* Baltimore, MD: John Hopkins University Press.

Schattschneider, E. E. 1960. *The semisovereign people: A realist's view of democracy in America.* Holt, Rinehart and Winston.

Scheve, K. 2010. "Envy and altruism in hard times." *Unpublished manuscript.*

Selb, P. 2009. "A deeper look at the proportionality-turnout nexus." *Comparative Political Studies* 42(4): 527–548.

Shayo, M. 2009. "A model of social identity with an application to political economy: Nation, class, and redistribution." *American Political Science Review* 103(2): 147–174.

Shugart, M. S., M. Ellis, and K. Suominen. n.d. "An open and closed case: Electoral rules, the personal vote, and the 'connectedness' of legislators." *Unpublished manuscript.*

Shugart, M. S. 2005. "Comparative electoral systems research: The maturation of a field and new challenges ahead." In M. Gallagher and P. Mitchell (Eds.), *The Politics of Electoral Systems.* Oxford: Oxford, 25–56.

Sigelman, L. 1982. "The nonvoting voter in voting research." *American Journal of Political Science* 26(1): 47–56.

Silver, B. D., B. A. Anderson, and P. R. Abramson. 1986. "Who over-reports voting?" *The American Political Science Review* 80(2): 613–624.

Sniderman, P. M. et al. 1991. *Reasoning and choice.* New York: Cambridge University Press.

Söderlund, P., H. Wass, and A. Blais. 2011. "The impact of motivational and contextual factors on turnout in first-and second-order elections." *Electoral Studies*, 30(4): 689–699.

Solt, F. 2008. "Economic inequality and democratic political engagement." *American Journal of Political Science* 52(1): 48–60.

———. 2009a. "Standardizing the World Income Inequality Database." *Social Science Quarterly* 90(2): 231–242.

———. 2009b. *The Standardized World Income Inequality Database.* V3 [Version] http://hdl.handle.net/1902.1/11992 (downloaded in July 2011).

———. 2011. "Does economic inequality depress electoral participation? Testing the Schattschneider hypothesis." *Political Behavior* 32(2): 285–301.

Sondheimer, R. M., and D. P. Green. 2010. "Using experiments to estimate the effects of education on voter turnout." *American Journal of Political Science* 54(1): 174–189.

Soroka, S. N., and C. Wlezien. 2008. "On the limits to inequality in representation." *PS: Political Science & Politics* 41(2): 319–327.

Steinbrecher, M., and G. Seeber. 2011. "Inequality and turnout in Europe." *Unpublished manuscript.*

Strom, K. 1985. "Party goals and government performance in parliamentary democracies." *The American Political Science Review* 79(3): 738–754.

Studlar, D. T., and S. Welch. 1986. "The policy opinions of British nonvoters: A research note." *European Journal of Political Research* 14(1–2): 139–148.

Svallfors, S. 1997. "Worlds of welfare and attitudes to redistribution: A comparison of eight western nations." *European Sociological Review* 13(3): 283–304.

Tan, A. C. 2009. "The 2008 Taiwan elections: Forward to the past?" *Electoral Studies* 28(3): 502–506.

Teixeira, R. A. 1992. *The disappearing American voter.* Washington: Brookings Institution Press.

Tenn, S. 2007. "The effect of education on voter turnout." *Political Analysis* 15(4): 446–464.

Teorell, J., Sum, P. and Tobiasen, M. 2007. "Participation and political equality: An assessment of large-scale democracy." In J. van Deth,

J. R. Montero, and A. Westholm (Eds.), *Citizenship and involvement in european democracies: A comparative perspective.* London: Routledge.

Thaler, R. H., and C. Sunstein. 2009. *Nudge: Improving decisions about health, wealth, and loss aversion.* London: Penguin.

The Comparative Study of Electoral Systems. 2011. www.cses.org (downloaded in May 2011).

Tichenor, P. J., G. A. Donohue, and C. N. Olien. 1970. "Mass media flow and differential growth in knowledge." *Public Opinion Quarterly* 34(2): 159–170.

Tingsten, H. 1937. *Political behavior.* Totowa, NJ: Bedminster.

Teorell, J., M. Samanni, S. Holmberg, and B. Rothstein. 2011. *The Quality of Government Dataset,* version 6Apr11. University of Gothenburg: The Quality of Government Institute, http://www.qog.pol.gu.se (downloaded in June 2011).

Tóka, G. 2002. "Voter Inequality, turnout and information effects in a cross-national perspective." *Helen Kellogg Institute Working Paper Series* No. 297. Notre Dame, IN.

Tomz, M., and R. P. V. Houweling. 2003. "How does voting equipment affect the racial gap in voided ballots?" *American Journal of Political Science* 47(1): 46–60.

Topf, R. 1995. "Electoral participation." In H. D. Klingemann, and D. Fuchs (Eds.), *Citizens and the state.* Oxford: Oxford University Press, 27–51.

Traugott, M. W., and J. P. Katosh. 1979. "Response validity in surveys of voting behavior." *Public Opinion Quarterly* 43(3): 359.

Uhlaner, C. J., B. E. Cain, and D. R. Kiewiet. 1989. "Political participation of ethnic minorities in the 1980s." *Political Behavior* 11(3): 195–231.

Ura, J. D., and C. R. Ellis. 2008. "Income, preferences, and the dynamics of policy responsiveness." *PS: Political Science & Politics* 41(4): 785–794.

Van der Eijk, C., and M. Van Egmond. 2007. "Political effects of low turnout in national and European elections." *Electoral Studies* 26(3): 561–573.

Van Egmond, M. 2003. *Rain falls on all of us (but some manage to get more wet than others): Political context and electoral participation.* Doctoral dissertation, University of Amsterdam.

Verba, S. 2003. "Would the dream of political equality turn out to be a nightmare?" *Perspective on Politics* 1(04): 663–679.

Verba, S., and N. H. Nie. 1972. *Participation in America: Social equality and political democracy.* New York: Harper & Row.

Verba, S., K. L. Schlozman, and H. E. Brady. 1995. *Voice and equality: Civic voluntarism in American politics*. Cambridge: Cambridge University Press.

Verba, S., N. H. Nie, and J. Kim. 1978. *Participation and political equality: A seven-nation comparison*. Chicago: University of Chicago Press.

Visser, J. 2006. "Union membership statistics in 24 countries." *Monthly Labor Review* 129(1): 38–49.

Voos, P. B. 2003. "Democracy and industrial relations." In *Proceedings of the Industrial Relations Research Association*.

Vowles, J. 2010. "Making a difference? Public perceptions of coalition, single-party, and minority governments." *Electoral Studies* 29(3): 370–380.

Warwick, P. V. 2011. "Government intentions and citizen preferences in dynamic perspective." *British Journal of Political Science* 41(3): 599–619.

Wattenberg, M. P. 2002. *Where have all the voters gone?* Cambridge: Harvard University Press.

———. 2006. *Is voting for young people?* New York: Longman Pub Group.

Western, B., and J. Rosenfeld. 2011. "Unions, norms, and the rise in US wage inequality." *American Sociological Review* 76(4): 513–537.

White, S., and I. McAllister. 2007. "Turnout and representation bias in post-communist Europe." *Political Studies* 55(3): 586–606.

Wilkinson, R. G. et al. 2009. *The spirit level: Why more equal societies almost always do better*. London: Allen Lane.

Wolfinger, R. E., and S. J. Rosenstone. 1980. *Who votes?* Yale: Yale University Press.

Zucco, C. 2007. "Where's the bias? A reassessment of the Chilean electoral system." *Electoral Studies* 26(2): 303–314.

Index

American National Election Studies,
125
Australia, 26, 29, 48, 53, 76, 121, 175
Austria, 15, 30, 121, 129

ballot structure, 57–59, 62–67, 70,
74, 79, 82–86, 112
closed party lists, 67, 71, 73–76,
82–83
flexible ballots, 62, 64, 75–76,
82–84
open ballots, 64, 67, 71, 73–76, 79,
82–84
Belarus, 173
Belgium, 29, 52–53, 121, 129, 131,
179, 185
Blais, André, 8, 17–18, 37–40, 42,
58–59, 69, 89, 92–93, 157
Brazil, 29, 52, 129
Bulgaria, 30, 129, 179

Canada, 17, 26, 29, 48, 173
Centro de Investigaciones
Sociológicas, xvi, 66
Chile, 26, 30
coalition governments, 89–92, 95
Comparative Study of Electoral
Systems, 4, 6, 9, 23–24, 74, 154,
176

compulsory voting, 9, 17, 33, 50–51,
53–55, 69, 79, 83, 140, 153, 175
concurrent elections, 76
costs of voting, cognitive, 8, 40–42,
44–45, 92, 112–113
costs of voting, non-cognitive, 40–41,
43, 57
Croatia, 30, 129
cross-national data, 9
Czech Republic, 26, 30, 121, 129,
179, 189, 191

Dahl, Robert, 1, 33, 168
Database of Political Institutions,
101–102
Denmark, 30, 53, 105, 121, 129,
185
Downs, Anthony, 37, 90–91

education, 14, 24
absolute education model, 18
age and voter turnout, 21
causal effect of, 20
relative education model, 18–19
effective number of electoral parties,
93, 109, 112
Egypt, 23
Elections and Democracy research
group, 66

electoral system, 58–59, 79, 82, 92
    Alternative Vote, 60, 76
    majoritarian, 75, 85, 92, 101
    mixed member, 75, 85
    PR, 75, 82–84, 92
    Single Transferable Vote, 60, 76
    Single-Non-Transferable-Vote, 76
equality, political, 1–2, 13, 204
European Social Survey, 118, 123,
    151, 172, 178–179
experiments, 9–10, 65–69, 71–72, 74,
    93–95, 99–100, 195, 197–198

Finland, 26, 29, 71, 105, 121, 129,
    189
fractionalization, government,
    101–103, 109
fragmentation, electoral, 94–95,
    99–100
France, 26, 30, 121, 129, 131, 189
Franklin, Mark, 21, 37, 42, 49,
    194
Freedom House, 23

Germany, 17, 48, 129, 179, 189
Gini coefficient, 151, 153
Greece, 179

Hungary, 26, 29, 121, 129

Iceland, 30
India, 15
inequality, economic, 146–147
    voter turnout, 150–151, 157
International Institute for Democracy
    and Electoral Assistance, 53
International Social Survey Program,
    118, 172
Inter-Parliamentary Union database,
    78
Ireland, 30, 76, 121
Israel, 30, 131, 185
Italy, 30, 127, 129, 131

Japan, 15, 30, 121, 129
Jusko, Karen, 31, 36, 40, 114,
    142–143, 178

Korea, 26, 30, 53, 129

Lijphart, Arendt, 3, 9, 17, 35, 43,
    51–52, 54, 59, 90, 92, 168, 198
Lithuania, 26, 30

media system, 103, 105–109, 112
Meltzer-Richard model, 147, 166,
    202
Mexico, 30, 53, 76, 129
mobilization, political, 8, 36, 114,
    116–117
multilevel models, 55–56

Netherlands, 15–16, 30, 51, 129
New Zealand, 30, 47, 53, 121, 129
Nigeria, 15
Norris, Pippa, 16, 60, 65, 74, 106,
    118, 121
Norway, 17, 30

participation, unequal 2–3, 5, 7, 13
    cross-national research, 15–16
    description of, 23–24, 26, 29–31
    in the US, 4, 14–16, 26, 36
    measurement of, 14, 17, 19, 26–27,
        31, 56
    over time, 16
Peru, 26, 30
Poland, 26, 29, 79, 83, 121, 129,
    179, 189
political efficacy, 146–147, 158
political parties
    mobilization, 141–143
Portugal, 30, 129
preferences
    economic issues, 179, 182,
        187–189
    social issues, 182, 187–189
preferences of voters and non-voters,
    169, 171–174, 178–179, 182
Putnam, Robert, 17, 123

redistribution, 147
    theories of, 147–148
representation, unequal, 3, 168–169,
    191, 203–204

resources, 3, 8, 18, 39–40,
146–147
responsiveness of politicians,
174
Romania, 30, 129, 179
Russia, 173

Slovakia, 121
Slovenia, 26, 30
socio-economic status, 3, 8, 14, 117
Solt, Frederick, 145, 146–147, 150,
153
Spain, 5, 6, 16, 26, 30, 64, 66–67, 70,
93–95, 100, 129, 185
Sweden, 17, 30, 121, 129, 165
Switzerland, 15–16, 26, 29, 60, 129,
189

Taiwan, 24, 30, 76, 101, 131
trade unions, 114, 117
education of members, 121–123,
125, 129, 131
effect on turnout, 120, 133
effects on policy, 122

membership, 115–116, 121, 127,
129, 131
mobilization, 117–120, 125
triangulation, 198

UK, 30, 105, 129
Ukraine, 173
unequal participation
election results, 169, 175–176
policy, 170, 177–178
US, 14–17, 26, 48, 129, 153, 172, 204

Verba, Sidney, 1–3, 7–8, 14–15,
17–18, 36, 39–40, 42, 50, 114,
116–117, 168
voter registration, 36, 45, 47–48, 50
voter turnout, 36–38
over-reporting, 24, 97

World Income Inequality Database,
153
World Values Survey, 150, 172

Yugoslavia, 15